America,

Have You Lost Your Mind, or Is it Your Soul?

Can't You Remember the Faith of Your Fathers, or Do You Want To?

ROBBIE TRUSSELL

WestBow Press
A Division of Thomas Nelson

WestBow Press books may be ordered through booksellers or by contacting:

WestBow Press
A Division of Thomas Nelson
1663 Liberty Drive
Bloomington, IN 47403
www.westbowpress.com
1-(866) 928-1240

ISBN: 978-1-4497-6666-5 (hc)
ISBN: 978-1-4497-6667-2 (sc)
ISBN: 978-1-4497-6668-9 (e)

Library of Congress Control Number: 2012916549

Printed in the United States of America

WestBow Press rev. date: 09/12/2012

Contents

Introduction

Dear Readers,

It is extremely important to me that everyone who reads this book knows who wrote it and why. I'm going to give you a brief autobiography to let you know where I'm coming from and why I love this country as I do—and also why I am so disturbed by what is happening to it.

This book is not coming from an academic setting where the author is sitting at his desk while students and others are scurrying around researching and gathering his material. I have lived and worked and observed attitudes and theories as they developed in this United States of America for almost three-quarters of a century. I have been a part of and understand the "work ethic" of the working class as well as the "professional ethics" and methods in the professions and the business world. I have also seen the once commonly held belief in the wonder and beauty of the "red, white, and blue" become an embarrassment to the enlightened elite.

Let's begin our journey with a brief, but detailed background story which hopefully will convince you that I am the "everyman of America" who can relate to the majority of US citizens.

My heritage mirrors that of our country. On my father's side, Scotch-Irish immigrants came to this continent and at some point brought a Native American (Cherokee) wife into the family. My mother's mother was part Mississippi Choctaw and was raised by a medicine man who taught her how to make several medicines that were like miracle cures. If some of her thirteen children had been able to get those formulas from her, I could have been an heir to a pharmaceutical fortune.

My paternal grandfather was the manager of a large farm in my home county and was also an elected constable, who in that very rural area had to perform some of the same tasks and duties of a sheriff or marshal. My dad told some colorful stories of some of my grandfather's escapades.

Unfortunately, both of my grandfathers died in their late thirties or early forties, and my paternal grandmother not long afterward. So my maternal grandmother was the only one I was able to spend time with.

I was born May 30, 1941, some seven months before the dreadful attack on Pearl Harbor, Hawaii. My brother, who was sixteen years older than me, joined the US Marines on December 14, 1942 at the age of seventeen. He saw the world in the very frightening South Pacific, from Hawaii to New Zealand, by way of Guam and Iwo Jima.

I was the only child to my mother, whom my father married after his first wife died. They had four children. The aforementioned brother was the oldest, followed by three girls almost exactly two years apart. All but the youngest were on their own by the time I came along.

We were not wealthy. My father was a sheet metal worker, and my mother was a seamstress. She worked from home and was very good at it. She could create simple things or pieces as complex as a man's suit or a wedding gown. She was always an inspiration to me. When she was about eighteen months old, she contracted polio, which affected her right leg. She was on crutches, but with the help of her twelve siblings, she learned to walk on one crutch. She did this until she was in her late fifties when she had a car accident that broke her back. It put her in a wheelchair, but that didn't slow her down. She would still drive her car to her office. I guess I neglected to mention that she went back to business school and became an accountant after I graduated from high school.

My dad had to quit school when his dad died—he was thirteen and in eighth grade. He was the oldest of four children and had to go to work to help support the family. He was self-educated as he became an avid reader of everything from the newspaper to series of books by Louis L'Amour and Zane Gray.

As I finished high school, my ambition was to follow my older brother's path and study business administration. He had come home from WWII and gone to the University of Mississippi on his GI Bill. Problem was, I had no money or other means to pay for tuition. Luckily I found out through an older cousin about a man who ran the barbershop on campus at Mississippi State University. He would send needy young men to the barber college in Memphis during the summer before they started college and let them work in the barbershop to pay their way through. I contacted him and we made a deal.

The summer seemed to fly by, and there I was enrolling. The university had both Army and Air Force ROTC (Reserve Officer Training Corps) which had inspection during drills every Tuesday afternoon, so all day Monday and Tuesday mornings the guys were lined up in the hall to get haircuts. This made me and the other young barbers very happy. I actually made almost as much doing this as my dad did at his full-time job.

As is true for so many young men, I didn't really know what I wanted to do and found myself just going through the motions. In the middle of the second semester of my sophomore year, I met a local girl and she became my total focus. If I wasn't in class or working, we were together. At the end of the semester, we were married, and I was back in my hometown looking for a job.

Over the years, I worked in retail, manufacturing, and sales (insurance, real estate, others). I always did well for a time, but then I would lose interest and move on. Unfortunately, I didn't know that I suffered with ADD (that was before they had a name for it).

When I went into law enforcement, I began to yearn to complete my education. I attended community college and, with my previous credits, I earned my degree in criminal justice in two semesters. I made near-perfect grades because I was focused. This really got me enthused, and I met with a couple of professors at the university and decided psychology was my cup of tea.

Again with the basics complete, I could concentrate on the primary psychology courses and earn my degree in three semesters—and I did this while I worked full-time. I later took advanced courses and, after working at a local hospital for a couple of years, went to work on a program for the Substance Abuse and Mental Health Administration. I did that for several years before I went into semiretirement.

I spend my time now studying the history of our great country and the Holy Bible. I haven't yet mentioned that I was ordained into the Christian ministry.

I hope this brief autobiography shows that there are few among us who have a more diverse and thorough connection with the history and workings of our republic. It is that fact, coupled with my deep love for our country and my sincere belief that Nikita Khrushchev's prediction from the 1960s is coming true, that compelled me to write this book. His statement, when questioned about the strained relations between the United States and what was then the Union of Soviet Socialist Republics, was, "Whether you like it or not, history is on our side. We will bury you."

His remark came at the Polish Embassy in Moscow. He later alluded to the downfall of the United States coming from within. And that possibility is certainly rearing its ugly head as we see so many who cannot or will not accept the true heritage of our once great country. Instead they want to tear it down and build a new one based on one of the failed models of the past.

I find myself suffering severe frustration over the misrepresentation of the true history of our country. Even as far back as when I started to school, the history books didn't tell the whole story of who our original settlers were. Granted, some of the teachers of the lower grades kept the Holy Bible on their desk or in a drawer, and some even read a "Bible story" to start the class.

Later, when we got into the actual study of the history of the United States of America—the original colonies and the people who came here—it was bland and void of the passion and determination, not to mention dedication, that these people showed. They were excited about the new life of liberty and freedom they saw before them.

And now we have sunk to a new low in our passion and level of appreciation for what those dedicated souls did for us. For quite a number of years now, the secularists and atheists have waged a campaign to take any reference to God or Christianity from the public discourse. They also want to challenge any mention of the Founding Fathers being people of faith. They started a list and continue to add names to it of the people who framed our Constitution that they claim are nonbelievers or, at best, Deists. Deists believe that some powerful figure (may have) created the earth but then left us on our own to run it the best we could. My purpose and desire is to show through documents and the actual words and thoughts of our Founding Fathers that the United States of America was founded on the principles of the Christian faith and with the purpose to grow and spread that faith.

One of the biggest misrepresentations has been the taking of a statement made by Thomas Jefferson in a letter he wrote to the Committee of the Danbury Baptist Association on January 1, 1802, where he talked about the First Amendment to the Constitution being a safeguard from the nation becoming a theocracy. It did not provide for the elimination of religious discussions, symbols, or activity from all public property as the ACLU and others claim. Anyone with common sense and an open mind could see that. Their steady propagation of that viewpoint has caused the general public to take it for granted.

My primary purpose for writing this book is to share just a portion of the truth about who our predecessors were and the true heritage that they left us. There are many books and artifacts out there that most of us have never seen, containing everything we need to prove who we are. Everyone should have the opportunity to see or hear the truth about who the original settlers of our country were and why they came here. It wasn't for riches and fame, although some attained both. They came here to escape persecution, primarily concerning their religious beliefs, in their home country.

My sincere desire is that when you read this presentation of the facts, you will have a real appreciation for what these people did for us, beginning with the earliest settlement four hundred years ago.

In closing, let me share a couple of quotes that state the case very well:

> "Those that fail to learn from history are doomed to repeat it."—Winston Churchill (former British politician and statesman, 1874-1965)
>
> "Those who ignore history are doomed to repeat it"—Edmund Burke (1729-1797)
>
> "My God! How little do my countrymen know what precious blessings they are in possession of, and which no other people on earth enjoy!"—Thomas Jefferson (1743-1826)
>
> "I like to see a man proud of the place in which he lives. I like to see a man live so that his place will be proud of him."—Abraham Lincoln (1809-1865)

These great men knew the blessings that this country offered. I wish all of our people felt that way today.

CHAPTER 1

"In the Beginning God . . ."

Anytime we delve into history, it would perhaps be a good idea to mention the One who is and was always there. A thorough and complete history of anything or any place would not be all that it could be without it.

> There is an exceptionally beneficial and fruitful advantage to be derived from a study of the past. There you see, set in the clear light of historical truth, examples of every possible type. From these you can select for yourself and your country what to imitate, and also what, as being mischievous in its inception and disastrous in its consequences, you should avoid. (Titus Livius [Livy], *Ab Urbe Condita,* preface)

Ignorance of the past is dangerous. We must be informed about our history and the world, otherwise, we can be manipulated by those who corrupt the truth and use it against us. Our past helps to guide our future, so we must be prepared to base our plan on the foundations laid before us.

I propose the true foundation and plan for the United States of America was in place centuries before Columbus, de Soto, or any of the other explorers set foot in this part of the world. As a matter of fact, I made a statement several years ago that, just as the land of Canaan was the Promised Land for the Jews, America was the "Promised Land" for Christians.

The search for a place where one could worship the Creator as described in John 1:1-3, in freedom and without fear of persecution, began in the early days of what we call the Common Era (CE), formerly anno Domini (AD), or "after death."

Jewish Christians were persecuted in their own country. One of their fiercest persecutors was a man named Saul of Tarsus, a member of the Pharisees and a Roman citizen. With the blessing of the leaders of the Jewish church, he hunted down Christian converts. He was present at the stoning and martyring of Stephen. Ironically, after his encounter with Jesus Christ when he was temporarily blinded, he became a powerful advocate of Christianity, evangelist, and church organizer. All of Christ's apostles, except John (the author of the books of St. John, 1 John, 2 John, 3 John, and Revelation), were martyred.

Long before this, starting with Adam and Eve, we find the main problem man had, and still has today, is a lack of respect for authority. God plainly told Adam and Eve they had full freedom to do as they pleased and to take full advantage of the bounty of their beautiful home in the garden of Eden. The only thing forbidden to them was to eat from the Tree of Knowledge of Good and Evil. But Eve was beguiled by the Serpent (Satan), took the fruit from the tree, and shared it with Adam.

Through the ages, the form or level of authority has varied, but there have always been those who rebelled. For many generations, God dealt with his creation directly, but eventually he delegated some responsibility to various entities. God chose Moses to lead the Jews out of Egypt, and they rebelled against him time and again. It was extremely frustrating trying to be the authority figure, dealing with the rebellious Israelites, so Moses went up on the mountain and asked for God's help in setting up some consistent and solid guidelines to present to the people. Out of this came the Ten Commandments. This gave the people a clear-cut, concise set of rules that applied equally to everyone. But people broke them and looked for exceptions to the rules. Does this sound familiar? Later, the tribe of Levi was designated as priests to help teach and counsel the people. Eventually, they were given judges, and then they insisted on having a king. Still, they always had a problem with authority.

The Roman Empire became a factor in the region, and it conquered Israel and most of the other countries. Jesus Christ had come in the meantime, and the Christian church had begun to grow. The Christians were persecuted at home, but they were also persecuted by their own people in Rome. It became so disruptive that the Jews were expelled from Rome in 51 CE.

But in the year 61, Emperor Nero blamed the fire that destroyed much of Rome on the Christians. He persecuted the churches ruthlessly and even used Christians as candles to light his garden. By the year 66, the Christians and Jews had separated into their own subcultures. The Palestinian Jews were still under Roman rule, and because they still resented it, they revolted.

At this time, there may have been more non-Jews or, as they were called then, Gentiles, than Jewish Christians. Wherever and whomever they were, they were persecuted—the Jewish Christians by their fellow Jews and the Gentiles by whatever authority they fell under: Greek, Roman, Persian, and so on.

This excerpt from the writings of Tacitus, from *Annals* 15.44, in the early second century, gives a description of some of the treatment at the hands of the Romans.

> To kill the rumours, Nero charged and tortured some people for their evil practices—the group popularly known as "Christians" . . . their deadly superstition had been suppressed temporarily, but was beginning to spring up again—not now just in Judea but even in Rome itself where all kinds of sordid and shameful activities are attracted and catch on.
>
> First, those who confessed to being Christians were arrested. Then, from information obtained from them, hundreds were convicted, more for their anti-social

> beliefs than for rebellion. In their deaths they were made a mockery. They were covered in skins of wild animals, torn to death by dogs, crucified or set on fire—so that when darkness fell they burned like torches in the night . . . . As a result, "although they were guilty of being Christians and deserved death, people began to feel sorry for them."
>
> There was a major change in the third century when the first recognized "church and state" incident was recognized. In AD 330 the subject on everyone's mind in the so-called Roman Empire was that Rome had fallen. But a New Rome, the city of Constantinople, stood firm. Here, the vision of the emperor Constantine—of a perfect Christian state, with the emperor presiding over civil and religious life—was realized.

From the founding of Constantinople by Constantine the Great to the fall of the city to the Ottomans in 1453, the Byzantine Empire endured for 1,123 years and 18 days. During this time, there was inevitable great change, both social and political, yet the degree of cultural uniformity throughout that time is striking. That was due in large part to the central role Christianity played in the empire.

In contrast to this was what transpired in old Rome and the surrounding areas of Spain, France, and Germany. In the year 800, Pope Leo III crowned Charlemagne head of the Holy Roman Empire (aka the Nominally Christian Germanic Kingdom). His dynasty is called the Carolingian Empire. His reign is the cultural high point of the early Middle Ages.

It also was the beginning of almost one thousand years of the blurred line between emperor and pope. There seemed to be no separation of church and state. There was a strained relationship between the people in power. The perceived need for a political leader and a religious leader led to an uneasy arrangement. When there was a powerful emperor, he chose and anointed the pope. When the standing pope was more powerful, he chose the next emperor.

The Crusades

There was something else during this time that deserves attention. Pope Urban II (1088-1099) called the Council of Clermont in 1095. He asked for Christians in Europe to assist the Byzantine Christians in the East. Men from all over the area responded in a series of crusades.

The Crusades were a series of military conflicts conducted by European Christian knights for control over the lucrative trade routes running through the Middle East and establishment of European, but not necessarily Christian, influence in the region. However, many historians write that its purposes were to defend Christians and expand Christian domains.

Generally, the Crusades refer to the campaigns in the Holy Land against Muslim forces sponsored by the papacy. There were other crusades against Islamic forces in southern Spain, southern Italy, and Sicily, as well as the campaigns of Teutonic knights against pagan strongholds in northeastern Europe. A few crusades, such as the Fourth Crusade, were waged within Christendom against groups that were considered heretical and schismatic. Krak des Chevaliers was built in the country of Tripoli by the Knights Hospitaller during the Crusades.

The Holy Land had been part of the Roman Empire, and thus Byzantine Empire, until the Islamic conquests of the seventh and eighth centuries. Thereafter, Christians had generally been permitted to visit the sacred places in the Holy Land until 1071, when the Seljuk Turks closed Christian pilgrimages and assailed the Byzantines, defeating them at the Battle of Manzikert. Emperor Alexius I asked for aid from Pope Urban II for help against Islamic aggression. He probably expected money from the pope for the hiring of mercenaries. Instead, Urban II called on the knights of Christendom in a speech made at the Council of Clermont on November 27, 1095, to combine the idea of pilgrimage to the Holy Land with that of waging a holy war against infidels.

The First Crusade captured Antioch in 1099 and then Jerusalem. The Second Crusade occurred in 1145, when Islamic forces retook Edessa. Jerusalem would be held until 1187 and the Third Crusade, famous for the battles between Richard the Lionheart and Saladin. The Fourth Crusade, begun by Innocent III in 1202, was intended to retake the Holy Land but was soon subverted by Venetians, who used the forces to sack the Christian city of Zara. Eventually, the crusaders arrived in Constantinople. Rather than proceeding to the Holy Land, the crusaders instead sacked Constantinople and other parts of Asia Minor, effectively establishing the Latin Empire of Constantinople in Greece and Asia Minor. This was effectively the last crusade sponsored by the papacy; individuals sponsored later crusades. Thus, though Jerusalem was held for nearly a century and other strongholds in the Near East would remain in Christian possession much longer, the crusades in the Holy Land ultimately failed to establish permanent Christian kingdoms.

Islamic expansion into Europe would renew and remain a threat for centuries, culminating in the campaigns of Suleiman the Magnificent in the sixteenth century. On the other hand, the crusades in southern Spain, southern Italy, and Sicily eventually lead to the demise of Islamic power in the regions; the Teutonic Knights expanded Christian domains in Eastern Europe, and the much less frequent crusades within Christendom, such as the Albigensian Crusade, achieved their goal of maintaining doctrinal unity.

There are many stories, both positive and negative, about the Crusades that we could discuss. We will move on, however, and come back to the subject of the Islamic story later.[1]

The Reformation

Western Europe had just gone through roughly a thousand years of Catholic culture, where the church dominated every facet of society. Now as the Middle Ages began the development of the early modern period, that dominance was broken and the most dramatic shake-up in religious history since Constantine imposed the Holy Roman mantle on the empire began.

The Reformation came about during the period known as the Renaissance, which lasted from about the fourteenth to the sixteenth century. Europe was devastated by plague during the fourteenth century and early fifteenth century. The whole area changed during the period.

Not only was the society affected by the sickness, death, and monetary hardships, but there was a religious change brewing. An information revolution was started where ideas could travel faster, which aided the Reformation. The Renaissance brought about an element of religious renewal. Christianity was reinterpreted with a Neoplatonic mysticism element. Ironically, the old traditions of philosophy and spirituality were still around, and the best description of this situation was found in *The Imitation of Christ* by Thomas à Kempis. This book came from a tradition of Christ-centered mysticism which came from the developments of the later Middle Ages. The book was deeply ingrained with the principles of personal integrity and devotion to Christ. Here is a sample of the work:

> If a man knows what it is to love Jesus, then he is really blessed. We have to abandon all we love for the one we love, for Jesus wants us to love him only above all things. Whether you will or no, you must one day leave everything behind. Keep yourself close to Jesus in life as well as death, commit yourself to his faithfulness, for he only can help you when everything else will fail.

There were many and varied causes for the Reformation and many people were involved, but the catalyst seemed to be Martin Luther. That's the name that most often comes to mind when this period is mentioned. Luther, sometimes called the German Hercules, was born in the village of Eisleben in 1483 and became an Augustinian monk at an unusually young age. He began to teach at the university at Wittenburg in 1508.

He began to have problems with the use of penance. He found that the practice of granting penance was being abused by certain figures in the church. They were actually putting a price on the indulgences. Initially Luther's intention was to bring the situation to a debate, but his Ninety-Five Theses started a storm in the church. He later wrote, "What I did toppled heaven and consumed earth by fire."

The hierarchy of the church turned Luther's concerns over corruption and misuse of indulgences into one about the authority of the pope. They insisted that the pope was divinely appointed and had divine authority. Luther wrote, in the preface to his complete works, "I began to understand that in this verse (Roman1:17) 'the righteousness of God' means the way in which a righteous person lives through a gift of God—that is, by faith. I began to understand that this verse means that the righteousness of God is revealed through the Gospel, but it is a passive righteousness—that is, it is that by which the merciful God makes us righteous by faith, as it is written, 'The righteous person lives by faith.' All at once I felt that I had been born again and entered into paradise itself through open gates. Immediately I saw the whole of Scripture in a different light."

Luther and his group of like thinkers felt compelled to clarify their views, hoping to create an agreed set of doctrines for all Protestants. In 1530, Philip Melanchthon worked with Luther to revise an earlier set of doctrinal statements that they had produced. This came to be known as the Augsburg Confession. Here is an excerpt from it:

> Also [we] teach that men cannot be justified before God by their own strength, merits, or works, but are freely justified for Christ's sake, through faith, when they believe that they are received into favour, and that their sins are forgiven for Christ's sake, who, by His death, has made satisfaction for our sins. This faith God imputes for righteousness in His sight.

And from the intro to his *Commentary on Galatians*:

> In my heart reigns this one article, faith in my dear Lord Christ, the beginning, middle, and end of whatever spiritual and divine thoughts I may have, whether by day or by night.

After Luther lead the first generation of Reformers, his successor was likely John Calvin. Calvin stayed mostly around Geneva, Switzerland, which became a kind of Protestant theocracy. Through Calvin's leadership, the city was transformed into the leading center of Protestant thought—some called it the Protestant Rome. Calvin developed a new understanding of the Protestant faith through his sermons and writings, including his *Institutes of the Christian Religion.* Through this work, he sought to offer the Christian faith in a systematic way, all based on the Holy Bible.

The movement and efforts of Calvin became the basis of the Reformed Church. The development of Calvinism—the movement started and inspired by his theology—spread into the whole area of Christian traditions. The Reformed Church in the end enjoyed more success than the Lutheran Church, which was mostly a German-speaking group in western Europe. It spread over most of Europe, including Scotland and the Netherlands. The theological tensions grew until not only the churches turned on each other, it spread to the general public and eventually into war. In 1572 alone, the civil war in France with different factions clashing over control resulted in the Catholic troops killing twenty thousand Protestant civilians in Paris and throughout France. At the Saint Bartholomew Massacre, as it was called, was the spark that later led to the Thirty Years War. It spread over most of Europe and it is estimated that between 1618 and 1648, the population of the Hapsburg empire, devastated by not only the fighting but by disease and the starvation that followed, dropped in population from 21 million to 13.5 million.

One of the great accomplishments of Calvin's group was the Geneva Bible. The Geneva translators produced a revised New Testament in English in 1557 that was essentially a revision of Tyndale's revised and corrected 1534 edition. Much of the work was done by William Whittingham, the brother-in-law of John Calvin. The Geneva New Testament was barely off the press when work began on a revision of the entire Bible, a process that took more than two years. The new translation was checked with Theodore Beza's earlier work and the Greek text.

After the death of Mary in England, Elizabeth was crowned queen in 1558, once again moving the country toward Protestantism. In 1560 a complete revised Bible was published, translated according to the Hebrew and Greek, and conferred with the best translations in diverse languages, and dedicated to Queen Elizabeth I. The Geneva Bible was finally printed in England in 1575 only after the death of Archbishop Matthew Parker, editor of the Bishop's Bible. [I have an edition of the 1599 Geneva Bible.]

It seemed that after the initial impact of the Reformation began to wane, the Protestant churches went into a long period of restructuring. During the latter section of the sixteenth century and most of the seventeenth, which was called the Age of Confessionalism, the different groups became more focused on their individual beliefs, or confessions, in contrast to the other churches. This practice has been called Protestant Scholasticism, where the churches concentrated more on outlining in more detail their own doctrines, developing terminology to describe them more accurately. This had been done centuries before to a different degree. Eventually, their discussions became dull and technical. Part of what Luther had tried to do was to overturn centuries of the medieval definitions and descriptions and focus more on the New Testament teachings. Calvin is normally thought of as a more "systematic" thinker and theologian. However, his *Institutes of the Christian Religion*, despite its precise topics, was supposed to be simply a faithful exposition of the Bible. Their followers were going further in their categorical definitions and specifications of the Protestant principle of the Scripture alone, but digging further for answers to questions not found in the Bible.

The prime example was the question of predestination and the relationship between grace and free will. This seemed to be the hottest topic being discussed at the time by both Protestants and Catholics. The Protestants were quite comfortable using Aristotle's terminology and held Aquinas in high regard as an authority on theological themes.

One of the key figures in these developments, although he isn't mentioned in a lot of stories on this period, is Theodore Beza. He was a Calvinist theologian and was quite active, writing profusely. Beza's New Testament went through five editions during his lifetime. In 1556 he published an annotated Latin translation of the New Testament, adding the Greek text in 1565. The work was intended to replace Eramus's Greek text, Latin translation, and annotations which Beza considered doctrinally and textually unsound.

Beza, an aristocratic Frenchman, who was only ten years younger than Calvin, outlived him by forty years and was widely regarded as the great man's natural successor. It was Beza, rather than Calvin, who was regarded by most Reformed theologians of the seventeenth century as *the* theological authority, and he was especially good at recasting the terminology of Aristotle and the medieval scholastics in disputing with his opponents, both Lutheran and Catholic. It was Beza who defined the doctrine of predestination and its role in the Reformed theology.

The Church of England

During this time of adjustment and search for definition, the church which played a great part in the formation of the American colonies was growing in the British Isles. The Anglican Church held a peculiar position in the midst of these church developments. Historically, it was a Protestant church, created in the 1530s when King Henry VIII essentially took control of the existing Catholic Church in England. The Lutheran sympathies of its advisers, such as Thomas Cranmer and Thomas Cromwell, had influenced the new church, but the Catholic tendencies of the later monarchs such as Charles I and churchmen such as William Laud had their effect also.

They fought over a number of things, such as the Prayer Book, switching from episcopacy to Presbyterianism, not to mention the long list of monarchs who took control of the church. Each one had their own leanings. One may favor the Roman Catholic while the next might claim the Protestant mantle.

The main thing that led to the numbers of citizens to flee to the Netherlands and later to America was the persecution of those who didn't adhere to the central Church's control. There was no opportunity to freely choose your own way to worship.

Exploration

During this period, some very important things were happening in the other parts of the world. Actually, a new world was being carved out of the wilderness. The European countries had burst into a very competitive quest for God, glory and gold. They had developed a thirst for exploration and the possible bounties that lay in the uncharted areas of the world. Adventurers such as Marco Polo had been to places such as Cathay (China), and they brought tales of riches and also spices, dyes, rugs, and silk. The only thing keeping everyone from running to these distant foreign lands to bring the bounty back was it required very long treks over land routes. Along the way they could expect to encounter bandits, and demands of tribute or exorbitant taxes from the rulers of the many lands they must cross.

Everyone was excited by the prospects, but the costs and perils made it almost impossible to pursue them. The answer had to be by way of the oceans. Sailing and shipbuilding methods had been progressing rapidly around the beginning of the tenth century, primarily because of the Arabs' development of the astrolabe. This was a device with a pivoted limb that established the sun's altitude above the horizon. During the tenth century, the technology made it to Spain.[2]

Meanwhile the Vikings to the north had been advancing new methods of hull construction for their boats. By overlapping the planks for internal support, they were able to withstand the violent storms sometimes encountered at sea. The sailors of the Hanseatic League states had been experimenting with larger ship designs that incorporated sternpost rudders for better control. Thanks to the Italian seamen generating more accurate maps, the pieces were falling into place to encourage long-distance voyages. A new generation of explorers was now equipped and ready for the opportunities that the various monarchs were eager to support.[3]

In addition, the Protestant Reformation fostered a fierce and bloody competition for power and territory between Catholic and Protestant nations. England competed for land with Spain, not just for economic and political reasons, but because the English feared the possibility that Spain might catholicize numbers of non-Christians in new lands, whereas Catholics feared the prospect of subjecting natives to Protestants heresies. For these reasons, even though the economic or political gains of discovery and colonization may have been marginal, monarchs had strong religious incentives to open their royal treasuries and support these missions.

Portugal and Spain had a very sharp competition going on for exploration. Ironically, Portugal's king had refused to support Christopher Columbus. Now, in August of 1492, Columbus departed from Spain, laying a course due west. A native of Genoa, Italy, Columbus represented the finest combination of the new group of navigators. He was bold and confident that he knew what he was after and was capable of completing his quest. Like anyone, he wanted glory, and after being denied an opportunity before, he was motivated by a sort of desperation to prove himself. At the same time, he was "earnestly desirous of taking Christianity to heathen lands."[4] Contrary to an old and often repeated story, he didn't originate the theory that the earth was round. Many people of the era thought the same way. He was the first to test the theory.

As we know, he took three boats, the *Nina*, the *Pinta*, and the *Santa Maria* with a crew of ninety men. They set sail in August 1492 with the plan of sailing to Japan. There was some anxiety and doubt amongst the crew after ten weeks, but Columbus managed to keep them together. At last on October 11, 1492, the weary, but excited crew began to see pieces of wood covered with barnacles, green bulrushes, and other vegetation.[5] The lookout spotted land, and on October 12, 1492, the courageous band walked ashore on Watling Island in the Bahamas, where the men begged Columbus's pardon for doubting him.[6]

Columbus then sailed on to Cuba, which he called Hispaniola. He thought he had actually reached the Far East, and described the dark-skinned people he found in Hispaniola as Indians. He found them to be "very well-formed, with handsome bodies and good faces," and hoped to convert them 'to our Holy Faith by love rather than by force' by giving them red caps and glass beads 'and many other things of small value.'"[7] He dispatched emissaries into the interior to contact the

Great Khan, but they returned with no reports of spices, jewels, silks, or other evidence of Cathay; nor did the Khan send his regards. In spite of these disappointments, Columbus returned to Spain confident he had found an ocean passage to the Orient.[8]

Columbus was gradually forced to face the reality the he had not reached India or China, and after a second voyage in 1493—still convinced he was in the Pacific Ocean—he admitted he had stumbled on a new landmass, perhaps even a new continent of astounding natural resources and wealth. In February 1493, he wrote his Spanish patrons that Hispaniola and all the other islands like it were "fertile to an endless degree," possessing mountains covered by "trees of a thousand kinds and tall, so that they seem to touch the sky."[9] He confidently promised gold, cotton, spices—as much as Their Highnesses should command—in return for only minimal continued support. Meanwhile, he continued to probe the *Mundus Novus* south and west. After returning to Spain, Columbus made two more voyages to the New World in 1498 and 1502.

Whether Columbus had found a route to the Far East or a whole new land was not as important to most Europeans as the political events of the day. Spain had just accomplished the eviction of the Muslims after the long Reconquista, and England's Wars of the Roses had scarcely ended. Only a few merchant explorers and dreamers were focused on Columbus's discoveries. The prospect of finding a water passage to Asia still infatuated sailors, however, and in 1501 a Florentine passenger on a Portuguese voyage, by the name of Amerigo Vespucci, wrote letters to his friends describing a New World.

His self-promoting letters circulated quicker than Columbus's written accounts and, as a result, the name *America* became the term geographers attached to the lands in the western hemisphere that should rightfully have been called Columbia.

But even though Columbus received only a relatively small monetary reward and little name recognition except the title from Spain of "Admiral of the Ocean Sea," he had someone who would take care of the historical register. Historian Samuel Eliot Morison, a worthy seaman in his own right, who reenacted the Columbian voyages in 1939 and 1940, described Columbus as "the sign and symbol [of the] new age of hope, glory and accomplishment."[10]

It was said of Columbus that, "He came as a religious man, an admiral of Christ, to find the continent, not for its material treasures, but because it held souls which he wished to bring as a trophy to the feet of Christ."[11]

Benjamin F. Morris had a much more detailed story to tell of Columbus:

> A deep religious feeling mingled with his meditations and gave them at times a tinge of superstition, but it was of a sublime and lofty kind. He looked upon it as being in the hand of Heaven, chosen from among men for the accomplishment of its high purpose; he read, as he supposed, his contemplated discoveries foretold in the mystic revelations of the prophets. The ends of the earth were to be brought together, and all nations and tongues and languages united under the banner of the Redeemer. This was to be the triumphant consummation of his enterprise, bringing the unknown regions of the earth into communion with Christian Europe—carrying the light of the true faith into benighted and pagan lands, and gathering their countless nations under the holy dominion of the Church. One of his principal objects was undoubtedly the propagation of the Christian faith. Columbus now considered himself about to effect this great work—to spread the light of revelation to the very ends of the earth, and thus to be the instrument of accomplishing one of the sublime predictions of Holy Writ.
>
> Whenever he made any great discovery, he celebrated it by solemn thanks to God. The voice of prayer and melody of praise rose from his ship when they first beheld the New World, and his first act on landing

> was to prostrate himself upon the earth and return thanksgiving. All his great enterprises were undertaken in the name of the Holy Trinity, and he partook of the communion before his embarkation. His conduct was characterized by the grandeur of his views and the magnanimity of his spirit. Instead of scouring the newly found countries, like a grasping adventurer, eager only for immediate gain, as was too general with contemporaneous discoverers, he sought to ascertain their soil and productions, their rivers and harbors: he was desirous of colonizing and cultivating them, conciliating and civilizing the natives, introducing the useful arts, subjecting everything to the control of law, order, and religion, and thus of founding regular and prosperous empires.
>
> In his will, Columbus enjoins on his son Diego, or whoever might inherit after him, "to spare no pains in having and maintaining in the island of Hispaniola four good professors of theology, to the end and aim of their studying and laboring to convert to our holy faith the inhabitants of the Indias; and, in proportion as by God's will the revenue of the estate shall increase, in the same degree shall the number of teachers and devout persons increase, who are to strive to make Christians of the natives."[12]

Noah Webster had this view of Columbus:

> The great epitaph, commemorative of the character and the worth, the discoveries and the glory of Columbus, was that he had given a new world to the crowns of Castile and Aragon. This is a great mistake. It does not come up to all the great merits of Columbus. He gave the territory of the Southern hemisphere to the crowns of Castile and Aragon; but, as a place for the plantation of colonies, as a place for the habitation of men, a place to which laws and religion, and manners and science,

were to be transferred, as a place where the creatures of God should multiply and fill the earth under friendly skies and with religious hearts, he gave it to the whole world, he gave it to universal man!

From this seminal principle, and from a handful, a hundred saints, blessed of God and ever honored of men, landed on the shores of Plymouth and elsewhere along the coast, united with the settlement of Jamestown, has sprung this great people.[13]

Notes

1. Jonathan Hill, History of Christianity, also called Zondervan, Handbook of Christianity, Grand Rapids (Lion Publishing (2006) 206-210.
2. Eric L. Jones, *The European Miracle* (Cambridge, MA: Cambridge University Press, 1981).
3. James Burke, *Connections* (Boston: Little, Brown, 1978), 122-23. Carlo Cipolla, *Guns, Sails and Empires: Technological Innovations and the Early Phases of European Expansion, 1400-1700* (New York: Pantheon Books, 1965).
4. Esmond Wright, *The Search for Liberty: From Origins to Independence* (Oxford: Blackwell, 1995), 15.
5. Christopher Columbus, *The Diario of Christopher Columbus's First Voyage to America, 1492-1493*, abstracted by Fray Bartolome de Las Casas, trans. Oliver Dunn and James E. Kelley, Jr. (Norman, OK: University of Oklahoma Press, 1989), 57-69, entry for October 11, 1492.
6. Oliver Perry Chitwood, *A History of Colonial America,* 3rd edition (New York: Harper & Row, 1961 [1931]), 24.
7. Columbus, *Diario,* 57-59.
8. Howard Zinn, *A People's History of the United States* (New York: Harper & Row, 1992, 7-11.
9. Christopher Columbus, *The Journal of Christopher Columbus,* trans. Cecil Jane (New York: Clarkson N. Potter, 1960), 191-201.

10. Samuel Eliot Morison, *Admiral of the Ocean Sea: A Life of Christopher Columbus* (Boston: Little, Brown, 1942), 5.
11. Benjamin F. Morris, *The Christian Life and Character of the Civil Institutions of the United States* (Powder Springs, GA: American Vision, Inc., 2007), 58.
12. Ibid., 58-59.
13. Ibid., 59-60.

CHAPTER 2

Colonization

"The whole of the sixteenth century was a period of active preparation for future times, and all that is great in modern science and art may be said to have received its foundation in the agitations that grew out of that period of the world. The twelve decades, from 1480 to 1600, form one of the grandest and richest eras in the history of humanity. It was in that period that the foundation of our liberty was laid—in that period that it became sure that this would be a land of civil and religious freedom. England during all that time was a great laboratory in which these principles were brought out; and from the views which prevailed at the time of Henry VII, and which had prevailed for ages, it required one whole century to advance the world to that position which was maintained by Pym and Hampden and Milton, and was seen in the principles of Winthrop, Robinson, and Brewster, of George Calvert, Roger Williams, and William Penn. Scarcely anything has occurred in history which is more remarkable or which has been more certainly indicative of the designs of Providence."[1]

Under the convictions of a strong Christian faith, the Puritans, in 1608, bade farewell to England, where they had been persecuted for their pure faith and simple forms of Christian worship, and emigrated to Holland, where they hoped to find a permanent asylum. The love of country; the ties of home and kindred; the prospect of suffering, trials, and unnumbered privations, did not deter them from this Christian enterprise: "For their desires were set on the ways of God, and to enjoy his ordinances. But they rested on his providence, and knew whom they had believed."[2]

Webster puts it this way:

> The embarkation of the Pilgrims for Holland . . . is deeply interesting from its circumstances, and also as a mark of the character of the times, independently of its connection with names now incorporated with the history of empires. Theirs was not the flight of guilt, but virtue. It was a humble and peaceable religion flying from causeless oppression. It was conscience attempting to escape from the arbitrary rule of the Stuarts. It was Robinson and Brewster leading off their little band from their native soil, at first to find a shelter on the shores of a neighboring continent, but ultimately to come to a new land, and, having surmounted all difficulties and braved a thousand dangers, to find here a place of refuge and rest. Thanks be to God that this spot was honored as the asylum of religious liberty! May its standard, reared here, remain forever! May it rise as high as heaven, till its banner shall fan the air of both continents, and wave as a glorious ensign of peace and prosperity to the nations![3]

Voyage to the New World

After remaining in Holland twelve years, the Puritans resolved to seek rest and enlargement, and to fulfill their Christian mission by immigrating to the North American continent. They had, as they affirmed, "a great hope and inward zeal of laying some good foundation, or at least to make some way, for the propagating and advancing of the kingdom of Christ unto those remote parts of the world; yea, though they should be but as stepping-stones unto others for performing so great a work."

The farewell scenes are described by Governor Bradford, of the colony, as follows:

So, being ready to depart, they had a day of solemn humiliation with their pastor—taking his text from Ezra 8: 21, "I proclaimed a fast there, at the river Ahava, that we might afflict ourselves before God, and seek of him a right way for our little ones and our substance"; upon which he spent a part of the day profitably, and very suitably to their present occasion. The rest of the time was spent in pouring out their prayers to the Lord with great fervency, mixed with abundance of tears. And the time being come when they must depart, they were accompanied with most of their brethren out of the city unto a town sundry miles off, called Delft Haven, where the ship lay ready to receive them. So they left that good and pleasant city, which had been their resting-place near twelve years. But they knew they were Pilgrims, and looked not much on those things, but lifted up their eyes to heaven, their dearest country, and so quieted their spirits. When they came to the ship, and all things ready, and such of their friends as could not come with them followed after them, and sundry also came from Amsterdam to see them shipped and to take their leave of them.

"Little sleep was there to most of them that night. Friendly entertainment, Christian discourse, and expressions of deep affection in parting," held their eyes waking. "Never," says Winslow, "I persuade myself, never people on earth lived more lovingly together, and parted more sweetly, than we, the church of Leyden, . . . seeking, not rashly, but deliberately, the mind of God in prayer, and finding his gracious presence with us, and his blessing upon us."

The next day—July 22, 1620—the wind being fair, they went on board, and their friends with them; "when truly doleful was the sight of that sad and mournful parting; to see what sighs, and sobs, and prayers, did sound amongst them; what tears did gush from every

> eye, and pithy speeches pierced each other's heart;—that sundry of the Dutch strangers that stood on the quay as spectators could not refrain from tears. Yet comfortable and sweet it was to see such lively and true expressions of dear and unfeigned love. But the tide, which stays for no man, calling them away that were thus loth to depart, their reverend pastor, falling down upon his knees, and they all with him, with watered cheeks commended them with most fervent prayers to the Lord and his blessing; and then, with mutual embraces and many tears, they took leave of one another, which proved their last leave to many of them."[4]

Before they sailed, on the deck of the ship, their pastor, John Robinson, gave them the following farewell charge:

> Brethren, we are now quickly to part from one another; and whether I ever live to see your faces on earth any more, the God of heaven only knows; but whether the Lord has appointed that or no, I charge you, before God and his blessed angels, that you follow me no further than you have seen me follow the Lord Jesus Christ. If God reveals anything to you by any other instrument of his, be as ready to receive it as ever you were to receive any truth by my ministry, for I am verily persuaded the Lord has more truth yet to break forth from his Holy Word. I charge you to take heed what you receive as truth; examine it, consider it, and compare it with the scriptures of truth before you receive it.[5]

The farewell scenes closed, and they set sail for the shores of the New World:

> "That embarkation," says Choate, "speaks to the nation as with the voices and melodies of an immortal hymn, which dilates and becomes actualized into the auspicious going forth of a colony whose planting has changed

> the history of the world—a noble colony of devoted Christians—educated, firm men, valiant soldiers, and honorable women—a colony on the commencement of whose heroic enterprise the selectest influences of religion seemed to be descending visibly, and beyond whose perilous path was hung the rainbow and the western star of empire."[6]

Webster says:

> The *Mayflower* sought our shores . . . under no high-wrought spirit of commercial adventure, no love of gold, no mixture of purpose warlike or hostile to any human being. Like the dove from the ark, she had put forth only to find rest. Solemn supplications on the shore of the sea in Holland had invoked for her, at her departure, the blessings of Providence. The stars which guided her were the unobscured constellations of civil and religious liberty. Her deck was the altar of the living God. Fervent prayers on bended knees mingled morning and evening with the voices of the ocean and the sighing of the winds in her shrouds. Every prosperous breeze, which, gently filling her sails, helped the Pilgrims onward in their course, awoke new anthems of praise; and when the elements were wrought into fury, neither the tempest, tossing their fragile bark like a feather, nor the darkness and howling of the midnight storm, ever disturbed, in man or woman, the firm and settled purpose of their souls to undergo all and to do all that the meekest patience, the boldest resolution, and the highest trust in God could enable human beings to endure or to perform.
>
> That *Mayflower* was a flower destined to be of perpetual bloom! Its verdure will stand the sultry blasts of summer and the chilling winds of autumn. It will defy winter; it will defy all climate, and all time, and will

> continue to spread its petals to the world, and to exhale an ever-living odor and fragrance to the last syllable of recorded time.[7]

On the 16th of September, 1620, they set sail from Southampton and, after a stormy and perilous voyage, they fell in with land on the American coast on the 9th of November, "the which being made and certainly known to be it, they were not a little joyful. On their voyage they would set apart whole days of fasting and prayer, to obtain from heaven a good success in their voyage, especially when the weather was much against them, whereunto they had remarkable answers; so much so that the sailors were astonished, and said they were the first sea-fasts ever held in the world."[8]

Arrival at Plymouth Rock

On the 22nd of December, 1620, the Puritans, 101 in number, landed from the *Mayflower* and planted their feet on the Rock of Plymouth, and began a new era in the history of the world. The day and the rock became canonized in American history, and emblems of the grandest Christian ideas and associations.

The first act of the Puritans, after landing, was to kneel down and offer their thanksgiving to God, and by a solemn act of prayer, and in the name and for the sake of Christ, to take possession of the continent. They thus repeated the Christian consecration which Columbus, more than a century before, had given to the New World, and so twice in the most formal and solemn manner was it devoted to Christ and Christian civilization. The seed thus planted bore an abundant harvest of Christian fruits, which have blessed the nation and enriched the world. How significant and sublime the lessons that gather round and flow from Plymouth Rock! How does it speak for God and of God! How grandly does it proclaim the Christian faith and fruits of those great and good men who, in prayer and faith, planted a Christian empire in the New World, and started a Christian nation on a noble career of progress and greatness![9]

English historian Thomas Macaulay said of the Puritans:

The Puritans were men whose minds derived a peculiar character from the daily contemplation of superior beings and eternal interests. Not content with acknowledging in general terms an overruling Providence, they habitually ascribed every event to that great Being for whose power nothing was too vast, for whose inspection nothing was too minute. To know him, to serve him, to enjoy him, was with them the great end of existence. They rejected with contempt the ceremonious homage which other sects substituted for the worship of the soul. Instead of catching occasional glimpses of the Deity through an obscuring veil, they aspired to gaze full on the intolerable brightness, and to commune with him face to face. Hence originated their contempt for terrestrial distinctions. The difference between the greatest and meanest of mankind seemed to vanish when compared with the boundless interval which separated the whole race from Him on whom their own eyes were constantly fixed.

They recognized no title to superiority but God's favor; and, confident of that favor, they despised all the accomplishments and all the dignities of the world. If they were unacquainted with the works of philosophers and poets, they were deeply read in the oracles of God. If their names were not found in the registers of heralds, they felt assured that they were recorded in the book of life. Their palaces were houses not made with hands; their diadems, crowns of glory which should not fade away. On the rich and the eloquent, on nobles and priests, they looked down with (comparative) contempt; for they esteemed themselves rich in more precious treasures, and eloquent in a more sublime language; nobles by the right of an earlier creation, and priests by the imposition of a mightier hand. The very meanest of them was a being to whose fate a mysterious and terrible importance belonged—on whose slightest action the spirits of light and darkness

> looked with anxious interest—who had been destined, before heaven and earth were created, to enjoy a felicity when heaven and earth should pass away. For his sake the Almighty had proclaimed his will by the pen of the evangelist and the harp of the prophet. He had been rescued by no common deliverer from the grasp of no common foe. He had been ransomed by the sweat of no vulgar agony, by the blood of no earthly sacrifice. It was for him the sun had been darkened, that the rocks had been rent, that the dead had arisen, that all nature had shuddered at the sufferings of an expiring God.
>
> Thus the Puritan was made of two different men: the one all self-abasement, penitence, gratitude, passion; the other, stern, calm, inflexible, sagacious. He prostrated himself in the dust before his Maker, but set his foot on the neck of his king. In his devotional retirement, he prayed with groans and tears; but when he took his seat in the council, or girt on his sword for war, these workings of the soul had left no perceptible trace behind them. The intensity of their feelings on one subject made them tranquil on all others.[10]

Webster says, "Our fathers had that religious sentiment, that trust in Providence, that determination to do right, and to seek, through every degree of toil and suffering, the honor of God, and the preservation of their liberties, which we shall do well to cherish, to imitate, to equal, to the utmost of our ability."[11]

As a tribute to this original settlement in the New England area, we find this:

> "On the rocky summit overlooking the bay where the *Mayflower* first anchored, a magnificent monument has been erected. That colossal statue is at once a miracle, a parable, and a prophecy—a miracle of artistic genius, a parable of Christian civilization, and a prophecy of increasing national glory. On the corners of the pedestal

are four figures in a sitting posture—representing Law, Morality, Freedom, and Education. Standing far above, on the lofty shaft of granite, is a majestic figure symbolizing Faith, holding an open Bible in one hand, and, with the other uplifted, pointing far away to the throne of God. What a sublime conception! How true to the facts of our heroic history! That open Bible is the Magna Charta of America, and that uplifted hand, symbolizing trust in the God of our fathers, is the condition of our national stability and continued prosperity."[12]

Notes

1. Benjamin F. Morris, *The Christian Life and Character of the Civil Institutions of the United States* (Powder Springs, GA: American Vision, Inc., 2007), 57.
2. Ibid., 62.
3. Ibid., 62-63.
4. Ibid., 63-64.
5. Ibid., 64-65.
6. Ibid., 65.
7. Ibid., 65-66.
8. Ibid., 66.
9. Ibid.
10. Ibid., 67-69.
11. Ibid., 69.
12. Charles B. Galloway, *Christianity and the American Commonwealth* (Powder Springs, GA: American Vision, Inc., 2005), 72

CHAPTER 3

A Surviving Colony

The Massachusetts colony had landed in the wrong place. They were in a no-man's-land outside the reach of the government and the laws of England, so they knew they must establish some formal plan for operating as a community. The men, other than the ship's crew, were assembled in the cabin and drew up what served as their constitution. This is an excerpt from the document:

> The Mayflower Compact: In the name of God, Amen. We whose names are underwritten . . . having undertaken, for the glory of God, and advancement of the Christian faith, and honor of our king and country, a voyage to plant the first colony in the northern parts of Virginia, do by these presents solemnly and mutually in the presence of God . . . covenant and combine ourselves together into a civil body politic . . . and by virtue hereof to enact, constitute, and frame such just and equal laws . . . as shall be thought most meet and covenant for the general good of the Colony, unto which we promise all due submission and obedience. In witness whereof we have hereunder subscribed our names.[1]

After the Compact was signed, John Carver was elected governor of the colony, but died a year later. William Bradford was elected to replace him and served for almost thirty years. Cotton Mather, a clergyman and eminent figure in the colony wrote of Bradford, "Latin and Greek he mastered, but the Hebrew he studied most of all. Because, he said he would see with his own eyes the ancient oracles of God in their native beauty . . . . But the crown of all was, his holy, prayerful, watchful, and fruitful walk with God, wherein he was exemplary."[2]

Of the 102 *Mayflower* colonists, 51 died during the first winter, mostly from what Bradford called "the general sickness." He had exclaimed, "What could sustain us in this winter season . . . but the Spirit of God and His grace?"[3] When winter had passed and the *Mayflower* returned to England, not one colonist returned with it.

The work required of those early settlers was demanding, arduous, and time-consuming. They had to make their own lumber for the building of their houses. They had to plant and tend crops, tend the livestock, make their own furniture, sew their own clothes. They had to fashion a lot of their own tools and other household and farming necessities. They had to teach their own children. And they faithfully observed the Sabbath. It takes a while to wrap your mind around all that, doesn't it?

Here is an excerpt from the book, *The Descendants of William Lamson of Ipswich, Massachusetts (1634-1917)*:

> The strict observance of the Sabbath was perhaps the most striking characteristic of this colony and of others of its time. Work ceased on Saturday at three o'clock, and the rest of the day was spent in learning the catechism and preparing for the Sabbath. The morning of the Sabbath was begun by home worship, and then at nine o'clock the meetinghouse bell summoned every citizen to public service, only the sick and disabled being excused. The meetinghouse was a crude, humble structure, built with logs chinked with clay or moss, with a thatched roof. It was surrounded by a stone wall or fort for protection against sudden attack by Indians. Every man above eighteen years of age brought his firearms to church, and sentinels paced their beat outside during service. There were no pews, only

> benches, and the men and women sat on different sides of the aisle . . . . The service was long and solemn.
>
> About two in the afternoon a second service was begun, followed by the baptism of children, which was an important ceremony, as Puritan babies were invariably taken to church for baptism on the first Sunday after birth, no matter how inclement the weather. At sunset the Sabbath was ended.
>
> Stern and forbidding as that old worship appears at the present day, yet beneath it all we discover that simple, unswerving fidelity to Conscience, and the Bible which compelled those men to make their Sabbath what it was. In that rugged spiritual soil were planted the seeds of a religious character which has exerted its influence on all their descendants, and we cannot help reverencing and respecting them for their consistency.[4]

After the Plymouth colony was established, people from England began to swarm to the new colony. In 1630 five ships, carrying nine hundred passengers ported at Massachusetts Bay. John Winthrop was governor. He preached a long sermon during the two-month voyage called, "A Model of Christian Charity." He focused on the tenets of Jesus Christ's teaching that should be applied in the everyday life of the people. Here is a portion of his closing remarks:

> The end is to improve our lives to do more service to the Lord . . . . We are entered into a covenant with Him to do this work . . . . We must delight in each other, make each other's condition our own, rejoice together, mourn together, labor together, suffer together . . . so shall we keep the unity of spirit in the bond of peace. The Lord will be our God and delight to dwell among us . . . . We must consider that we shall be as a city upon a hill. The eyes of all people are upon us.[5]

In just ten years, the population of the Massachusetts Bay colony rose to sixteen thousand. The people realized the need for schools and churches if the Christian purpose was to be accomplished. In 1636, the Massachusetts legislature authorized the establishment of a college, and two years later Harvard College began enrolling students. The purpose was "to train a literate clergy."[6]

In 1642, Harvard published "The Rules and Precepts" governing student life. Here is an excerpt:

> Let every student be plainly instructed, and earnestly pressed to . . . consider well the main end of his life and studies is to know God and Jesus Christ which is eternal life (John 17:3), and therefore to lay Christ in the bottom as the only foundation of all sound knowledge and learning.[7]

The centrality of Christianity in Harvard's deliberations was evident in the dismissal of its first president, Henry Dunster. He "was forced to resign . . . indicted, tried, convicted and publicly admonished for opposing the church ordinance on infant baptism."[8]

For many years, most of the Congressional ministers in New England were Harvard graduates. In 1642, the legislature threatened town leaders with fines if they did not see that all children were educated about the laws and the Christian religion. It is not surprising that the first English language book published in North America was religious. *The Whole Book of Psalms Faithfully Translated into English Meter* appeared in 1640. It was so much in demand that there were twenty editions of it and seventy printings. Below the title was printed, "Whereunto is prefixed a discourse declaring not only the lawfulness, but also the necessity of the heavenly Ordinance of singing Scripture Psalms in the churches of God."

The majority of settlers that had come to the New England section of America were Puritans, and they had fled the oppression of the Church of England. They still hoped to be able to reform the Church rather than defect from it. The population grew rapidly, and other colonies were established. In 1643 the colonies of Massachusetts, Connecticut, Plymouth, and New Hampshire joined into the United Colonies of New England for protection against Indian attacks and to provide a united front against the growing Dutch settlements in New York. Their devotion to Christianity had caused them to come to the New World and was the continuing influence in New England well into the future. Church historian Mark Noll wrote:

> At the heart of the Puritan experiment in New England was the weekly gathering in church for worship, fellowship and instruction . . . . Because the sermon was the common form of communication in colonial New England, its history is in many ways the history of New England . . . . Most New Englanders who lived a full life would have heard seven thousand sermons (averaging nearly two hours each).[9]

Here are two examples of the religious dedication:

> We celebrated Mass . . . . We took on our shoulders a great cross, which we had hewn out of a tree, and advancing in order to the appointed place, with the assistance of the Governor and his associates . . . we erected a trophy to Christ the Savior. *Father White, an original colonist of Maryland, upon arrival on March 25, 1634.*[10]

> Our end in leaving our native country is not to gain riches and honor, but singly this: to live wholly to the glory of God. *Declaration made by the original settlers of Georgia in 1732.*[11]

In the colonies of Virginia, (mostly Church of England), Maryland (Catholic and Church of England), Pennsylvania (many denominations including Quaker, Mennonite, Baptist, Presbyterian, Lutheran, Calvinist, Dutch Reformed, and German Reformed), and in New York (Dutch Reformed and Calvinist), the religious intensity was generally less than in the Puritan colonies. But in the eighteenth century, Christianity's claim on all the colonies was evident when revivalist movements spread among all the colonies until after the Civil War. The synod of the New England churches met at Cambridge, Massachusetts, September 30, 1648, and defined the nature of civil government, the functions of the civil magistrate, and the duties of the citizens as follows:

> I. God, the Supreme Lord and King of all the world, hath ordained civil magistrates to be under him, over the people, and for his own glory and the public good; and to this end hath armed them with the power of the sword for the defence and encouragement of them that do well, and for the punishment of evil doers.
>
> II. It is lawful for Christians to accept and execute the office of magistrate when called thereunto. In the management thereof, as they ought especially to maintain piety, justice and peace, according to the wholesome laws of each Commonwealth, so for that end they may lawfully now, under the New Testament, wage war on just and necessary occasions.
>
> III. They who, upon pretence of Christian liberty, shall oppose any lawful power, or the lawful exercises of it, resist the ordinances of God; and for their publishing of those opinions or maintaining of such practices as are contrary to the light of nature, or the known principles of Christianity, or to the power of godliness, or such erroneous opinions and practices as either in their own nature, or in the manner of publishing or maintaining them, are destructive to the external peace and order which Christ hath established in the church, they may be called to account and proceeded against by the censure of the church and by the power of the civil magistrate; yet in such differences about the doctrines of the gospel,

> or the ways of the worship of God, as may befall men exercising a good conscience, manifesting it in their conversation, and holding the foundation and duly observing the rules of peace and order, there is no warrant in the magistrate to abridge them of their liberty. From which ecclesiastical persons are not exempted; much less has the Pope any power or jurisdiction over them in their dominions, or over any of their people; and least of all to deprive them of their dominions and lives, if he shall judge them to be heretics, or upon other pretext whatsoever.[12]

Cotton Mather, in his work on New England, makes the following statements concerning the motives and reasons the Puritans had for coming to the New World:

> The God of heaven served, as it were, a summons upon the spirits of his people in the English nation, stirring up the spirits of thousands which never saw the faces of each other, with a most unanimous inclination to leave the pleasant accommodations of their native country, and go over a terrible ocean into a more terrible desert, for the pure enjoyment of all his ordinances. It is now fit that the reasons for this undertaking should be more exactly made known unto posterity; especially unto the posterity of those who were the undertakers, lest they come at length to forget and neglect the true interests of New England. Wherefore I shall transcribe some of them from a manuscript wherein they were tendered unto consideration.
>
> First. It will be a service unto the church of great consequence, to carry the gospel into those parts of the world and raise a bulwark against the kingdom of the Antichrist, which the Jesuits labor to rear up in all parts of the world.

Second. All other churches of Europe have been brought under desolations; and it may be feared that the like judgments are coming upon us; and who knows but God has provided this place to be a refuge for many whom he means to save out of the general destruction?

Thirdly. The land grows weary of her inhabitants, inasmuch that man, which is the most precious of all creatures, is here (in Europe) more vile and base than the earth he treads upon. Children, neighbors and friends, especially the poor, are counted the greatest burdens; which, if things were right, would be counted the chiefest of earthly blessings.

Fourthly. We are grown to that intemperance in all excess of riot, as no mean establishment will suffice a man to keep sail with his equals, and he that fails in it must live in scorn and contempt. Hence it comes to pass that all arts and trades are carried in that deceitful manner and unrighteous course, as it is almost impossible for a good, upright man to maintain his constant charge and live comfortably in them.

Fifthly. The schools of learning and religion are so corrupted as (beside the unsupportable charge of education) most children, even the best, wittiest, and of the fairest hopes, are perverted, corrupted and utterly overthrown by the multitudes of evil examples and licentious behavior in these seminaries.

Sixthly. The whole earth is the Lord's garden, and he hath given it to the sons of Adam, to be tilled and improved by them; why then should we stand starving here for places of habitation, and in the meantime suffer whole countries, as profitable for the use of man, to be waste without improvement

> Seventhly. What can be better and nobler work, and more worthy of a Christian, than to erect and support a reformed particular church in its infancy, and unite our forces with such a company of faithful people, as by timely assistance may grow stronger and prosper, but for want of it may be put to great hazards, if not wholly ruined?
>
> Eightly. If any such are known to be godly, and live in wealth and prosperity here, shall forsake all this to join with this reformed church, and with it run the hazard of a hard and mean condition, it will be an example of great use, both for removing of scandal and to give more life unto the faith of God's people in their prayers for the plantation, and also to encourage others to join the more willingly in it.[13]

In 1629, an Emigrant Aid Society was formed in England to promote the more rapid settlement of the North American Colonies; and in the instructions of John Endicott, who was to be in charge of the emigration, it is declared that the purpose is:

> "for propagating of the gospel in these things we do profess ABOVE ALL to be our ayme in settling this plantacion."
>
> "In 1643, a confederation between the colonies Massachusetts, New Plymouth, Connecticut, and New Haven was formed, in which it is affirmed that "wee all came into these parts of America with the same end and ayme, namely, to advance the Kingdom of our Lord Jesus Christ, and to enjoy the liberties thereof with puritie and peace, and for preserving and propagating the truth and liberties of the gospel."
>
> In the charter granted to Massachusetts, in 1640, by Charles I, the colonies are enjoined by "their good life and conversation to winne and invite the natives of the

> country to the knowledge of the only true God and savior of mankind and the Christian faith which, in our royal intention and the adventurer's free possession, is the principal end of this plantation.[14]

In 1658, John Eliot, pastor of Roxbury, Massachusetts, and afterwards a devoted and distinguished missionary, completed the translation of the entire Bible, including the Old and New Testaments, for the use of the Indians. This fact having been communicated to the corporation established in London for the propagation of the gospel among the Indians of New England, the body declared, that 'wee conceive' (the printing of the work) will not only be acceptable unto God, but very profitable to the poor heathen, and will much tend to the promotion of the spiritual part of this worke amongst them. And therefore wee offer it not only as our owne, but as the judgment of others, that the New Testament bee first printed in the Indian language."

The New Testament was, accordingly, printed at Cambridge, Massachusetts, in 1660; and its preface contained the following "Epistle Dedicatory":

> To the High and Mighty Prince, Charles the Second, by the Grace of God, King of *England, Scotland, France,* and *Ireland,* Defendre of the faith, &c. The Commissioners of the United Colonies in New England wish increase of all happiness, &c.
>
> The people of these four colonies (confederate for mutual defence in the time of the late distractions of our dear native country), your Majestie's natural born subjects, by the Favor and Grant of Your Royal Father and Grandfather of Famous Memory, put themselves upon this great and hazardous undertaking, of planting themselves at their own Charge in these remote ends of the Earth, that, without offence or provocation to our dear Brethren and Countrymen, we might enjoy the liberty to worship God, which our own Consciences informed us was not only Right, but Duty; As also

that we might (if it so pleased God) be instrumental to spread the light of the Gospel, the knowledge of the Son of God our Savior, to the poor barbarous Heathen, which by His late Majesty, in some of our patents, is declared to be His principle aim.

Our Errand hither hath been Endeavors and blessings; many of the wild *Indians* being taught, and understanding the Doctrine of the Christian Religion, and with much affection tending such Preachers are sent to teach them. Many of their Children are instructed to Write and Reade, and some of them have proceeded further, to attain the knowledge of the Latine and Greek tongues, and are brought up with our English youth in University learning. There are divers of them that can and do reade some parts of the Scripture, and some catechisms, which was formerly Translated into their own language, which hath occasioned the undertaking of a greater Work, *viz,*: The Printing of the whole Bible, which being Translated by a painful Labourer [Eliot] amongst them, who as desirous to see the Work accomplished in his dayes, hath already proceeded to the finishing of the New Testament, which we here humbly present to Your Majesty, for the first fruits and accomplishment of the Pious Design of your Royal Ancestors.

And we do most humbly beseech your Majesty, that a matter of so much Devotion and Piety, tending so much to the Honour of God, may Suffer no disappointment. As this Book was begun, and now finished, in the first Year of your Establishment; which doth not only presage the happy success of your Highness' Government, but will be a perpetual Monument, that, by your Majestic Favour, the Gospel of our Lord and Savour *Jesus Christ* was first made known to the Indians.[15]

Notes

1. John A. Howard, *Christianity: Lifeblood of America's Free Society* (Manitou Springs, CO: Summit Press, 2008), 30.
2. Daniel Marsh, *Unto the Generations* (New Canaan, CT: The Log House, 1968), 18.
3. Edwin Gaustad and Leigh Schmidt, *The Religious History of America* (San Francisco, CA: Harper, 2002), 52.
4. William J. Lamson, *Descendants of William Lamson of Ipswich, Massachusetts* (New York, NY: Tobias A. Wright, 1917), 33
5. William J. Federer, *God and Country: Encyclopedia of Quotations* (St. Louis, MO: Amerisearch, 2000), 214.
6. Tim LaHaye, *Faith of Our Founding Fathers* (Brentwood, TN: Wolgemuth & Hyatt, Publishers, Inc., 1987), 32.
7. Federer, *God and Country*, 281.
8. *Webster's Biographical Dictionary* (Springfield, MA: G. and C. Merriam Co., 1958), 453.
9. Mark A. Noll, *A History of Christianity in the United States and Canada* (Grand Rapids, MI: Eerdmans Publishing Co., 1992), 199.
10. David Barton, *The Myth of Separation* (Aledo, TX: Wallbuilder Press, 1991), 86.
11. Stephen K. McDowell and Mark A. Beliles, *America's Providential History* (Charlottesville, VA: Providence Press, 1988), 55.
12. Benjamin F. Morris, *The Christian Life and Character of the Civil Institutions of the United States* (Powder Springs, GA: American Vision, Inc., 2007), 73-74.
13. Ibid., 75-76.
14. Ibid., 76.
15. Ibid., 77-78.

ACTS, Chap. 9, &c.

Pub. by Hogg & Co. Paternoster row.

CHAPTER 4

The Coincidence of the Reformation and the Colonization of America

The history of the changing of the views of the church, the tremendous surge of Christianity, and the colonization of America all together is almost mind-boggling. When the Reformation started, people began an awakening to the knowledge of the freedoms they had lost to dictators and monarchs. The religious controversy of this period changed society as well as religion.

All the colonies, having been educated under the teachings of Christianity, were also indoctrinated into the knowledge of the principles of just civil governments as laid out in the civil systems of the Bible (specifically in Romans 13:1-7). The colonists then made its truths the cornerstone of all their institutions. We've seen that plainly in all the quotations from the last chapter. The fundamental doctrine of the men who planted each colony was that the legislation of the Bible must be supreme and universal. They rejected the idea that civil governments could be rightly instituted or wisely administered without Christianity.

We see in the beginnings of this country that once this system assumed the form of the Christian model and the order that it provided, the system grew into a greatly admired symmetry and completeness. The local democracies, including the townships, counties, and colonies, became the nurseries of freedom. The schools were models of learning, and the ring of freedom was everywhere.

> "The settlement of New England," said John Trumbull, "purely for the purposes of religion and the propagation of civil and religious liberty, is an event which has no parallel in the history of modern ages. The piety, self-denial, suffering, patience, perseverance and magnanimity of the first settlers of the country are without a rival. The happy and extensive consequences of the settlements which they made, and the sentiments which they were careful to propagate to their posterity, to the Church and to the world, admit of no description. They are still increasing, spreading wider and wider, and appear more and more important."[1]

Massachusetts, as an independent colony, was the first and the most memorable of the Puritan family by many accounts. Its Christian history and bold enunciation and vindication of the pure doctrines of Christianity and their incorporation into forms of civil government and social life is one of the most remarkable and instructive for the world to see.

The New England colonies had begun to grow, and the population had increased substantially by 1660, when Charles II rescinded the throne. They had all grown strong in Christian faith and their love for liberty, and they enjoyed the freedom from the despotic atmosphere of the king. So, naturally, when Charles II was restored to the throne in 1664, they feared their newfound freedom and rights would be taken from them.

The people from the Massachusetts colony sent a formal message to the king, stating their allegiance would be subject to him unless it came in conflict with their homage to Jesus Christ. It stated:

> Your servants are true men, fearing God and the king. We could not live without the public worship of God; and we, therefore, might enjoy divine worship, without

> human mixtures, we, not without tears, departed from our country, kindred, and fathers' houses. To enjoy our liberty, and to walk according to the faith and order of the gospel, was the cause of transporting ourselves, our wives, our little ones and our substance, choosing the pure Christian worship, with a good conscience, in this remote wilderness, rather than the pleasures of England with submission to the imposition of the hierarchy, to which we could not yield without an evil conscience.

This presentation of good faith and loyalty did not set well with Charles II, and he demanded they surrender their charter and with it their independence as a free Christian commonwealth. This encounter is a great example of a vindication of the axiom "resistance to tyrants is obedience to God." In their address they had also stated they were "resolved to act for the glory of God, and for the felicities of his people," and that "having now above thirty years enjoyed the privilege of government within themselves, as their undoubted right in the sight of God and man, to be governed by rulers of their own choosing, and laws of our own, is the fundamental privilege of our charter."

The colony's civil court, when convened for official business, spent a portion of each day in prayer—six elders praying, and a minister preaching a sermon. "We must," said they, "as well consider God's displeasure as the king's, the interest of ourselves and of God's things, as his majesty's prerogative; for our liberties are of concernment, and to be regarded as to preservation."

> "Religion," says Bancroft, "had been the motive of settlement; religion was now its counselor. The fervors of the most ardent devotion were kindled; a more than usually solemn form of religious observance was adopted; a synod of all the churches in Massachusetts was convened to inquire into the causes of the dangers to New England liberty, and the mode of removing the evils.
>
> "Submission," said they, "would be an offence against the majesty of Heaven. Blind obedience to the pleasure

> of the king cannot be without great sin, and incurring the high displeasure of the King of kings. Submission would be contrary unto that which has been the unanimous advice of the ministers, given after a solemn day of prayer. The ministers of God in New England have more of the spirit of John the Baptist in them, than now, when a storm hath overtaken them, to be reeds shaken with the wind. The priests were to be the first that set their foot in the water, and there to stand till the danger be past. Of all men, they should be an example to the Lord's people, of faith, courage, and constancy.
>
> "The civil liberties of New England are part of the inheritance of their fathers; and shall we give that inheritance away? Is it objected that we shall be exposed to great suffering? Better suffer than sin. It is better to trust the God of our fathers than to put confidence in princes. If we suffer because we dare not comply with the wills of men, against the will of God, we suffer in a good cause, and shall be accounted martyrs in the next generation and at the great day."

These words were spoken by solemn Christian men and showed the nature of the principles that guided them in all they did, regardless of the circumstances. They stood firm on their Christian faith and civil rights, and by doing so they demonstrated the inseparable union between Christianity and civil liberty. If only our people today understood that. These are the principles that maintained the heroism that sustained them in their fight for independence.

This Christian commonwealth declared that those "who should go about to subvert and destroy the Christian faith and religion by broaching and maintaining damnable heresies, as denying the immortality of the soul or the resurrection of the body, or denying that Christ gave himself a ransom for our sins, or shall deny the morality of the 4th Commandment, or shall deny the ordinance of the civil magistrate, shall be banished."

> "Were a council," said Wise, in 1669, "called of all the learned heads of the whole universe, could they dictate better laws and advise better measures for the acquirement of learning, the increase of virtue and good religion, than are in the royal province of Massachusetts? If we take a survey of the whole land, we shall find religion placed in the body politic as the soul in the body natural. That is, the whole soul is in the whole body while it is in every part."[2]

Colony of Connecticut

The aim of the crown and of the colonists in planting Connecticut was to establish and extend the reign of the Christian religion. For this purpose, the General Assembly of the Colony were instructed to govern the people "so as their good life and orderly conversation may win and invite the natives of the country to the knowledge and obedience of the only true God and Saviour of mankind, and the Christian faith; which, in our royal intentions and the adventurer's free possession, is the only and principal end of this plantation."

The first organization of civil society and government was made, in 1639, at Quinipiack, now the beautiful city of New Haven. The emigrants, men of distinguished piety and ability, met in a large barn, on the 4th of June, 1639, and, in a very formal and solemn manner, proceeded to lay the foundations of their civil and religious polity.

I know you are probably in a daze or a rage right now, depending on your own personal beliefs, at the unashamed way the colonists blended the church and government together. Well, that is just the way it was back then. Here is presented another blockbuster.

Government Instituted by the Church

The subject was introduced by a sermon from Mr. Davenport, the pastor, from the words of Solomon, "Wisdom hath builded her house, she hath hewn out her seven pillars" (Proverbs 9:1 KJV). After a solemn invocation to Almighty God, he proceeded to represent to the Plantation that they were met to consult respecting the setting up of civil government according to the will of God, and for the nomination of persons who, by universal consent, were in all respects the best qualified for the Foundation work of a church. He enlarged on the great importance of thorough action, and exhorted every man to give his vote in the fear of God. A constitution was formed, which was characterized as "the first example of a written constitution; as a distinct organic act, constituting a government and defining its powers." The preamble and resolutions connected with its formation are as follows:

> Forasmuch as it hath pleased the Almighty God, by the wise disposition of his divine providence, so to order and dispose of things that we, the inhabitants of Windsor, Hartford, and Wethersfield, are now cohabiting and dwelling in and upon the river of Connecticut, and the lands thereunto adjoining, and well knowing where a people are gathered together the word of God requireth that, to maintain the peace and union of such a people, there should be an orderly and decent government established according to God, to order and dispose of the affairs of the people at all seasons as occasion should require; do, therefore, associate and conjoin ourselves to be as one public State or Commonwealth, and do enter into combination and confederation to maintain and preserve the liberty and purity of the gospel of our Lord Jesus, which we now profess, as also the discipline of the churches, which, according to the truth of said gospel, is now practised amongst us; as also in our civil affairs to be guided and governed according to such laws, rules, orders, and decrees as shall be made.
>
> I. That the Scriptures hold forth a perfect rule for the direction and government of all men in all duties which they are to perform to God and men, as well in families and commonwealths as in matters of the church.

II. That as in matters which concerned the gathering and ordering of a church, so likewise in all public offices which concern civil order—as the choice of magistrates and officers, making and repealing laws, dividing allotments of inheritance, and all things of like nature—they would all be governed by those rules which the Scripture held forth to them.

III. That all those who had desired to be received free planters had settled in the plantation with a purpose, resolution, and desire that they might be admitted into church fellowship according to Christ.

IV. That all the free planters held themselves bound to establish such civil order as might best conduce to the securing of the purity and peace of the ordinance to themselves, and their posterity according to God.

When these resolutions had been passed, and the people had bound themselves to settle civil government according to the divine word, Mr. Davenport proceeded to state what men they must choose for civil rulers according to the divine word, and that they might most effectually secure to themselves and their posterity a just, free, and peaceable government. After a full discussion, it was unanimously determined—

V. That church members only should be free burgesses; and that they only should choose magistrates among themselves, to have power of transacting all the public civil affairs of the plantation, of making and repealing laws, dividing inheritances, deciding of differences that may arise, and doing all things and businesses of a like nature.[3]

Bancroft comments again on the colony:

> "Religion," says Bancroft, "united with the pursuits of agriculture to give to the land the aspect of salubrity; religious knowledge was carried to the highest degree of refinement, alike in its application to moral duties, and to the mysterious questions on the nature of God, of liberty, and of the soul. Civil freedom was safe under the shelter of a masculine morality, and beggary and crime could not thrive in the midst of the severest manners. The government was in honest and upright hands; the state was content with virtue and single-mindedness; and the public welfare never suffered at the hands of plain men."

Under this Christian government, "Connecticut was long the happiest state in the world." "The contentment of Connecticut was full to the brim. In a public proclamation, under the great seal of the colony, it told the world that its days, under the charter, were the 'halcyon days of peace.'"

> "In an age," says Trumbull, "when the light of freedom was but just dawning, the illustrious men of the colony of Connecticut, by voluntary compact, formed one of the most free and happy constitutions of government which mankind has ever adopted. Connecticut has ever been distinguished by the free spirit of its government, the mildness of its laws, and the general diffusion of knowledge among all classes of its inhabitants. They have been no less distinguished for their industry, economy, purity of manners, prosperity, and spirit of enterprise. For more than a century and a half they have had no rival as to the steadiness of their government, their internal peace and harmony, their love and high enjoyment of domestic, civil, and religious order and happiness. They have ever stood among the most illuminated, fervent, and boldest defenders of the civil and religious rights of mankind."

Rhode Island Colony

Rhode Island became a distinct colony in 1662, by the grant of a charter from Charles II. This charter gave the utmost Christian liberty in the exercise of the rights of conscience in religion. The object of colonizing Rhode Island is thus expressed in the charter:

> The colonists are to pursue with peace and loyal minds their sober, serious, and religious intentions of godly edifying themselves and one another in the holy Christian faith and worship, together with the gaining over the conversion of the poor ignorant Indians to the sincere profession and obedience of the same faith and worship.

Roger Williams, a Baptist minister, and among the first emigrants to the colony of Massachusetts, was the founder of the Rhode Island Colony. Having seen and felt the evils of an intolerant spirit in matters of religion, he obtained a charter that granted freedom in religious matters to all denominations. "No person," declared the charter, "within the said colony, at any time hereafter, shall be in any wise molested or punished, disquieted or called in question, for any difference in opinion in matters of religion; every person may at all times freely and fully enjoy his own judgment and conscience in matters of religious concernments." This organic law was confirmed by the first legislative Assembly declaring, in 1665, that "liberty to all persons as to the worship of God had been a principle maintained in the colony from the very beginning thereof; and it was much in their hearts to preserve the same liberty forever." In 1680 the same fundamental law was re-enacted—"We leave every man to walk as God persuades his heart: all our people enjoy freedom of conscience."

> "Roger Williams," says Bancroft, "asserted the great doctrine of intellectual liberty. It became his glory to found a state upon that principle, and to stamp himself upon its rising institutions so deeply that the impress can never be erased without the total destruction of the work. He was the first person in

> modern Christendom to assert in its plenitude the doctrine of the liberty of conscience, the equality of opinions before the law; and in its defence it was the harbinger of Milton, the precursor and the superior of Jeremy Taylor. Williams would permit persecutions of no opinion, of no religion, leaving heresy unharmed by law, and orthodoxy unprotected by the terrors of penal statutes." He had the honor of enunciating that fundamental principle of the Bible and of American institutions, "that the civil power has no jurisdiction over the conscience," a doctrine which, Bancroft says, "secures him an immortality of fame, as its application has given religious peace to the American world."

The colony, like the others, was founded on a Christian basis with a Christian democracy, and this original charter of civil and religious liberty continued as the organic government of Rhode Island till 1842, "the oldest constituted charter in the world. Nowhere in the world were life, liberty, and property safer than in Rhode Island."

> "Rhode Island," says Arnold, in his history of that commonwealth, "was a State whose founders had been doubly tried in the purifying fire; a State which more than any other has exerted, by the weight of its example, an influence to shape the political ideas of the present day, whose moral power has been in the inverse ratio with its material importance; of which an eminent historian of the United States has said, that, had its territory 'corresponded to the importance and singularity of the principles of its early existence, the world would have been filled with wonder at the phenomena of its history.'"

New Hampshire Colony

In 1679, New Hampshire was separated from Massachusetts and organized as an independent province. The colonists, having been so long a part of the Christian commonwealth of Massachusetts, constituted their institutions on the same Christian basis. Its legislature was Christian, and the colony greatly prospered and increased in population. It nourished a class of Christian men who loved liberty, and who have always exerted a prominent influence on the civil and religious interests of the American nation.

January 1, 1680, a royal decree declared New Hampshire an independent province; and the policy of the king was to smooth the way to an unjust and an unconstitutional government. The colonists, in their remonstrances, declared that the policy "struck liberty out of existence, by denying them the choice of their own rulers; and they viewed the loss of liberty as a precursor to an invasion of their prosperity." A civil assembly was convened, and a solemn public fast proclaimed and observed to propitiate the favor of Heaven, and the continuance of their "precious and pleasant things."

In an address to the king, the colonists of New Hampshire said, "that your petitioners' predecessors removed themselves, and some of us, into this remote region and howling wilderness, in pursuance of the glorious cause proposed, viz.: The glory of God, the enlarging of his majesty's dominions, and spreading the gospel among the heathen."

The influence and results of the Christian constitutions and governments of New England are stated by Rev. John Wise, in a work on the Government of the New England Churches, as follows:

1. Legislative power (that civil omnipotence) is doing very great things for religion, by their proclamations, and all penal laws enacted for the crushing of immorality and vice, and all their wise and exact precepts for the support of justice and piety. They are opening many civil channels, whereby they are conveying judgment, justice, and righteousness down our streets from the great fountain. Nay, this great and dread assembly puts awe upon all mankind. And the more daring and desperate are kept within compass, from a sense of this most terrible seat of thunder hanging over their heads,

> and upon every affront ready to break in strokes of vengeance and woes upon them, especially if they grow beyond the reach of common law.
>
> 2. The executive power, or ministers of the law, are like a standing camp to awe, and a flying army to beat off, the enemy: they have their spies and scouts out in every quarter to observe his motions and break his measures, namely, in the innumerable number of all sorts of civil officers; and thus by the sword of justice they hunt down sin and impiety in the land. They are a terror to evil-doers, and a praise to them that do well; for the civil authority, by their wise and just precepts, their personal and noble examples and zealous administrations, outdo Plato himself, with all his moral reasons; for they can turn a Sodom into a Sion, and keep Sion to be Sion, evident by the history and chronicles of several governments of God's ancient people. For chief rulers, by their good or bad measures, can make or mar, kill or cure, a nation in a moral sense.[4]

Early Christian Systems of Education

The settlers of the New England colonies believed that education, next to the Christian religion, was an indispensable element of a republican institution.

> The state must rest upon the basis of religion, and it must preserve this basis, or itself must fall. But the support which religion gives to the state will obviously cease the moment religion looses its hold upon the popular mind. The very fact that the state must have religion as a support for its own authority demands that some means for teaching religion be employed. Better for it to give up all other instruction than that religion should be disregarded in its schools. The state itself

> has a more vital interest in this continued influence of religion over its citizens than in their culture in any other respect.

From the very beginning of the New England colonies, the Puritans were aware of the importance of instructing the children in every part of human and religious knowledge. One of the early leaders, Cotton Mather, in presenting the considerations for the plantation of the colonies, says—"The schools of learning and religion are so corrupted as (besides the unsupportable charge of education) most children, even the best and wittiest, and of the fairest hopes, are perverted, corrupted, and utterly overthrown by the multitude of evil examples and licentious behavior in these seminaries."

John Eliot, the apostle to the Indians, in a prayer before the Civil Court, in Massachusetts, in 1645, uttered the following sentiments: "Lord! for schools everywhere among us! That our schools may flourish! That every member of this Assembly may go home and procure a good school to be encouraged in the town where he lives! That before we die we may be so happy as to see a good school encouraged in every plantation in the country!"

Formal Establishment of Schools

In 1644, the Christian colonists, "to the end that all learning may not be buried in the graves of our forefathers, ordered," that every township, "after the Lord hath increased them to fifty householders, shall appoint one to teach all children to read and write; and where any town shall increase to the number of one hundred families, they shall set up a grammar school; the master thereof being able to instruct youth so far as they may be fitted for the university."

Actual laws were passed to assure education of the children. One of the earliest legislative acts of the Massachusetts colony was the following:

> Forasmuch as the good education of children is of singular behoofe and benefit to any commonwealth;

> and whereas parents and masters are too indulgent and negligent of their duty in that kind—
>
> "It is therefore ordered by this courte and authority thereof that the selectmen of every towne, in the several precincts and quarters where they dwell, shall have a vigilent eye over theire brethren and neighbours; to see, first, that none of them shall suffer so much barbarisme in any of their familyes, as not to endeavor to teach, by themselves or others, theire children and apprentices, so much learning as may inable them perfectly to read the English tongue, and knowledge of the capitall lawes."

As early as 1635, free schools were commenced in Boston. The union of the Massachusetts and New Hampshire colonies continued till 1680, and during this time the example of Boston was rapidly followed by smaller towns in both colonies. "In the subject of schools both rulers and ministers felt a deep interest, and schoolmasters were a commodity in great demand, and eagerly sought." As early as 1644, one town devoted a portion of its lands to the support of schools; but, before the lands could be productive, they raised in various ways the sum of twenty pounds to hire a schoolmaster.

The following was passed by the General Court, in the year 1647, for the promotion of common education:

> It is therefore ordered by this courte and authority thereof, That every towneshipp within this jurisdiction, after that the Lord hath increased them to the number of fifty howsholders, shall then forthwith appointe one within theire towne, to teach all such children as shall resorte to him, to write and read; whose wages shall be paid either by the parents or masters of such children, or by the inhabitants in generall, by way of supplye, as the major parte of those who order the prudentials of the towne shall appointe.

> And it is further ordered, That where any towne shall increase to the number of one hundred families or howsholders, they shall sett up a grammar schoole, the masters thereof being able to instruct youths so far as they may bee fitted for the university.

In 1636, the colonists began at Cambridge, Massachusetts, the first college on the American continent. Its commencement was as follows:

> "The magistrates led the way by a subscription among themselves of two hundred pounds, in books for the library. The comparatively wealthy followed with gifts of twenty and thirty pounds. The needy multitude succeeded, like the widow of old, casting their mites into the treasury. A number of sheep was bequeathed by one man; a quantity of cotton cloth, worth nine shillings, presented by another; a pewter flagon, worth ten shillings, by a third; a fruit-dish, a sugar-spoon, a silver-tipt jug, one great set, and one smaller trencher set, by others.
>
> "The ends," says Cotton Mather, "for which our fathers chiefly erected a college were that scholars might there be educated for the service of Christ and his churches, in the work of the ministry, and that the youth might be seasoned in their tender years with such principles as brought their blessed progenitors into this wilderness. There is no one thing of greater concernment to these churches, in present and after times, than the prosperity of that society. We cannot subsist without a college."

The Founding of Harvard College

According to this proposal, a college was established in 1636, and in 1638 Rev. John Harvard, a learned and wealthy minister, died, and by his will gave one-half of his property and his entire library to the college at Boston; and hence it is called Harvard College, and later, Cambridge University was begun.

Christian tenants were invoked as was the custom:

> According to the rules for the government of this college, the president or professor, on being inaugurated, must first, "repeat his oath to the civil government; then he must declare his belief in the scriptures of the Old and New Testaments, and promise to open and explain the Scriptures to his pupils with integrity and faithfulness, according to the best light God shall give him." He also must promise "to promote true piety and godliness by his example and instruction."
>
> The rector or president shall also cause the Scriptures daily, except on the Sabbath mornings and evenings, to be read by the students at the times of prayer in the school; and upon the Sabbath he shall either expound practical theology, or cause the non-graduating students to repeat sermons; so that, through the blessing of God, it may be conducive to their establishment in the principles of the Christian Protestant religion.
>
> The exercises of the students had the aspect of a theological in reading the Scriptures, giving an account of their proficiency in practical and spiritual truths, accompanied by theoretical observations on the language and logic of the sacred writings. They were carefully to attend God's ordinances, and be examined on their profiting; commonplacing the sermons, and repeating them publicly in the hall. In every year and every week of the college course, every class was practised in the Bible and catechetical divinity.

Rev. Thomas Shepard, D.D., a learned divine, and laborious minister of God, conceived the design of procuring voluntary contributions of corn—money being out of the question—from all parts of New England, for the purpose of maintaining poor students. He laid the following memorial before the commissioners of the united colonies of

Plymouth, Connecticut, and New Haven, Massachusetts which met at Hartford, in 1644.

> To the Honored Commissioners—
>
> Those whom God hath called to attend the welfare of religious commonwealths have been prompt to extend their care for the good of public schools, by means of which the commonwealth may be furnished unto knowing and understanding men in all callings, and the church with an able minister in all places; without which it is easy to see how both these estates may decline and degenerate into gross ignorance, and, consequently, into great and universal profaneness. May it please you, therefore, among other things of common concernment and public benefit, to take into your consideration some way of comfortable maintenance for that school of the prophets that now is established . . . . If, therefore, it were recommended by you to the freedom of every family that is able and willing to give, throughout the plantations, to give but the fourth part of a bushel of corn, or something equivalent thereto, &c.

This memorial was received, and its policy cordially carried out by the commissioners, who recommended to the deputies of the several General Courts, and to the elders within the four colonies, to call for a voluntary contribution of one peck of corn, or twelve pence in money, or its equivalent in other commodities, from every family—a recommendation which was adopted and very generally responded to.

The constitution of Massachusetts, of 1780, thus refers to Harvard College:

> Whereas our wise and pious ancestors, so early as they of great eminence have, by the blessing of God, been initiated into those arts and sciences which qualified them for public employment, both in Church and State; and whereas the encouragement of arts and

> sciences, and all good literature, tends to the honor of God, the advantage of the Christian religion, and the great benefit of this and the other United States of America, it is declared, that the President and Fellows of Harvard College, &c.

Yale College

At New Haven, Connecticut, the second successful effort was made to found a permanent college of learning. Common schools, where the elements of education were widely diffused among the rising population, did not satisfy the enlarged views of literary men, and the plan of an institution of higher learning and more extended scope occupied the thoughts of the first settlers of Connecticut.

After various consultations, chiefly in reference to the interests of the Church, and confined in a great measure to the liberal and enlightened clergy of the times, a definite proposition was at length submitted with regard to the establishment of a college in New Haven.

The following resolution is the earliest record on the subject:

> At a General Court, held at Guilford, June 28th, A.D. 1652, Voted, the matter about a college at New Haven was thought to be too great a charge for us of this jurisdiction to undergo alone, especially considering the unsettled state of New Haven town, being publicly declared, from the deliberate judgment of the most understanding men, to be a place of no comfortable subsistence for the present inhabitants there. But, if Connecticut do join, the planters are generally willing to bear their just proportion for erecting and maintaining of a college there.

In 1700, ten of the principal ministers in the colony were nominated and agreed upon, by a general consent, both of the ministers and people, to stand as trustees or undertakers to found, erect, and govern a college. They soon met at Branford and laid the foundation of Yale

College. Each member brought a number of books and presented them to the body, and, laying them on the table, said—"I give these books for the founding of a college in this colony." The object of a college at New Haven was stated by a large number of ministers and laymen, who petitioned the Colonial Assembly for a charter.

They said that, "from a sincere regard to, and zeal for upholding the Protestant religion by a succession of learned and orthodox men, they had proposed that a collegiate school should be erected in this colony, wherein youth should be instructed in all parts of learning, to qualify them for public employment in Church and civil State."

The legislature of the colony promptly responded to the application, and a charter was granted, in which it was said:

> Whereas, several well-disposed and public-spirited persons, out of their sincere regard to, and zeal for upholding and propagating the Christian Protestant religion by a succession of learned and orthodox men, have expressed by petition their earnest desire that full liberty and privilege be granted unto certain undertakers for the founding, suitably endowing and ordering a Collegiate School within his Majesty's Colony of Connecticut, wherein youth may be instructed in the arts and sciences, who, through the blessing of Almighty God, may be fitted for public employment both in Church and State. To the intent, therefore, that all due encouragement be given to such pious resolutions, and that so necessary and religious an undertaking may be set forward and well managed, be it enacted, &c.

The charter being granted, at a meeting of the collegiate undertakers, held at Saybrook, November 11, A.D. 1701, they sent out the following circular:

> "Whereas, it was the glorious public design of our now blessed fathers in their removal from Europe into these parts of America, both to plant, and (under the Divine

blessing) to propagate in this wilderness, the blessed Reformed Protestant religion, in the purity of its order and worship, not only to their posterity, but also to the barbarous natives; in which great enterprise they wanted not the royal commands and favor of his Majesty King Charles the Second to authorize and invigorate them.

We, their unworthy posterity, lamenting our past neglect of this grand errand, and sensible of the equal obligations better to prosecute the same end, are desirous in our generation to be serviceable thereunto. Whereunto the religious and liberal education of suitable youth is, under the blessing of God, a chief and most probable expedient:

Therefore, that we might not be wanting in cherishing the present observable and pious disposition of many well-minded people to dedicate their children and substance unto God in such a good service, and being ourselves with sundry other reverend elders, not only desired by our godly people to undertake, as Trustees, for erecting, forming, ordering, and regulating a Collegiate School, for the advancement of such an education; but having also obtained of our present religious government both full liberty and assistance by their donation to such use; tokens, likewise, that particular persons will not be wanting in their beneficence; do, in duty to God and the weal of our country, undertake in the aforesaid design.

For the orderly and effectual management of this affair, we agree to, and hereby appoint and confirm, the following rules—

1st. That the Rector take special care, as of the moral behavior of the students, at all times, so with industry to instruct and ground them well in theoretical divinity; and to that end shall take effectual measures

> that the said students be weekly caused memoriter to recite the Assembly's Catechism in Latin; and he shall make, or cause to be made, from time to time, such explanations as may (through the blessing of God) be most conducive to their establishment in the principles of the Christian Protestant religion.
>
> 2d. The Rector shall also cause the Scriptures daily (except on the Sabbath), morning and evening, to be read by the students, at the times of prayer in the school, according to the laudable order and usage of Harvard College, making expositions upon the same; and upon the Sabbath shall either expound practical theology, or cause the non-graduating students to repeat sermons; and in all other ways, according to his best discretion, shall at all times studiously endeavor, in the education of the students, to promote the power and purity of religion and the best edification of these New England churches.

Rev. Henry B. Smith, of the Union Theological Seminary at New York, in behalf of the Society for the Promotion of Collegiate and Theological Education at the West, presents the following view of the history and fruits of the colleges at Cambridge and New Haven:

> For our encouragement it may be said that no people ever began its institutions under better auspices or with ampler promise. This we owe, under God, to the pious zeal of our Pilgrim Fathers, many of them eminent in learning as well as faith. John Cotton, of Boston, had been the head-lecturer and dean of Immanuel College in Cambridge, England. John Newton, of Ipswich, afterwards of Boston, was offered a fellowship in the same college. John Davenport, of New Haven, was termed a "universal scholar." Thomas Hooker, of Hartford, was a fellow of Cambridge, and was here called the "light of the Western churches." Thomas Thatcher, of Weymouth, composed a Hebrew lexicon. Charles

Chauncey, president of Harvard, had been Professor of Greek in Cambridge, England. Cotton Mather was the author of three hundred and eighty-two publications, including the "Magnalia."

The Influence of the Christian Colleges

"Established under such auspices, it is no wonder that all our earlier colleges, and, following in their train, most of the later, have been animated by the conviction that institutions of learning are needed by Christianity, and should have this faith as the basis of all their instructions. The earliest were not so much colleges as schools for the training of the ministry. The Pilgrims, when they numbered only five thousand families, founded the University of Cambridge, in 1636, with its perennial motto, 'Christo et Ecclesiae;' and Cotton Mather says that this university was 'the best thing they ever thought of.' In 1696, there were one hundred and sixteen pastors in the one hundred and twenty-nine churches, and one hundred and nine of these were from Harvard. Harvard has educated one thousand six hundred and seventy-three ministers: three hundred and fifty-one were still living in 1850. Yale College dates from 1700, and in its earlier years the Assembly's Catechism in Greek was read by the freshmen; the sophomores studied Hebrew; the juniors, sophomores, and the seniors, both at Harvard and Yale, were thoroughly instructed in divinity in the admirable compend of Wollebius.

"Yale has given to our churches one thousand six hundred and sixty-one ministers, of whom seven hundred and forty-one were still living during the mid 1850's. In the State of Connecticut, down to 1842, out of nine hundred and forty-seven ministers, only thirty-three were not graduates. Princeton was started in 1741, one of the fruits of the great revival, and by

> the New Side of that day. Dartmouth was a missionary school from its inception in 1769; and its catalogue gives the names of more than seven hundred ministers, a quarter-part of all its graduates. And almost all of our later colleges are the fruit of Christian beneficence, and their foundations have been laid with the prayers of our churches; and He who heareth prayer has breathed upon them his divine blessing, and through their influence sanctified our youth for the service of Christ and his Church. They have aspired to realize that ideal of education which Milton had in vision when he said, 'The end of learning is to repair the ruins of our first parents by regaining to know God aright, and out of that knowledge to love him, to imitate him, to be like him, as we may the nearest by possessing our souls of true virtue, which, being united to the heavenly grace of faith, makes up the highest perfection.'"
>
> "Yale College," says Benson John Lossing, "aside from its intrinsic worth as a seminary of learning, is remarkable for the great number of the leading men of the Revolution who were educated within its walls. That warm and consistent patriot, President Daggett, gave a political tone to the establishment favorable to the republican cause, and it was regarded as the nursery of Whig principles during the Revolution. When New Haven was invaded by Tryon, Yale College was marked for special vengeance; but the invaders retreated hastily, without burning the town. There were very few among the students, during our war for independence, who were imbued with tory principles, and they were generally, if known, rather harshly dealt with."

A statement of the times sums it up well:

> "In these measures," says Bancroft, "especially in the laws establishing common schools, lies the secret of the success and character of New England. Every child, as

> it was born into the world, was lifted from the earth by the genius of the country, and in the statutes of the land received, as its birthright, a pledge of the public care for its morals and its mind."[5]

From the book of Deuteronomy we find, "Teach it to the children of Israel; put it in their mouths" (31:19). The people of the New England colonies were dedicated to seeing that their children were educated properly. There were numerous innovative methods and materials that came to life during this time. For example:

> *The New England Primer* was one of these inventions. It was first published between 1688 and 1690 by Benjamin Harris of Boston. It was the first reading primer designed for the American colonies and became the most successful educational textbook published in the early days of U.S. history. The 90-page work contained religious maxims, woodcuts, alphabetical assistants, catechisms, and moral lessons. Many of its selections were drawn from the King James Bible.
>
> The listing below will show how the primer blends alphabetical and religious instruction.

A In ADAM'S Fall
We sinned all.
B Heaven to find,
The Bible Mind.
C CHRIST crucify'd
For sinners dy'd.
D The DELUGE drown'd
The Earth around.
E ELIJAH hid
BY Ravens fed.
F The judgment made
FELIX afraid.
G As runs the GLASS,
Our Life doth pass.

N NOAH did view
The old world & new.
O Young OBADIAS,
David, Josias
All were pias.
P PETER deny'd
His Lord and cry'd

Q Queen Esther sues
And saves the Jews.
R Young pious RUTH,
Left all for Truth.
S Young SAM'L dear
The Lord did fear.

H My book and HEART
Must never part.
J JOB feels the Rod,
Yet blesses God.
K Proud KORAH'S troop
Was swallowed up.
L LOT fled to *Zoar*
Saw fiery Shower
On *Sodom* pour.
M MOSES was he
Who *Israel's* Host
Led thro' the Sea.
T Young TIMOTHY
Learnt sin to flee.
V VASHTI for Pride,
Was set aside.
W WHALES in the Sea,
God's Voice obey.
X XERXES did die
And so must I.
Y While YOUTH do chear
Death may be near.
Z ZACCHEUS he
Did climb the Tree
Our Lord to see.[6]

The book of Proverbs tells us that "the fear of the Lord is the beginning of knowledge" (1:7). The American founders certainly understood this truth, and from the beginning stressed the relationship between a sound education based upon biblical absolutes and the future of the nation. We can certainly see that both sides of this equation have been neglected today.

In 1776, the future president John Adams said, "Statesmen . . . may plan and speculate for liberty, but it is *religion* and *morality* alone, which can establish the principles upon which freedom can securely stand." That mindset was widely held among the Founders who helped shape the political, educational and legal foundations of the new nation. Men such as Daniel Webster, Benjamin Franklin, Benjamin Rush, Samuel Adams, and George Washington echoed these same sentiments, believing that the strength of the republic was dependent on the morality of her people, and that religion must undergird it. They saw that the education of young minds being at the heart of it. Now you see the educators trying to destroy this mindset.

It may be a surprise to many, who have been brought up in our religion-free schools, that most of our oldest universities were started by preachers and churches. Harvard, William and Mary, Yale, Princeton, King's College, Brown, Rutgers, and Dartmouth were all founded by Christian preachers and church affiliations.

As we have seen, Harvard, for example, which was founded in 1636 by the Puritans, adopted the "Rules and Precepts" of the university that stated, "Let every student be plainly instructed, and earnestly pressed to consider well, the main end to his life and studies is, to know God and Jesus Christ which is eternal life (John 17:3) and therefore lay Christ at the bottom, as the only foundation of all sound knowledge and learning." Even Harvard's original seal, which can be seen etched in the walls of the campus today, states upon it these words: "Truth for Christ and the Church."

> Yale College was established in 1701 with a stated goal that "every student shall consider the main end of his study to wit to know God in Jesus Christ and answerably to lead a godly and sober life." The College of William and Mary was founded in 1693 to supply the church of Virginia "with a seminary of ministers" that the Christian faith may be propagated." And King's College, known today as Columbia University, purposed to "inculcate upon [students'] tender minds the great principles of Christianity and morality." Princeton had as one of its founding statements: "Cursed is all learning that is contrary to the Cross of Christ."
>
> In 1836, Noah Webster, often called "The Father of American Education," expressed the purpose of schools was meant for the advancement of the Christian faith: "In my view, the Christian religion is the most important and one of the first things in which all children, under a free government ought to be instructed . . . No truth is more evident to my mind than that the Christian religion must be the basis of any government intended to secure the rights and privileges of a free people."[7]

Unfortunately, over the last century at least, the mind-set of the American people has changed. The biblical principles and moral compass that goes with it has been tossed aside, in favor of "let's just all get along," and "let's not be intolerant of anything or anybody's attitude." John Dewey, often referred to as "The Architect of Modern Education," once said, "There is no God, and there is no soul. Hence there are no needs for the props of traditional religion." It seems that those props have been knocked away as the moral fiber of this country is in tatters and the main god being worshipped and taught about in schools is the god of material wealth.

This was the view of one Founding Father on the purpose of public education:

> William Samuel Johnson (1727-1819), president of Columbia University (as we stated earlier, formerly King's College), said to the first graduating class after the Revolutionary War:
>
> "You have . . . received education, the purpose whereof hath been to qualify you the better to serve your Creator and your country . . . Your first great duties . . . are those you owe to Heaven, to your Creator and Redeemer. Let these be forever present to your minds and exemplified in your lives and conduct. Imprint deep upon your minds the principles of piety toward God, and a reverence and fear of His holy name. The fear of God is the beginning of wisdom, and its consummation is everlasting felicity . . . Remember too, that you are redeemed of the Lord, that you are bought with a price, even the inestimable price of the precious blood of the son of God. Adore Jehovah, therefore, as your God and your Judge. Love, fear, and serve Him as your Creator, Redeemer, and Sanctifier. Acquaint yourselves with Him in His Word and holy ordinances. Make Him your friend and your protector and your felicity is secured both here and hereafter. And with respect to particular duties to Him, it is your happiness that you are well assured that he best serves his Maker, who does most good to his country and to mankind."[8]

Can you see someone making a statement like that to the graduating class of a major university today? I think not.

Notes

1. Benjamin F. Morris, *The Christian Life and Character of the Civil Institutions of the United States* (Powder Springs, GA: American Vision, Inc., 2007), 84-85.
2. Ibid., 86-87.
3. Ibid., 88-89.
4. Ibid., 90-94.
5. Ibid., 95-105.
6. Richard Lee, *The American Patriot's Bible* (Nashville,TN: Thomas Nelson, 2009), 29.
7. Ibid., I21-I24.
8. Ibid., 206.

CHAPTER 5

More Colonies Formed[1]

[We have covered the New England colonization and now it is time to look at other early colonies and their establishment. The year 1682 was significant in that it was a continuation of the Christian foundation of our country.]

William Penn fit the mold of a Christian leader of the time. He had been educated under the influence of the gospel. He had studied the origin of government, the nature of civil liberty, and the rights of man, in the light of the pure word of God, and formed the purpose of founding a Christian empire on the free and peaceful precepts of Christianity. He had a firm faith in the great American idea that man, educated by Christianity, was capable of self-government. Finding no place in Europe to try the experiment of a Christian government, he resolved to seek it in America.

The settlement of the province of Pennsylvania by William Penn formed a new era in the liberties of mankind. It afforded a resting-place where the conscientious and oppressed people of Europe might repose, and enjoy the rights of civil and religious freedom which mankind had derived as an inheritance from the Creator.

King Charles II granted him a large section of territory that now embraces the States of Pennsylvania, New Jersey, and Delaware. He was legally inducted to the governorship of this immense domain, in England, by the officers of the crown, and in 1682 arrived in the New World and assumed the civil government of the colony. He avowed his purpose to be to institute a civil government on the basis of the Bible and to administer it in the fear of the Lord. The acquisition and government of the colony, he said, was "so to serve the truth and the people of the Lord, that an example may be set to the nations."

Penn completed a structure in 1682 for the government of Pennsylvania that was derived from the Bible. He deduced from various passages "the origination and descent of all human power from God; the divine right of government, and that for two ends—first, to terrify evil doers; secondly, to cherish those who do well"; so that government, he said, "seems to me to be a part of religion itself,"—"a thing sacred in its institutions and ends." "Let men be good, and the government cannot be bad." "That, therefore, which makes a good constitution must keep it—namely, men of wisdom and virtue—qualities that, because they descend not with worldly inheritance, must be carefully propagated by a virtuous education of youth." We again can see that the people who came to America during the colonization knew who had provided this new world for them and, in turn who they should worship and adore for such a gift.

The first legislative act, passed at Chester, the seventh of the twelfth month, December, 1682, announced the ends of a true civil government. The preamble recites, that, "Whereas the glory of Almighty God and the good of mankind is the reason and end of government, and, therefore, government in itself is a venerable ordinance of God, and forasmuch as it is principally desired and intended by the proprietary and governor, and the freemen of Pennsylvania and territories thereunto belonging, to make and establish such laws as shall best preserve true Christian and civil liberty, in opposition to all unchristian, licentious, and unjust practices, whereby God may have his due, Caesar his due, and the people their due, from tyranny and oppression."

The structure of their government contained the following article on religious rights—"That all persons living in this province who confess and acknowledge the one almighty and eternal God to be the creator, upholder, and ruler of the world, and who hold themselves obliged in conscience to live peaceably and justly in civil society, shall in no wise be molested or prejudiced for their religious persuasion or practice in matters of faith and worship; nor shall they be compelled at any time to frequent or maintain any religious worship, place, or ministry whatsoever."

William Penn, who went about planting his colony and establishing his government in Pennsylvania, in 1682, caused the following law to be made—"To the end that looseness, irreligion, and atheism may not creep in under the pretence of conscience in this province, be it further enacted by the authority aforesaid, That, according to the good example of the primitive Christians, and for the ease of the creation, every first day of the week, called the Lord's day, people shall abstain from their common toil and labor, that, whether masters, parents, children, or servants, they may better dispose themselves to read the Scriptures of truth at home or to frequent such meetings of religious worship abroad, as may best suit their respective persuasions."

"The judgment of this Quaker patriarch and legislator," says Bancroft, "professes the government derived neither its obligations nor powers from man. God was to him the beginning and the end of government. He thought of government as a part of religion itself. Christians should keep the helm and guide the vessel of state."

Penn's main object also was to carry the Christian religion to the natives. This Christian design is expressed in the charter granted by Charles II. It says, "Whereas our trusty and beloved William Penn, out of a commendable desire to enlarge the British empire, as also to reduce the savages, by just and gentle measures, to the love of civil society and the Christian religion, hath humbly besought our leave to translate a colony." This purpose was expressed by Penn in the petition he sent to the king. He says he "should be able to colonize the province, which might enlarge the British empire, and promote the glory of God by the civilization and conversion of the Indian tribes."

He urged all who proposed to join the colony "to have especial respect to the will of God." He continued to act as Governor of Pennsylvania till June, 1684, when he returned to England. Before his embarkation, he uttered these farewell words to the colony, as his parting benediction—"I bless you in the name and power of the Lord;

and may God bless you with his righteousness, peace, and plenty, all the land over. Oh that you would eye God in all, through all, and above all the works of his hand."

One of the great features of the Christian polity of Penn was his faith and fair dealings with the Indians. Every portion of land he obtained by honest purchase, and his integrity and frankness won for him and his colony the confidence and friendship of the Indian race. Treaties of mutual advantage were entered into between them, in which it was covenanted that as long as the grass grew and the waters ran, the links in the chain of their mutual friendship should be kept bright and strong. His transactions with the Indian tribes were marked with Christian integrity, and added new luster to his fame.

Priorities of Education

Penn, as the wise founder of a civil commonwealth, provided measures for the general diffusion of the blessings of a Christian education. "Let men," he says, "be good, and the government cannot be bad. That, therefore, which makes a good constitution must keep it—namely, men of wisdom and virtue, qualities that, as they descend not with worldly inheritance, must be carefully propagated by a virtuous education of the youth."

One of the last acts of William Penn on leaving the country for England was to grant a charter to the public school in Philadelphia, in order to secure good school instruction equally to all the children of the community. On the seal of this institution he placed the motto, "GOOD EDUCATION IS BETTER THAN RICHES;" with the impressive adage, "Love ye one another."

Christians Come to New York

Starting with its first settlement, commerce and Christianity were always in a mode of cooperation; and as commerce, from the very beginning of the colony in 1609, was a leading motive of the first settlers, so the Christian religion pioneered its way side by side with commerce. As early as 1613, four years after the discovery of Manhattan by Hudson,

Holland merchants had established several trading-posts, and in 1623 measures were taken to found an agricultural and Christian settlement. The first emigrants were those who had fled from the severity of religious persecution in the seventeenth century in the French Belgic provinces, and came with a faith tried in a fiery furnace.

The East India Company, formed in 1621, stipulated that "where emigrants went forth under their auspices, and that of the States-General of Holland, it should be their duty to send out a schoolmaster, being a pious member of the church, whose office it was to instruct the children, and preside in their religious meetings on the Sabbath and other days, leading in the devotions, and reading a sermon, until the regular ministry should be established over them. An individual was often designated as a Zickentrooster, (comforter of the sick), who for his spiritual gifts was adapted to edify and comfort the people."

In 1633 the first minister came over, and associated with him was a schoolmaster, who organized a church school. The introduction, at this early period of the settlement of the colony, of the church and school combined, cannot, therefore, be claimed as the peculiar distinction of the Puritan emigrants, as the direct aim and the provision made in the early settlements by the Dutch was to extend and preserve in the midst of them the blessings of education and religion.

First Church in the Colonial Era

The Collegiate Reformed Dutch Church of New York was the first founded in North America, and dates from the first settlement on Manhattan Island. The first religious meetings were held in a temporary building, till in 1626 an emigrant, in building a horse-mill, provided a spacious room above it for the congregation.

At an interview, in 1642, between a famous navigator, Captain David De Vries, and the Governor of the Colony, the former remarked "that it was a shame that the English when they visited Manhattan saw only a mean barn in which we worshipped. The first they built in New England, after their dwelling-houses, was a fine church: we should do the same."

This led to the erection of a new and spacious church-edifice. In a letter written on the 11th of August, 1628, by Rev. Jonas Michaëllus, the first minister of the Dutch Reformed Church in the United States, made this statement—

"We have established the form of a church, and it has been thought best to choose two elders for my assistance, and for the proper consideration of all such ecclesiastical matters as might occur. We have had at the first administration of the Lord's Supper full fifty communicants, not without great joy and comfort for so many—Walloons and Dutch; of whom a portion made their first confession, and others exhibited their church certificates. We administer the Holy Sacrament of the Lord's Supper once in four months.

"We must have no other object than the glory of God in building up his kingdom and the salvation of many souls. As to the natives of this country, I find them entirely savage and wild, proficient in all wickedness, who serve nobody but the devil. Let us then leave the parents in their condition, and begin with the children who are still young, and place them under the instruction of some experienced and godly schoolmaster, where they may be taught especially in the fundamentals of our Christian religion. In the meantime it must not be forgotten to pray to the Lord, with ardent and continual prayers, for his blessing."

Other Denominational Church Groups

In 1636, the Puritans of New England began to add largely to the New York colony. In ten years after the Puritan emigration began, "there were so many at Manhattan as to require preachers who could speak in English as well as Dutch."

"Whole towns," says Bancroft, "had been settled by New England men, who had come to America to serve God with a pure conscience, and to plant New England liberties in a congregational way."

The colony of New York, after being under the jurisdiction of the Dutch for fifty years, passed, in 1664, to that of England. This political revolution secured a rapid colonization from various quarters.

"English, Irish, Scotch, French, and Dutch, chiefly Presbyterians and Independents," now began to emigrate to the colony of New York. The Episcopalians claimed "that the province was subject to the ecclesiastical government of the Church of England, and that theirs was the religion of the state." The Duke of York, afterwards James II, maintained an Episcopal chapel in New York at his own private expense. "Ministers," said Andros, the civil Governor of the colony, in 1683, "are scarce, and religion wanes. There were about twenty churches, of which half were destitute of ministers. But the Presbyterians and Independents, who formed the most numerous and thriving portions of the inhabitants, were the only class of the people who showed much willingness to procure and support ministers."

The Huguenots Influence

The seventeenth century, constituting an important era of Christian colonization of the New World, brought to the North American colonies the rich Christian contribution from the Huguenots of France. All the colonies gave them a hearty welcome as refugees from a frenzied and cruel religious persecution. They were ardent lovers of liberty, and declared that, with "their ministers, they had come to adore and serve God with freedom." These Christian exiles were warmly welcomed to the colony of New York, and became one of the richest portions of the population. In 1682 they had become so numerous that the colonial laws and official papers were published in French as well as in Dutch and English. The French church in the city of New York became the metropolis of Calvinism, where the Huguenot emigrants of the city came to worship.

"The character of the first Huguenot settlers," says Dr. De Witt, "was eminently worthy, both here and in other parts of the State and the United States. An interesting fact is related concerning the first settlers of New Rochelle, in Westchester county. When they entered the forests, and with serious labor engaged in clearing and cultivating the fields, they resolved, in the spirit of deep piety which they brought with them, to unite with their brethren in New York in the public worship of the Sabbath, though at a distance of twenty miles. In their sincere reverence for the sanctification of the Sabbath that they would take up their march on foot in the afternoon of Saturday, and reach New York by midnight, singing the hymns of Clement Marot on the way. Engaging in the worship of the Sabbath, they remained here till after midnight, and then they marched back to New Rochelle, relieving the fatigue along the way by singing Marot's hymns."

"Happy and proud," says Bancroft, "in the religious liberty they enjoyed, they ceased not to write to their brethren in France of the grace which God had shown them."

More Christian-Based Legislation

In 1665, the colonial legislature of New York passed the following act in reference to Christianity and its ordinances—

"Whereas, The public worship of God is much discredited for want of painful [laborious] and able ministers to instruct the people in the true religion, it is ordered that a church shall be built in each parish, capable of holding two hundred persons; that ministers of every church shall preach every Sunday, and pray for the king, queen, the Duke of York, and the royal family; and to marry persons after legal publication of license."

It was also enacted that "Sunday is not to be profaned by travelling, by laborers, or vicious persons," and "church-wardens to report twice a year all misdemeanors, such as swearing, profaneness, Sabbath-breaking, drunkenness, fornication, adultery, and all such abominable Sins." "Persons were punished with death who should in any wise deny the true God or his attributes." These were the laws of the colony of New York until 1683.

The following paper will give a better picture of the attention that the early settlers of New York paid to education, and is an amusing relic of colonial antiquity. It belongs to the ancient local history of Flatbush, Long Island—

A School Relic

Art. 1. The school shall begin at 8 o'clock and go outt att 11; shall begin again att 1 o'clock and ende att 4. The bell shall bee rung before the school begins.

Art. 2. When school opens, one of the children shall reade the morning prayer as it stands in the catechism, and close with the prayer before dinner; and inn the afternoon the same. The evening school shall begin with the Lord's prayer and close by singing a psalm.

Art. 3. Hee shall instruct the children inn the common prayers and the questions and answers off the catechism on Wednesdays and Saturdays, too enable them too say them better on Sunday inn the church.

Art. 4. Hee shall bee bound too keep his school nine months in succession, from September too June, one year with another, and shall always bee present himself.

Art. 5. Hee shall bee choirister off the church; ring the bell three tymes before service, and reade a chapter off the Bible inn the church between the second and third ringinge off the bell; after the third ringinge he shall reade the ten commandments and the twelve articles off ffaith and then sett the psalm. In the afternoone after the third ringinge off the bell hee shall reade a short chapter or one off the psalms off David as the congregatione are assemblinge; afterwards he shall again sett the psalm.

Art. 6. When the minister shall preach at Broockland or Utrecht he shall be bounde to reade twice before the congregatione from the booke used for the purpose. Hee shall heare the children recite the questions and answers off the catechism on Sunday and instruct them.

Art. 7. Hee shall provide a basin off water for the baptism, ffor which hee shall receive twelve stuyvers in wampum ffor every baptism from parents or sponsors. Hee shall furnish bread and wine ffor communion att the charge off the church. Hee shall also serve as messenger ffor the consistories.

Art. 8. Hee shall give the funerale invitations and toll the bell; and ffor which hee shall receive for persons off fifteen years off age and upwards twelve guilders; and ffor persons under fifteen, eight guilders; and if hee shall cross the river to New York hee shall have four guilders more.

[The compensation of the schoolmaster was as follows:]

1st. Hee shall receive ffor a speller or reader three guilders a quarter; and for a writer ffour guilders for the daye school. Inn the evening four guilders for a speller or reader, and five guilders for a writer per quarter.

2nd. The residue off his salary shall bee four hundred guilders in wheat (of wampum value) deliverable at Broockland Fferry with the dwellinge, pasturage and meadowe appurtaininge to the school.

Done and agreede on inn consistorie, in the presence off the Honourable Constable and Overseers, this 8th daye off October, 1682.

Constable and Overseers	*The Consistorie*
Cornelius Berrian,	Casparus Vanzuren,
Ryniere Aertsen,	*Minister.*
Jan Remben.	Adriaen Ryerse,
	Cornelius B. Vanderwyck

I agree to the above articles, and promise to observe them.
Johnnes Von Echkellen

The Birth of New Jersey

New Jersey became an independent colony in 1664. "Its moral character was moulded by New England Puritans, English Quakers, and Dissenters from Scotland." An association of church-members from the New Haven colony resolved with one heart "to carry on their spiritual and town affairs according to Godly Government;" and in 1668 the colonial legislative Assembly, under Puritan influence, transferred the chief features of the New England codes to the statute book of New Jersey. New Jersey increased in population and prosperity under the genial presence of Christian institutions, and became distinguished for intelligence, industry, and enterprise. "The people," says Bancroft, "rejoiced under the reign of God, confident that he would beautify the meek with salvation."

More Christian-Influenced Law

The Christian teachings of the Quakers, in union with Presbyterian and Anabaptist influences, made New Jersey, in its colonial structure, a model Protestant republic. "These were interwoven into the earliest elements of the political society of New Jersey, and constitute one of the beautiful historical incidents of the age. The people have always enjoyed a high reputation for piety, industry, economy, and good morals."

They received and practiced such Christian lessons as the following, given by their friends in England, in 1681—

"Friends that are gone to make plantations in America, keep the plantations in your own hearts, that your own vines and lilies be not hurt. You that are governors and judges, you should be eyes to the blind, feet to the lame, and fathers to the poor, that you may gain the blessing of those who are ready to perish, and cause the widow's heart to sing for gladness. If you rejoice because your hand hath gotten much, if you say to the fine gold, Thou art my confidence, you will have denied the God that is above. The Lord is ruler among nations; he will crown his people with dominion."

The high standard of Christian morality in the colony of New Jersey was indicated by the motto on the provincial seal—"Righteousness exalteth a nation." A proclamation made by Governor Basse, in 1697, contains the following Christian record—"It being very necessary for the good and prosperity of this province that our principal care be, in obedience to the laws of God, to endeavor as much as in us lyeth the extirpation of all sorts of looseness and profanity, and to unite in the fear and love of God and one another, that, by the religious and virtuous carriage and behavior of every one in his respective station and calling, the blessing of Almighty God may accompany our honest and lawful endeavors, I do therefore, by and with the advice of the Council of this province, strictly prohibit cursing, swearing, immoderate drinking, Sabbath-breaking, and all sorts of lewdness and profane behavior in word and action; and do strictly charge and command all justices of the peace, sheriffs, constables, and all other officers within the province, that they take due care that all laws made and provided for the suppression of vice and encouraging of religion and virtue, particularly the observance of the Lord's day, be duly put into execution."

Delaware Colony

Gustavus Adolphus, born into the royal family of Sweden, wanted to be a part of the Christian settlement of the New World. His plan was, through a combination of business enterprise and settlement, as he described it, to be for the benefit of the "whole Protestant world." In 1637, two vessels, fitted out by the Government of Sweden, carried a band of emigrants with their Christian teachers, and in the spring of 1638 they sailed into Delaware Bay and began the Christian colonization of that region. In 1640 the colony received Christian emigrants from New England. It continued a political connection with the colony of Pennsylvania till 1704, when it became an independent commonwealth.

Virginia, Another Christian Colony

Even before the Puritans settlements began in New England, the grant from King James in April, 1606, brought about the origins of the Virginia colony. It was to be located on the coastline between the 34th and 45th latitudes and include any islands within those boundaries. That charter declared the design of the colonists to be "to make habitation and plantation and to deduce a colony of sundry of our people into that part of America commonly called Virginia; and that so noble a work may, by the providence of Almighty God, hereafter tend to the glory of his divine majesty in propagating of the Christian religion to such people as yet live in darkness and in miserable ignorance of the true knowledge and worship of God, and may, in time, bring the infidels and savages living in those parts to human civility and a quiet government."

It is, in the Virginia charter of 1609 declared "that it shall be necessary for all such as inhabit within the precincts of Virginia to determine to live together in the fear and true worship of Almighty God, Christian peace, and civil quietness;" and that "the principal effect which we [the crown] can desire or expect of this action is the conversion and reduction of the people in those parts unto the true worship of God and the Christian religion."

The Official Beginning of Preaching the Gospel

In a code of laws for the government of the Virginia colony, which the king helped to frame, were "enjoined the preaching of the gospel in America, and the performance of divine worship in conformity with the doctrines and rites of the Church of England." In 1619, twelve years after the first settlement of Virginia, "The King of England having formerly issued his letters to the bishops of the kingdom, for collecting money to erect a college in Virginia for the education of Indian children, nearly fifteen hundred dollars had been already paid to this benevolent and pious design, and Henrico had been selected as a suitable place for the seminary. The Virginia Company granted ten thousand acres of land to be laid off for the University at Henrico. The first design was to erect and build a college in Virginia for the training up and educating infidel [Indian] children in the true knowledge of God." The principal design of William and Mary College was to instruct and Christianize the Indians.

Thomas Jefferson, in his "Notes on Virginia," says, "The purposes of the institution would be better answered by maintaining a perpetual mission among the Indian tribes, the object of which, besides instructing them in the principles of Christianity, as the founder required, should be to collect their traditions, laws, customs, languages, and other circumstances which might lead to a discovery of their relation with one another or descent from other nations. When these objects are accomplished with one tribe, the missionary might pass to another."

"The colony of Virginia consisted of Church-of-England men, and many of their first acts related to provision for the Church. The ministers were considered, not as pious and charitable individuals, but as officers of state, bound to promote the true faith and aid sound morality by authority of the community by which they were paid, and to which they were held responsible for the performance of their duty. The very first act of the Assembly required every settlement in which the people worship God to build a house to be appropriated exclusively for that purpose; the second act imposed a penalty of a pound of tobacco for absence from divine service on Sunday; and another act prohibited any man from disposing of his tobacco until the minister's portion was paid."

When the population had increased to fifty thousand, in 1668, there were "nearly fifty Episcopal parishes, with as many glebes, church edifices, and pastors. Episcopacy was established by law; attendance was enforced by penalties: even religion was the underlying basis and the pervading element of all the social and civil institutions of the Virginia colony.

In 1662, the Assembly of Virginia passed an act to make permanent provision for the establishment of a college. The preamble of the act establishing it recites "that the want of able and faithful ministers in this country deprives us of those great blessings and mercies that always attend upon the service of God"; and the act itself declares "that for the advancement of learning, education of youth, supply of the ministry, and promotion of piety, there be land taken up and purchased for a college and free school, and that with all convenient speed there be buildings erected upon it for the entertainment of students and scholars." In 1693 the College of William and Mary was founded.

Maryland Is Founded

In 1632, the colony of Maryland is started under the auspices of Lord Baltimore, a British nobleman and a Roman Catholic. His object was to "people a territory with colonists of his own religious faith, and to erect an asylum in North America for the Catholic religion."

He obtained a charter from Charles I, in which it was declared that the "grantee was actuated by a laudable zeal for extending the Christian religion and the territory of the British empire; and if any doubt should ever arise concerning the true meaning of the charter, there should be no construction of it derogatory to the Christian religion." The first band of colonists, consisting of two hundred men of rank, led by Leonard Calvert, brother of Lord Baltimore, sailed from England in November, 1632, and landed on the coast of Maryland early in 1633. As soon as they landed, the governor erected a cross, and took possession of the country "for our Lord Jesus Christ, and for our sovereign lord the King of England."

"To every emigrant fifty acres of land were given in absolute fee; and the recognition of Christianity as the established faith of the land, with an exclusion of the political predominance or superiority of any particular sect or denomination of Christians was enacted." The colonists "soon converted a desolate wilderness into a flourishing commonwealth enlivened by industry and adorned by civilization."

Religious toleration was, from the beginning, proclaimed as one of the fundamental laws of the colony. The Assembly, mostly of the Roman Catholic faith, passed, in 1650, a memorable Christian act, entitled, an "Act concerning Religion." The preamble declared that "the enforcement of the conscience had been of dangerous consequence in those countries where it had been practiced;" and therefore it was ordained "that no person professing to believe in Jesus Christ should be molested on account of their faith, or denied the free exercise of their particular modes of worship."

This act of religious toleration was as honorable to the first Catholic colony as it was a fitting tribute to the genius and sanction of the Christian religion. "It was the earliest example," says Judge Story, "of a legislator inviting his subjects to the free indulgence of religious opinion."

"With all that was excellent and grand and far-reaching in the principles of the Pilgrims, and with all the mighty influences of the religion of the Pilgrims in its bearing on the liberties of this nation—ultimately infinitely more far-reaching than those which had gone out from Maryland—still, it cannot be denied that the principles adopted in that colony were in advance of those which were held by the settlers of either Plymouth or Jamestown; and though coming short of those held by Roger Williams and William Penn, yet they were such as the age, in its progress, was carrying to that result." This beneficent and fundamental law exerted a highly favorable influence on the prosperity of the Maryland colony, and largely increased its population. It was, in time, incorporated in the legislation of the less tolerant colonies, and finally became the supreme law in all the State Constitutions, as well as in the Constitution of the United States.

Colonization of South Carolina

South Carolina began her colonial existence and history under the auspices of the Christian religion. In 1662, a company of emigrants, generally grandees of England and courtiers of Charles II, obtained a charter and settled in South Carolina. In the charter, it was stated that the colonists, "excited with a laudable and pious zeal for the propagation of the gospel, have begged a certain country in the parts of America, not yet cultivated and planted, and only inhabited by some barbarous people, who have no knowledge of God."

Government Foundation by Locke

In 1669, a second charter was obtained, and the outlines of its government, under the title of "the Fundamental Constitution of Carolina," was drawn up by John Locke, the great Christian philosopher, who declared that Christianity had "God for its Author, salvation for its end, and truth without any mixture of error for its matter." [You will learn a lot more about John Locke in the next chapter.]

In that constitution it is declared that—

"Since the natives of the place, who will be concerned in our plantations, are utterly strangers to Christianity, whose idolatry, ignorance, or mistake gives us no right to expel or treat them ill, and those who remove from other parts to plant there will undoubtedly be of different opinions concerning matters of religion, the liberty whereof they will expect to have allowed them, and it will not be reasonable on this account to keep them out; that civil peace may be maintained amidst the diversity of opinions, and our agreement and compact with all men may be duly and faithfully observed; the violation whereof, upon what pretence soever, cannot be, without great offence to Almighty God, and great scandal to the true religion which we profess; and also that Jews, heathens, and dissenters from the purity of the Christian religion may not be scared and kept at a distance from it, but, by having opportunity of acquainting themselves with the truth and reasonableness of its doctrines and the peaceableness and inoffensiveness of its professors, may by good usage and persuasion, and all those convincing methods of gentleness and meekness suitable to the rules and designs of the gospel, be won over to embrace and unfeignedly to receive the truth: therefore any seven or more persons, agreeing in any religion, shall constitute a Church or profession, to which they shall give some name, to distinguish it from others."

In the terms of communion of every such Church or profession, it was required that the three following articles should appear—that there is a God; that public worship is due from all men to this Supreme Being; and that every citizen shall, at the command of the civil magistrate, deliver judicial testimony with some form of words indicating a recognition of divine justice and human responsibility.

Only the acknowledged members of some Church or profession were capable of becoming freemen of Carolina, or of possessing any estate or habitation within the province; and all persons were forbidden to revile, disturb, or in any way persecute the members of any religious association allowed by law. What was enjoined to freemen was permitted to slaves, by an article which declared that "since charity obliges us to wish well to the souls of all men, and religion ought to alter nothing in any man's civil estate or right, it shall be lawful for slaves, as well as others, to enter themselves and be of what Church or profession any of them shall think best and thereof be as fully members as any freeman."

In another of the articles of "the Fundamental Constitution" it was declared that "whenever the country should be sufficiently peopled and planted, the provincial parliament should enact regulations for the building of churches, and the public maintenance of divines, to be employed in the cause of religion according to the canons of the Church of England; which, being the only true and orthodox and the national religion of all the king's dominions, is so also of Carolina; and therefore it alone shall be allowed to receive public maintenance by grant of parliament."

After twenty years of experiment, the form of government instituted by Locke was abolished. The French Protestants, and Dissenters from England, became the ruling power, and established a more just and liberal system of government.

The Huguenots formed an important part of the colony of South Carolina. The same lovely picture of piety as in the New York colony was presented by these Christian refugees who had settled in South Carolina. "There it was," says Bancroft, "that these Calvinist exiles could celebrate their worship, without fear, in the midst of the forests, and mingle the voice of their psalms with the murmur of the winds which sighed among the mighty oaks. Their church was in Charleston. They repaired thither every Sunday from their plantations, which were scattered in all directions on the banks of the Cooper."

The descendants of these Christian colonists became distinguished in American history, and exerted a prominent influence in achieving the independence of the nation. American patriotism, eloquence, oratory, and jurisprudence are adorned by many noble names, descendants of the Huguenots.

Colonization of North Carolina

The North Carolina colony, from the beginning of her colonial history, laid the basis of her institutions on Christianity. The first permanent settlements were made by fugitives from Virginia, who sought refuge from the rigid, intolerant laws of that colony, which bore so heavily on all that could not conform to the ceremonies of the established Church. When the Puritans were driven from Virginia, some eminently pious people settled along the seaboard, where they might be free from the oppression of intolerant laws and bigoted magistrates. About the year 1707, a colony of Huguenots located on the Trent River, and one of

Palatines at Newbern, each maintaining the peculiar religious services of the fatherland.

The Quakers were, like other sects, compelled to flee from the severe laws passed against them in Virginia, and sought refuge in Carolina. As early as 1730, scattered families of Presbyterians from the north of Ireland were found in various parts of the colony.

In 1736 a colony of Presbyterians came from the province of Ulster, Ireland, and made a permanent settlement. Subsequently several other colonies of Presbyterians came from Ireland, and settled in different sections of the colony. These Presbyterian bands rapidly increased, and formed numerous large congregations, which multiplied into other congregations; and thus the colony became thoroughly Christian, and the people imbued with a fervent love of liberty.

In 1746 and 1747 a large emigration of Scotch came into the colony of North Carolina. In the efforts of Prince Charles Edward to obtain the crown of England, the Scotch were in sympathy with him. George II granted pardon to a large number on condition of their emigration and taking the oath of allegiance. This is the origin of the Scotch settlements in North Carolina. A large number who had taken up arms for the Pretender preferred exile to death or to subjugation in their native land, and during the years 1746 and 1747 emigrated with their families and those of many of their friends, to North Carolina. In the course of a few years, large companies of industrious Highlanders joined their countrymen.

This Christian people, both in Scotland and this country, contended "that obligation to God was above all human control, and for the government of their conscience in all matters of morality and religion the Bible is the storehouse of information—acknowledging no Lord of the conscience but the Son of God, the head of the Church, Jesus Christ, and the Bible as his divine communication for the welfare and guide of mankind."

The Scotch-Irish Presbyterians, who formed so large a proportion of the people of North Carolina, and moulded its religious and political character, were eminently pious and ardent lovers of liberty. "Their religious principles swayed their political opinions; and in maintaining their form of worship and their creed they learned republicanism before they emigrated to America."

The religious creed of these Christian emigrants formed a part of their politics so far as to lead them to decide that no law of human government ought to be tolerated in opposition to the expressed will of God. Their ideas of religious liberty have given a coloring to their political notions on all subjects—have been, indeed, the foundation of their political creed. The Bible was their text-book on all subjects of importance, and their resistance to tyrants was inspired by the free principles which it taught and enforced.

The following instructions to the delegates of Mecklenburg County exhibit the sentiments of the people on the Christian religion as the basis of civil government. It bears the date September 1, 1775. The first Provincial Congress of North Carolina was then in session.

"13th. You are instructed to assent and consent to the establishment of the Christian religion, as contained in the Scriptures of the Old and New Testament, to be the religion of the state, to the utter exclusion forever of all and every other (falsely so called) religion, whether pagan or papal; and that a full and free and peaceable enjoyment thereof be secured to all and every constituent member of the state, as their individual right as freemen, without the imposition of rites and ceremonies, whether claiming civil or ecclesiastical power for their source; and that a confession and profession of the religion so established shall be necessary in qualifying any person for public trust in the state.

"14th. You are also to oppose the establishment of any mode of worship to be supported to the oppression of the rights of conscience, and at the destruction of private judgment."

This political paper declares that the people of North Carolina believed the Bible, and from it drew their principles of morals, religion, and polities. To abjure the Christian religion would have been, with them, to abjure freedom and immortality. They asserted in every political form the paramount authority of the Christian religion as the sole acknowledged religion of the state and community.

These Christian men, and others like them, constituted the celebrated Mecklenburg Convention of North Carolina convened in 1775. The convention was composed largely of Presbyterians, the most distinguished of whom were ministers. The delegates met on the 15th of May, 1775, and during their sittings news arrived of the battle of Lexington. Every delegate felt the value and importance of the prize of liberty, and the awful and solemn crisis which had arrived. Every bosom swelled with indignation at the malice, inveteracy, and insatiable revenge developed in the late attack at Lexington. After a full and free discussion of various subjects, it was unanimously—

"2. Resolved, That we, the citizens of Mecklenburg county, do hereby dissolve the political bands which have connected us with the mother-country, and hereby absolve ourselves from allegiance to the British crown, and abjure all political connection, contract, and association, with that nation which has wantonly trampled on our rights and liberties, and inhumanly shed the innocent blood of American patriots at Lexington.

"3. Resolved, That we do hereby declare ourselves a free and independent people—that we are, and of right ought to be, a sovereign and self-governing association, under the control of no power other than that of God and the general government of the Congress; to the maintenance of which independence we solemnly pledge to each other our mutual co-operation, our lives, our fortunes, and our most sacred honor."

This declaration of independence preceded the one made by Congress in 1776 more than a year, and is a noble monument of the patriotism and piety of the people of North Carolina. The colony of North Carolina is particularly distinguished for the large number of able and patriotic ministers who were diligent laborers in the fields of intellectual and Christian culture and in sowing broadcast the seeds of liberty and of future independence. The annals of Biblical learning and of freedom are adorned with the names of Campbell, Hall, Hunter, McAden, Craighead, Alexander, McWhorter, McCane, Petillo, and others, who were master-workmen in their department of Christian labor, and ardent and fearless patriots. These men were the pioneers of freedom and independence, and in all the measures preparatory to the coming revolution they were the foremost leaders.

Georgia Colonized

Georgia has a suggestive Christian history. James Oglethorpe, a member of the British Parliament, imbued with the philanthropic spirit of the gospel, obtained in 1732 a charter from George II to establish a colony in North America. He had in former years devoted himself to the benevolent work of relieving multitudes in England who were imprisoned for debt and suffering in loathsome jails. Actuated by Christian motives, he desired to see these poor sufferers placed in an independent condition, and projected a colony in America for that purpose.

"For them, and for persecuted Protestants," says Bancroft, "he planned an asylum and a destiny in America, where former poverty would be no reproach, and where the simplicity of piety could indulge the spirit of devotion without fear of persecution from men who hated the rebuke of its example." This Christian enterprise enlisted "the benevolence of England; the charities of an opulent and enlightened nation were to be concentrated on the new plantation; the Society for Propagating the Gospel in Foreign Parts sought to promote its interests; and Parliament showed its good will by contributing ten thousand pounds."

In January, 1732, Oglethorpe, with one hundred and twenty emigrants, landed in America, and on the basis of the Christian religion laid the future commonwealth of Georgia. The Christian liberality and philanthropy of the founder of the colony spread its fame far and wide; for it was announced that the rights of citizenship and all the immunities of the colony "would be extended to all Protestant emigrants from any nation of Europe, desirous of refuge from persecution, or willing to undertake the religious instruction of the Indians." The Moravians, or United Brethren—a denomination of Christians founded by Count

Zinzendorf, a German nobleman of the fifteenth century—were invited to emigrate to the colony of Georgia. They accepted the invitation, and arrived in the winter of 1736. Their object was to Christianize and convert the Indians, and to aid in planting the institutions of the New World on the basis of Christianity.

The journal of John Wesley during the voyage exhibits the godly manner of the emigrants. "Our common way," says he, "of living was this. From four of the morning till five, each of us used private prayer. From five to seven we read the Bible together, carefully comparing it (that we might not lean to our own understanding) with the writings of the earliest ages. At eight were public prayers. At four were the evening prayers—when either the second lesson was explained, or the children were catechized and instructed before the congregation. From five to six we again used private prayer. At seven I joined with the Germans in their public service. At eight we met again, to exhort and instruct one another. Between nine and ten we went to bed, where neither the roaring of the sea nor the motion of the ship could take away the refreshing sleep which God gave us."

What a Christian way of spending the time, for emigrants sailing over the mighty deep to aid in founding a Christian empire on the shores of a new world! When these Christian emigrants touched the shore, their first act was "to kneel and return thanks to God for their having safely arrived in Georgia." "Our end in leaving our native country," said they, "is not to gain riches and honor, but singly this—to live wholly to the glory of God." Their object was "to make Georgia a religious colony, having no theory but devotion, no ambition but to quicken the sentiment of piety."

The Christian founder of the commonwealth of Georgia carried his Christian principles into all the official transactions of the colony. The survey and division of the lots in the city of Savannah were conducted under the sanctions of religion. On the 7th of July, 1733, the emigrants met in a body upon the bluff of the river, before Oglethorpe's tent, and, having returned thanks to Almighty God and joined in prayer for his blessing to rest upon the colony and city they were about to found, they proceeded to lay out the lots and divide them in a Christian manner.

They felt and said, "Except the Lord keep the city, the watchman waketh but in vain."

Under the administration of Oglethorpe, the colony greatly prospered and increased in numbers. "His undertaking will succeed," said Johnson, Governor of South Carolina; "for he nobly devotes all his powers to serve the poor and rescue them from wretchedness." "He bears a great love to the servants and children of God," said the pastor of a Moravian church. "He has taken care of us to the utmost of his ability. God has so blessed us with his presence and his regulations in the land, that others would not in many years have accomplished what he has brought about in one."

In 1734, after a residence of fifteen months in Georgia, Oglethorpe returned to England. He succeeded in obtaining additional patronage for the colony, and in October, 1735, set sail with three hundred emigrants, and after a long and stormy voyage they reached the colony of Georgia in February, 1736, where they were joined a few days after by a band of Christian emigrants from the highlands of Scotland.

These colonists were accompanied by John and Charles Wesley, the founders of the Methodist Episcopal Church. Their purpose was to aid Oglethorpe in his philanthropic labors and to convert the Indians to Christianity. Charles Wesley held the office of Secretary for Indian Affairs, and also that of a chaplain to Governor Oglethorpe.

Rev. Mr. Stevens, a historian of Georgia, says that "John Wesley established a school of thirty or forty children, and hired a teacher, in which he designed to blend religious instruction with worldly wisdom; and on Sunday afternoon Mr. Wesley met them in the church before evening service, and heard the children recite their catechism, questioned them as to what they had learned in the Bible, instructed them still further in the Bible, endeavoring to fix the truth in their understandings as well as in their memories. This was a regular part of their Sunday duties; and it shows that John Wesley, in the parish of Christ's Church, in Savannah, had established a Sunday-school nearly fifty years before Robert Raikes originated his noble scheme of Sunday instruction in Gloucester, England, and eighty years before the first school in America on Mr. Raikes's plan was established in New York."

George Whitefield visited Georgia, and preached with wonderful eloquence and zeal, and labored with apostolic faith and perseverance in founding an Orphan Asylum, a "Bethesda," a "House of Mercy," for orphan children. His fame and influence soon spread over the colonies, and wherever he went tens of thousands of people hung with breathless interest on his preaching. He made a number of voyages to England and back to America, and died in Newburyport, Massachusetts, in 1770. In consequence of his Christian services to Georgia, and especially his efforts for the orphans, the legislature of the colony proposed to remove his remains to Savannah and to bury them at public cost.

Dr. Ben Franklin wrote to Dr. Jones, of Georgia, on the subject as follows—"I cannot forbear expressing the pleasure it gives me to see an account of the respect paid to Whitefield's memory, by your Assembly. I knew him intimately upwards of thirty years: his integrity, disinterestedness, and indefatigable zeal in prosecuting every good work I have never seen equaled, I shall never see excelled." And such was the effect of Whitefield's preaching in Philadelphia that Franklin said, "It was wonderful to see the change soon made in the manner of our inhabitants. From being thoughtless or indifferent about religion, it seemed as if all the world were growing religious, so that one could not walk through the town in an evening without hearing psalms sung in different families in every street."

"It is a matter of great interest," says the historian of Georgia, "that religion was planted with the first settlers, and that the English, the Salzburgers, the Moravians, the Methodists, the Presbyterians, and the Israelites severally brought with them the ministers or the worship of their respective creeds. The Christian element of colonization—that without which the others are powerless to give true and lasting elevation—entered largely into the colonization of Georgia, and did much for her prosperity and glory. No colony can point to a leader or founder in whose character meet more eminent qualities or more enduring worth than in that of James Oglethorpe, the father of Georgia."

There are a lot of lessons to be learned and facts to write down, concerning to truths of our American history. These Christian facts in the colonial history of our country suggest the following lessons—

1. The faith of the Puritans, and of the founders of the various colonies, in the divine origin and authority of civil government. They held firmly to the declarations of the Bible, that "there is no power but of God: the powers that be are ordained of God. Whosoever therefore resisteth the power, resisteth the ordinance of God." And the doctrine of the divine origin of civil government led these Christian men to regard the civil ruler as the "minister of God to the people for good; and that he that ruleth should rule in the fear of God." This true and noble faith in reference to civil government and the character of the men who administered it placed the entire administration of government under the direction of God and in harmony with his will. The results of this faith and practice will always be in perfect harmony with the just ends of government and with the highest political and moral propriety of a nation. This grand idea was one that was always supreme in the minds and purposes of the Puritan and other colonial legislators in respect to civil government.

They ever regarded government as from God; and this view invested it with all the dignity and authority of a divine institution. "The first settlers," says Lord Brougham, "of all the colonies, were men of irreproachable character. Many of them fled from persecution; others on account of honorable poverty; and all of them with their expectations limited to the prospect of a bare subsistence in freedom and peace. All idea of wealth or pleasure was out of the question. The greater part of them viewed their emigration as a taking up the cross, and bounded their hopes of riches to the gifts of the Spirit, and their ambition to the desire of a kingdom beyond the grave. A set of men more conscientious in their doings, or simpler in their manners, never founded an empire. It is indeed the peculiar glory of North America that, with very few exceptions, its empire was founded in charity and peace."

2. The subordination of civil government to the power of the Christian religion. "They looked upon their commonwealths as institutions

for the preservation of the Churches, and the civil rulers as both members and fathers of them." Hence it was a favorite doctrine with the first settlers of the colonies of Massachusetts and Connecticut, that all freemen and civil rulers must be in communion with the Churches, and so promote the interest and spread of Christianity.

This doctrine had an eminent advocate in the celebrated John Cotton, the first minister of Boston. "The government," says he, "might be considered as a theocracy, wherein the Lord was judge, lawgiver, and king; that the laws which he gave Israel might be adopted so far as they were of a moral and perpetual equity; that the people might be considered as God's people in covenant with him; that none but persons of approved piety and eminent gifts should be chosen rulers." At the desire of the court, he compiled a system of laws, which were considered by the legislative body as the general standard.

The same fact was stated by President Ezra Stiles, of Yale College, in 1783. "It is certain," said he, "that civil dominion was but the second motive, religion the primary one, with our ancestors in coming hither and settling this land. It was not so much their design to establish religion for the benefit of the state, as civil government for the benefit of religion, and as subservient and even necessary towards the peaceable and unmolested exercise of religion—of that religion for which they fled to these ends of the earth. They designed, in thus laying the foundations of a new state, to make it a model for the glorious kingdom of Christ."

Rev. John Norton, in 1661, declared, in an election sermon, that they came into this wilderness to live under the order of the gospel; "that our policy may be a gospel policy, and may be complete according to the Scriptures, answering fully to the word of God: this is the work of our generation, and the very work we engaged for in this wilderness; this is the scope and end of it, that which is written upon the forehead of New England, viz., the complete walking in the faith of the gospel according to the order of the gospel."

3. The end and operations of civil government to propagate and subserve the Christian religion. "The Pilgrims," says Rev. R. S.

Storrs, "would have held that state most imperfect which contented itself and complacently rested in its own advancement and special prosperities, without seeking to benefit others around it. They esteemed that progress to be radically wanting in greatness and value which was a mere progress in power and wealth and in physical success; which gained no results of great character and culture, and blossomed out to no wealthy fruits of enlarged Christian knowledge. The moral, to them, was superior to the physical; the attainments of Christian wisdom and piety, above accumulations of worldly resources; the alliance of the soul with God, through faith, above the conquest and mastery of nature. And to these they held the state to be tributary, as they held all things else that existed on the earth—the very earth itself and its laws.

"Not a mere police establishment was the state, on their theory, accomplishing its office in protecting its subjects and punishing criminals. It was to them a place and a power of the noblest education; a teeming nursery of all good influences and heavenly growths, from which letters, charities, and salvation should proceed, and in which they should perpetually be nourished. Philanthropic endeavors, and missionary enterprises, were to be its results, the proofs of its prosperity, the real and imperishable rewards of its founders. It existed in order that characters might be formed, commanding, large, and full of light, whose record should make all history brighter, whose influence should link the earth with the skies. And they expected the Millennium itself, with its long eras of peace and of purity, of tranquil delight and illuminated wisdom, to spring as the last and crowning fruitage from the states they were founding, and from others like them."

4. The position and influence of the ministers of the gospel in the civil affairs of the state. They were consulted on all matters pertaining to the civil affairs of the New England colonies, and had the controlling influence in forming and directing the civil government. The very first written code of laws for Massachusetts, under the charter of 1629, was drawn up by a minister. And the instruction of the civil court, appointed to frame the laws of the commonwealth, was to make them "as near the law of God as they

can." "They had great power in the people's heart," says Winthrop. "Religion ruled the state through its ministers."

Ministers were selected as agents to obtain charters and petition the king and Parliament, as well as to direct the character of the civil government at home. "The clergy were generally consulted on civil matters, and the suggestions they gave from the pulpit on election days and other special occasions were enacted into laws." [Today, some protest having chaplains in government proceedings!]

Prophecy of an English Bishop

Before the Declaration of Independence, the Bishop of St. Asaph, in England, published a discourse, in which are found the following remarkable passages in reference to the North American colonies—

"It is difficult," says he, "for man to look into the destiny of future ages: the designs of Providence are vast and complicated, and our own powers are too narrow to admit of much satisfaction to our curiosity. But when we see so many great and powerful causes constantly at work, we cannot doubt of their producing proportional effects.

"The colonies in North America have not only taken root and acquired strength, but seem hastening with an accelerated progress to such a powerful state as may introduce a new and important change in human affairs.

"Descended from ancestors of the most improved and enlightened part of the Old World, they receive as it were by inheritance all the improvements and discoveries of their mother-country. And it happens fortunately for them to commence their flourishing state at a time when the human understanding has attained to the free use of its powers and has learned to act with vigor and certainty. And let it be well understood what rapid improvements, what important discoveries, have been made, in a few years, by a few countries, with our own at the head, which have at last discovered the right method of using their faculties.

"May we not reasonably expect that a number of provinces possessed of these advantages and quickened by mutual emulation, with only the progress of the human mind, should very considerably enlarge the boundaries of science? It is difficult even to imagine to what height of improvement their discoveries may extend.

"And perhaps they may make as considerable advances in the arts of civil government and the conduct of life. May they not possibly be more successful than their mother-country has been in preserving that reverence and authority which are due to the laws—to those who make them, and to those who execute them? May not a method be invented of procuring some tolerable share of the comforts of life to those inferior useful ranks of men to whose industry we are indebted for the whole? Time and discipline may discover some means to correct the extreme inequalities between the rich and the poor, so dangerous to the innocence and happiness of both. They may, fortunately, be led by habit and choice to despise that luxury which is considered with us the true enjoyment of wealth. They may have little relish for that ceaseless hurry of amusements which is pursued in this country without pleasure, exercise, or employment. And perhaps, after trying some of our follies and caprices, and rejecting the rest, they may be led by reason and experiment to that old simplicity which was first pointed out by nature, and has produced those models which we still admire in arts, eloquence, and manners."

A New Sense of Providence in the Colonies

"The diversity of the new scenes and new situations, which so many growing states must necessarily pass through, may introduce changes in the fluctuating opinions and manners of men which we can form no conception of; and not only the gracious disposition of Providence, but the visible preparation of causes, seems to indicate strong tendencies towards a general improvement."

John Adams, in contemplating the Christian colonization of the American continent, uttered the following views of the design of Providence—"I always consider," said he, "the settlement of America with reverence and wonder, as the opening of a grand scheme and design of Providence for the illumination of the ignorant and the emancipation of the slavish part of mankind all over the earth."

Notes

1. Benjamin F. Morris, *The Christian Life and Character of the Civil Institutions of the United States* (Powder Springs, GA: American Vision, Inc., 2007), 106-13.

CHAPTER 6

Influences on the New Republic

I think it would only be fitting to take a portion of this story of the United States to acknowledge some of the major influential figures on our founders. We will start with one of the earliest:

John Locke

John Locke (1632-1704) is one of the most important, but largely unknown names in American history today. A celebrated English philosopher, educator, government official, and theologian, it is not an exaggeration to say that without his substantial influence on American thinking, there might well be no United States of America today—or at the very least, America certainly would not exist with the same level of rights, stability of government, and quality of life that we have enjoyed for well over two centuries.

Historians—especially of previous generations—were understandably effusive in their praise of Locke. For example:

> In 1833, Justice Joseph Story, author of the famed *Commentaries on the Constitution*, described Locke as "a most strenuous asserter of liberty"[1] who helped establish in this country the sovereignty of the people over the government,[2] majority rule with minority protection,[3] and the rights of conscience.[4]

> In 1834, George Bancroft, called the "Father of American History," described Locke as "the rival of 'the ancient philosophers' to whom the world had 'erected statues,'"[5] and noted that Locke esteemed "the pursuit of truth the first object of life and . . . never sacrificed a conviction to an interest."[6]
>
> In 1872, historian Richard Frothingham said that Locke's principles—principles that he said were "inspired and imbued with the Christian idea of man"—produced the "leading principle [of] republicanism" that was "summed up in the Declaration of Independence and became the American theory of government."[7]
>
> In the 1890s, John Fiske, the celebrated nineteenth-century historian, affirmed that Locke brought to America "the idea of complete liberty of conscience in matters of religion" allowing persons with "any sort of notion about God" to be protected "against all interference or molestation,"[8] and that Locke should "be ranked in the same order with Aristotle."[9]

Such acknowledgments continued across the generations; and even over the past half century, U. S. presidents have also regularly acknowledged America's debt to John Locke:

> President Richard Nixon affirmed that "John Locke's concept of 'life, liberty and property'" was the basis of "the inalienable rights of man" in the Declaration of Independence.[10]
>
> President Gerald Ford avowed that "Our revolutionary leaders heeded John Locke's teaching, 'Where there is no law, there is no freedom.'"[11]
>
> President Ronald Reagan confirmed that much in America "testif[ies] to the power and the vision of free

> men inspired by the ideals and dedication to liberty of John Locke . . ."[12]

> President Bill Clinton reminded the British Prime Minister that "Throughout our history, our peoples have reinforced each other in the living classroom of democracy. It is difficult to imagine Jefferson, for example, without John Locke before him."[13]

President George W. Bush confessed that "We're sometimes faulted for a naive faith that liberty can change the world, [but i]f that's an error, it began with reading too much John Locke . . ."[14]

The influence of Locke on America was truly profound; he was what we now consider to be a renaissance man—an individual skilled in numerous areas and diverse subjects. He had been well-educated and received multiple degrees from some of the best institutions of his day, but he also pursued extensive self-education in the fields of religion, philosophy, education, law, and government—subjects on which he authored numerous substantial works, most of which still remain in print today more than three centuries after he published them.

One of Locke's earliest writings was his 1660 "First Tract of Government" followed by his 1662 "Second Tract of Government." Neither was published at that time, but they later appeared in 1689 as his famous *Two Treatises of Government.* The first treatise (i.e., a thorough examination) was a brilliant Biblical refutation of Sir Robert Filmer's *Patriarcha* in which Filmer had attempted to produce Biblical support for the errant "Divine Right of Kings" doctrine. Locke's second treatise set forth the fundamental principles defining the proper role, function, and operation of a sound government. Significantly, Locke had ample opportunity to assert such principles, for he spent time under some of England's worst monarchs, including Charles I, Charles II, and James II; but he also saw many of his principles enacted into policy during the rule of Lord Cromwell and then William and Mary.

In 1664, Locke penned "Questions Concerning the Law of Nature" in which he asserted that human reason and Divine revelation were fully compatible and were not enemies—that the Law of Nature actually came from God Himself. (This work was not published, but many of its concepts appeared in his subsequent writings.)

In 1667, he privately penned his "Essay Concerning Toleration," first published in 1689 as *A Letter Concerning Toleration*. This work, like his *Two Treatises*, was published anonymously, for it had placed his very life in danger by directly criticizing and challenging the frequent brutal oppression of the government-established and government-run Church of England. (Under English law, the Anglican Church and its 39 Doctrinal Articles were the measure for all religious faith in England; every citizen was required to attend an Anglican Church. Dissenters who opposed those Anglican requirements were regularly persecuted or even killed. Locke objected to the government establishing specific church doctrines by law, argued for a separation of the state from the church, and urged religious toleration for those who did not adhere to Anglican doctrines.) When Locke's position on religious toleration was attacked by defenders of the government-run church, he responded with *A Second Letter Concerning Toleration* (1690), and then *A Third Letter for Toleration* (1692)—both also published anonymously.

In 1690, Locke published his famous *Essay Concerning Human Understanding*. This work resulted in him being called the "Father of Empiricism," which is the doctrine that knowledge is derived primarily from experience. Rationalism, on the other hand, places reason above experience; and while Locke definitely did not oppose reason, his approach to learning was more focused on the practical, whereas rationalism was more focused on the theoretical.

In 1693, Locke published *Some Thoughts Concerning Education*. Originally a series of letters written to his friend concerning the education of a son, in them Locke suggested the best ways to educate children. He proposed a three-pronged holistic approach to education that included (1) a regimen of bodily exercise and maintenance of physical health (that there should be "a sound mind in a sound body"[15]), (2) the development of a virtuous character (which he considered to be the most important element of education), and (3) the training of the mind through practical and useful academic curriculum (also encouraging students to learn a practical trade). Locke believed that education made the individual—that "of all the men we meet with, nine parts of ten are what they are, good or evil, useful or not, by their education."[16] This book became a run-away best-seller, being printed in nearly every European language and going through 53 editions over the next century.

Locke's latter writings focused primarily on theological subjects, including *The Reasonableness of Christianity as Delivered in the Scriptures* (1695), *A Vindication of the Reasonableness of Christianity* (1695), *A Second Vindication of the Reasonableness of Christianity* (1697), *A Common-Place-Book to the Holy Bible* (1697), which was a re-publication of what he called *Graphautarkeia, or, The Scriptures Sufficiency Practically Demonstrated* (1676), and finally *A Paraphrase and Notes on the Epistles of St. Paul to the Galatians, 1 and 2 Corinthians, Romans, Ephesians* (published posthumously in 1707).

In his *Reasonableness of Christianity*, Locke urged the Church of England to reform itself so as to allow inclusion of members from other Christian denominations—i.e., the Dissenters. He recommended that the Church place its emphasis on the major things of Christianity (such as an individual's relationship with Jesus Christ) rather than on lesser things (such as liturgy, church hierarchy and structure, and form of discipline). That work also defended Christianity against the attacks of skeptics and secularists, who had argued that Divine revelation must be rejected because truth could be established only through reason. Locke's defense evoked strong criticism from rationalists, thus causing him to pen two additional works defending the reasonableness of Christianity.

(While these are some of Locke's better known works, he also wrote on many other subjects, including poetry and literature, medicine, commerce and economics, and even agriculture.)

The impact of Locke's writings had a direct and substantial influence on American thinking and behavior in both the religious and the civil realms—an influence especially visible in the years leading up to

America's separation from Great Britain. In fact, the Founding Fathers openly acknowledged their debt to Locke:

> John Adams praised Locke's *Essay on Human Understanding*, openly acknowledging that "Mr. Locke . . . has steered his course into the unenlightened regions of the human mind, and like Columbus, has discovered a new world."[17]
>
> Declaration signer Benjamin Rush said that Locke was not only "an oracle as to the principles . . . of government"[18] (an "oracle" is a wise authority whose opinions are not questioned) but that in philosophy, he was also a "justly celebrated oracle, who first unfolded to us a map of the intellectual world,"[19] having "cleared this sublime science of its technical rubbish and rendered it both intelligible and useful."[20]
>
> Benjamin Franklin said that Locke was one of "the best English authors" for the study of "history, rhetoric, logic, moral and natural philosophy."[21]
>
> Noah Webster, a Founding Father called the "Schoolmaster to America," directly acknowledged Locke's influence in establishing sound principles of education.[22]
>
> James Wilson (a signer of the Declaration and the Constitution, and an original Justice on the U. S. Supreme Court) declared that "The doctrine of toleration in matters of religion . . . has not been long known or acknowledged. For its reception and establishment (where it has been received and established), the world has been thought to owe much to the inestimable writings of the celebrated Locke . . . ."[23]
>
> James Monroe, a Founding Father who became the fifth President of the United States, attributed much of our

> constitutional philosophy to Locke, including our belief that "the division of the powers of a government . . . into three branches (the legislative, executive, and judiciary) is absolutely necessary for the preservation of liberty."[24]
>
> Thomas Jefferson said that Locke was among "my trinity of the three greatest men the world had ever produced."[25]

And just as the Founding Fathers regularly praised and invoked John Locke, so, too, did numerous famous American ministers in their writings and sermons.[26] Locke's influence was substantial; and significantly, the closer came the American Revolution, the more frequently he was invoked.

For example, in 1775, Alexander Hamilton recommended that anyone wanting to understand the thinking in favor of American independence should "apply yourself without delay to the study of the law of nature. I would recommend to your perusal . . . Locke."[27]

And James Otis—the mentor of both Samuel Adams and John Hancock—affirmed that:

> The authority of Mr. Locke has . . . been preferred to all others.[28]

Locke's specific writing that most influenced the American philosophy of government was his *Two Treatises of Government*. In fact, signer of the Declaration Richard Henry Lee saw the Declaration of Independence as being "copied from Locke's Treatise on Government"[29]—and modern researchers agree, having authoritatively documented that not only was John Locke one of three most-cited political philosophers during the Founding Era[30] but that he was by far the single most frequently-cited source in the years from 1760-1776 (the period leading up to the Declaration of Independence).[31]

Among the many ideas articulated by Locke that subsequently appeared in the Declaration was the theory of social compact, which, according to Locke, was when:

> Men . . . join and unite into a community for their comfortable, safe, and peaceable living one amongst another in a secure enjoyment of their properties and a greater security against any that are not of it.[32]

Of that theory, William Findley, a Revolutionary soldier and a U. S. Congressman, explained:

> Men must first associate together before they can form rules for their civil government. When those rules are formed and put in operation, they have become a civil society, or organized government. For this purpose, some rights of individuals must have been given up to the society but repaid many fold by the protection of life, liberty, and property afforded by the strong arm of civil government. This progress to human happiness being agreeable to the will of God, Who loves and commands order, is the ordinance of God mentioned by the Apostle Paul and . . . the Apostle Peter.[33]

Locke's theory of social compact is seen in the Declaration's phrase that governments "derive their just powers from the consent of the governed."

Locke also taught that government must be built firmly upon the transcendent, unchanging principles of natural law that were merely a subset of God's greater law:

> [T]he Law of Nature stands as an eternal rule to all men, legislators as well as others. The rules that they make for other men's actions must . . . be conformable to the Law of Nature, i.e., to the will of God.[34]

> [L]aws human must be made according to the general laws of Nature, and without contradiction to any positive law of Scripture, otherwise they are ill made.[35]

The Declaration therefore acknowledges "the laws of nature and of nature's God," thus not separating the two but rather affirming their interdependent relationship—the dual connection between reason and revelation which Locke so often asserted.

Locke also proclaimed that certain fundamental rights should be protected by society and government, including especially those of life, liberty, and property[36]—three rights specifically listed as God-given inalienable rights in the Declaration. As Samuel Adams (the "Father of the American Revolution" and a signer of the Declaration) affirmed, man's inalienable rights included "first, a right to life; secondly, to liberty; thirdly, to property"[37]—a repeat of Locke's list.

Locke had also asserted that:

> [T]he first and fundamental positive law of all commonwealths is the establishing of the Legislative power . . . [and no] edict of anybody else . . . [can] have the force and obligation of a law which has not its sanction [approval] from that Legislative which the public has chosen.[38]

The Founders thus placed a heavy emphasis on preserving legislative powers above all others. In fact, of the 27 grievances set forth in the Declaration of Independence, 11 dealt with the abuse of legislative powers—no other topic in the Declaration received nearly as much attention. The Founders' conviction that the Legislative Branch was above both the Executive and Judicial branches was also readily evident in the U. S. Constitution, with the Federalist Papers affirming that "the legislative authority necessarily predominates"[39] and "the judiciary is beyond comparison the weakest of the three departments of power."[40]

Locke also advocated the removal of a leader who failed to fulfill the basic functions of government so eloquently set forth in his *Two*

Treatises;[41] the Declaration thus declares that "whenever any form of government becomes destructive of these ends, it is the right of the people to alter or to abolish it and to institute new government."

In short, when one studies Locke's writings and then reads the Declaration of Independence, they will agree with John Quincy Adams' pronouncement that:

> The Declaration of Independence [was] . . . founded upon one and the same theory of government . . . expounded in the writings of Locke.[42]

But despite Locke's substantial influence on America, today he is largely unknown; and his *Two Treatises* are no longer intimately studied in America history and government classes. Perhaps the reason for the modern dismissal of this classic work is because it was so thoroughly religious: Locke invoked the Bible in at least 1,349 references in the first treatise, and 157 times in the second[43]—a fact not lost on the Founders. As John Adams openly acknowledged:

> The general principles on which the Fathers achieved independence . . . were the general principles of Christianity . . . Now I will avow that I then believed (and now believe) that those general principles of Christianity are as eternal and immutable as the existence and attributes of God . . . In favor of these general principles in philosophy, religion, and government, I [c]ould fill sheets of quotations from . . . [philosophers including] Locke—not to mention thousands of divines and philosophers of inferior fame.[44]

Given the fact that previous generations so quickly recognized the Christian principles that permeated all of Locke's diverse writings, it is not surprising that they considered him a theologian.[45] Ironically, however, many of today's writers and so-called professors and scholars specifically call Locke a deist or a forerunner of Deism.[46] But since Locke included repeated references to God and the Scriptures throughout his writings, and since he wrote many works specifically in defense of religious topics, then why is he currently portrayed as being anti-religious? It is because in the past fifty years, American education has become thoroughly infused with the dual historical malpractices of Deconstructionism and Academic Collectivism.

Deconstructionism is a philosophy that "tends to deemphasize or even efface [i.e., malign and smear] the subject" by posing "a continuous critique" to "lay low what was once high"[47] and "tear down the ancient certainties upon which Western Culture is founded."[48] In other words, it is a steady flow of belittling and negative portrayals about the heroes, institutions, and values of Western civilization, especially if they reflect religious beliefs. The two regular means by which Deconstructionists accomplish this goal are (1) to make a negative exception appear to be the rule, and (2) deliberate omission.

These harmful practices of Deconstructionists are exacerbated by the malpractice of Academic Collectivism, whereby scholars quote each other and those from their group rather than original sources. Too many writers today simply repeat what other modern writers say, and this "peer-review" becomes the standard for historical truth rather than an examination of actual original documents and sources.

Reflecting these dual negative influences of Deconstructionism and Academic Collectivism in their treatment of John Locke, many of today's "scholars" simply lift a few short excerpts from his hundreds of thousands of written words and then present those carefully selected extracts in such a way as to misconstrue his faith and make it seem that he was irreligious. Or more frequently, Locke's works are simply omitted from academic studies, being replaced only with a professor's often inaccurate characterization of Locke's beliefs and writings.

Significantly, the charge that Locke is a deist and a freethinker is not new; it has been raised against him for over three centuries. It first originated when Locke advocated major reforms in the Church of England (such as the separation of the state from the church and the extension of religious toleration to other Christian denominations); Anglican apologists who stung from his biting criticism sought to malign him and minimize his influence; they thus accused him of irreligion and deism. As affirmed by early English theologian Richard Price:

> [W]hen . . . Mr. Locke's *Essay on the Human Understanding* was first published in Britain, the persons readiest to attend to it and to receive it were those who have never been trained in colleges, and whose minds, therefore, had never been perverted by an instruction in the jargon of the schools. [But t]o the deep professors [i.e., clergy and scholars] of the times, it appeared (like the doctrine taught in his book, on the *Reasonableness of Christianity*) to be a dangerous novelty and heresy; and the University of Oxford in particular [which trained only Anglicans] condemned and reprobated the author.[49]

The Founding Fathers were fully aware of the bigoted motives behind the attacks on Locke's Christian beliefs, and they vigorously defended him from those false charges. For example, James Wilson (signer of the Declaration and Constitution) asserted:

> I am equally far from believing that Mr. Locke was a friend to infidelity [a disbelief in the Bible and in Christianity[50]] . . . The high reputation which he deservedly acquired for his enlightened attachment to the mild and tolerating doctrines of Christianity secured to him the esteem and confidence of those who were its friends. The same high and deserved reputation inspired others of very different views and characters . . . to diffuse a fascinating kind of lustre over their own tenets of a dark and sable hue. The consequence has been that the writings of Mr. Locke, one of the most able, most sincere, and most amiable assertors of Christianity and true philosophy, have been perverted to purposes which he would have deprecated and prevented [disapproved and opposed] had he discovered or foreseen them.[51]

Thomas Jefferson agreed. He had personally studied not only Locke's governmental and legal writings but also his theological ones; and his summary of Locke's views of Christianity clearly affirmed that Locke was not a deist. According to Jefferson:

> Locke's system of Christianity is this: Adam was created happy and immortal . . . By sin he lost this so that he became subject to total death (like that of brutes [animals])—to the crosses and unhappiness of this life. At the intercession, however, of the Son of God, this sentence was in part remitted . . . And moreover to them who believed, their faith was to be counted for righteousness [Romans 4:3,5]. Not that faith without works was to save them; St. James, chapter 2 says expressly the contrary [James 2:14-26] . . . So that a reformation of life (included under repentance) was essential, and defects in this would be made up by their faith; i. e., their faith should be counted for righteousness [Romans 4:3,5] . . . The Gentiles; St. Paul says, Romans 2:13: "the Gentiles have the law written in their hearts," [A]dding a faith in God and His attributes that on their repentance, He would pardon them; (1 John 1:9) they also would be justified (Romans 3:24). This then explains the text "there is no other name under heaven by which a man may be saved" [Acts 4:12], i. e., the defects in good works shall not be supplied by a faith in Mahomet, Fo [Buddha], or any other except Christ.[52]

In short, Locke was not the deist thinker that today's shallow and often lazy academics so frequently claim him to be; and although Locke is largely ignored today, his influence both on American religious and political thinking was substantial, directly shaping key beliefs upon which America was established and under which she continues to operate and prosper.

Americans need to revive a widespread awareness of John Locke and his specific ideas that helped produce American Exceptionalism so that we can better preserve and continue the blessings of prosperity, stability, and liberty that we have enjoyed for the past several centuries.

Quotes:

Education:
—"Good and evil, reward and punishment, are the only motives to a rational creature: these are the spur and reins whereby all mankind are set on work, and guided." (*Some Thoughts Concerning Education*, 1693, sec. 54.)
—"Virtue is harder to be got than knowledge of the world; and, if lost in a young man, is seldom recovered." (*Some Thoughts Concerning Education*, sec. 64.)
—"The only fence against the world is a thorough knowledge of it." (*Some Thoughts Concerning Education*, sec. 88.)

Error:

—"All men are liable to error; and most men are, in many points, by passion or interest, under temptation to it." (*Essay Concerning Human Understanding*, bk. IV, ch. 20, sec. 17.)
—"It is one thing to show a man that he is in error, and another to put him in possession of truth." (*Essay Concerning Human Understanding*, bk. IV, ch. 7, sec. 11.)

Ideas:
—"There seems to be a constant decay of all our Ideas, even of those which are struck deepest." (*Essay Concerning Human Understanding*, ii. x. 5.)

Law:
—"Wherever Law ends, Tyranny begins." (*Second Treatise of Government*, sec. 202.)
—"Law, in its proper Notion, is the Direction of a free and intelligent Agent to his proper Interest." (*Government*, ii. vi. 57.)
—"The Legislative cannot transfer the Power of making Laws to any other hands." (*Government*, ii. 141 xi. [1694] 276.)

—"We must, wherever we suppose a Law, suppose also some Reward or Punishment annexed to that Rule." (*Essay Concerning Human Understanding*, ii. xxviii. [1695] 192.)

Opinions:
—"New opinions are always suspected, and usually opposed, without any other reason but because they are not already common." (*Essay Concerning Human Understanding*, dedicatory epistle.)

Property:
—"He is willing to join in Society with others for the mutual Preservation of their Lives, Liberties and Estates, which I call by the general Name, Property." (*Government*, ii. ix. 123.)

Understanding:
—"He is certainly the most subjected, the most enslaved, who is so in his Understanding." (*Essay Concerning Human Understanding*, iv. xix. 6.)
—"'Tis Ambition enough to be employed as an Under-Labourer in clearing the Ground a little." (*Essay Concerning Human Understanding*.)
" . . . we are utterly uncapable of universal and certain Knowledge." (*Essay Concerning Human Understanding*, iv. iii. 28.)

Notes

1. Joseph Story, *Commentaries on the Constitution of the United States* (Boston: Hilliard, Gray, and Company 1833), Vol. I, p. 299, n2.
2. Joseph Story, *Commentaries on the Constitution of the United States* (Boston: Hilliard, Gray, and Company 1833), Vol. II, p. 57, n2.
3. Joseph Story, *Commentaries on the Constitution of the United States* (Boston: Hilliard, Gray, and Company 1833), Vol. I, p. 293, n2; p. 299, n2; pp. 305-306.
4. Joseph Story, *Commentaries on the Constitution of the United States* (Boston: Hilliard, Gray, and Company 1833), Vol. III, p. 727.
5. George Bancroft, *History of the United States of America* (Boston: Little, Brown, and Company, 1858; first edition Boston: Charles Bowen, 1834), Vol. II, p. 150.

6. George Bancroft, *History of the United States of America* (Boston: Little, Brown, and Company, 1858; first edition Boston: Charles Bowen, 1834), Vol. II, p. 144.
7. Richard Frothingham, *The Rise of the Republic of the United States* (Boston: Little, Brown, and Company, 1872), p. 165.
8. John Fiske, *Old Virginia and Her Neighbors* (New York: Houghton, Mifflin and Company, 1897), Vol. II, p. 274.
9. John Fiske, *Critical Period of American History: 1783-1789* (New York: Mifflin and Company, 1896), p. 225.
10. Richard Nixon, "Message to the Congress Transmitting the Report of the American Revolution Bicentennial Commission," *The American Presidency Project*, September 11, 1970 (at: http://www.presidency.ucsb.edu/ws/index.php?pid=2658&st=John+Locke&st1=#ixzz1Vm7XvNfc).
11. Gerald Ford, "Address at the Yale University Law School Sesquicentennial Convocation Dinner," *The American Presidency Project*, April 25, 1975 (at: http://www.presidency.ucsb.edu/ws/index.php?pid=4869&st=John+Locke&st1=#ixzz1Vm8RSZb1).
12. Ronald Reagan, "Toasts of the President and Queen Elizabeth II of the United Kingdom at a Dinner Honoring the Queen in San Francisco, California," *The American Presidency Project*, March 3, 1983 (at: http://www.presidency.ucsb.edu/ws/index.php?pid=40996&st=John+Locke&st1=#ixzz1VmAxJTEw).
13. William Clinton, "Remarks at the State Dinner Honoring Prime Minister Tony Blair of the United Kingdom," *The American Presidency Project*, February 5, 1998 (at: http://www.presidency.ucsb.edu/ws/index.php?pid=55226&st=John+Locke&st1=#ixzz1VmCqe1mq).
14. George W. Bush, "Remarks at Whitehall Palace in London, United Kingdom," *The American Presidency Project*, November 19, 2003 (at: http://www.presidency.ucsb.edu/ws/index.php?pid=812&st=John+Locke&st1=#ixzz1VmDpUlFV).
15. John Locke, *The Works of John Locke* (London: Arthur Bettesworth, John Pemberton, and Edward Simon, 1722), Vol. III, p. 1, "Some Thoughts Concerning Education."
16. John Locke, *The Works of John Locke* (London: Arthur Bettesworth, John Pemberton, and Edward Simon, 1722), Vol. III, p. 1, "Some Thoughts Concerning Education."

17. John Adams, *The Works of John Adams*, Charles Francis Adams, editor (Boston: Little, Brown and Company, 1856), Vol. I, p. 53, to Jonathan Sewall on February 1760.
18. Benjamin Rush, *The Selected Writings of Benjamin Rush*, Dagobert D. Runes, editor (New York: The Philosophical Library, Inc., 1947), p. 78, "Observations on the Government of Pennsylvania."
19. Benjamin Rush, *Medical Inquiries and Observations* (Philadelphia: T. Dobson, 1793), Vol. II, p. 17, "An Inquiry into the Influence of Physical Causes upon the Moral Faculty."
20. Benjamin Rush, *Medical Inquiries and Observations* (Philadelphia: Thomas Dobson, 1794), Vol. I, p. 332, "Duties of a Physician."
21. Benjamin Franklin, *The Works of Benjamin Franklin*, Jared Sparks, editor (Boston: Tappan & Whittemore, 1836), Vol. II, p. 131, "Sketch of an English School."
22. Noah Webster, *A Collection of Papers on Political, Literary and Moral Subjects* (New York: Webster & Clark, 1843), p. 308, "Modes of Teaching the English Language."
23. James Wilson, *The Works of the Honourable James Wilson*, Bird Wilson, editor (Philadelphia: Lorenzo Press, 1804), Vol. 1, pp. 6-7, "Of the Study of the Law in the United States."
24. James Monroe, *The Writings of James Monroe*, Stanislaus Murray Hamilton, editor (New York: G. P. Putnam's Sons, 1898), Vol. I, p. 325, "Some Observations on the Constitution, &c."
25. Thomas Jefferson, *The Writings of Thomas Jefferson*, Henry Augustine Washington, editor (Washington, D. C.: Taylor & Maury, 1853), Vol. V, p. 559, to Dr. Benjamin Rush on January 16, 1811.
26. See, for example, REV. JARED ELIOT IN 1738 Jared Eliot, *Give Caesar His Due. Or, Obligation that Subjects are Under to Their Civil Rulers* (London: T. Green, 1738), p. 27, Evans # 4241. REV. ELISHA WILLIAMS IN 1744 Elisha Williams, *The Essential Rights and Liberties of Protestants. A Seasonable Plea for the Liberty of Conscience, and the Right of Private Judgment, in Matters of Religion* (Boston: S. Kneeland and T. Gaben, 1744), p. 4, Evans # 5520. Rev. JONATHAN EDWARDS IN 1754 Jonathan Edwards, *A Careful and Strict Inquiry into the Modern Prevailing Notions of That Freedom of Will, which is Supposed to be Essential to Moral Agency, Virtue and Vice, Reward and Punishment, Praise and Blame* (Boston: S. Kneeland, 1754), pp. 138-140, 143, 164,

171-172, 353-354 (available online at: http://edwards.yale.edu/archive?path=aHR0cDovL2Vkd2FyZHMueWFsZS5lZHUvY2dpLWJpbi9uZXdwaGlsby9uYXZpZ2F0ZS5wbD93amVvLjA=). REV. WILLIAM PATTEN, 1766 William Patten, *A Discourse Delivered at Hallifax in the County of Plymouth, July 24th, 1766* (Boston: D. Kneeland, 1766), pp. 17-18n, Evans # 10440. REV. STEPHEN JOHNSON, 1766 Stephen Johnson, *Some Important Observations, Occasioned by, and Adapted to, the Publick Fast, Ordered by Authority, December 18th, A. D. 1765. On Account of the Peculiar Circumstances of the Present Day* (Newport: Samuel Hall, 1766), pp. 22n-23n, Evans # 10364. REV. JOHN TUCKER, 1771 John Tucker, *A Sermon Preached at Cambridge Before His Excellency Thomas Hutchinson, Esq., Governor; His Honor Andrew Oliver, Esq., Lieutenant-Governor; the Honorable His Majesty's Council; and the Honorable House of Representatives of the Province of the Massachusetts-Bay in New England, May 29th, 1771* (Boston: Richard Draper, 1771), p. 19, Evans # 12256. REV. SAMUEL STILLMAN, 1779 Samuel Stillman, *A Sermon Preached before the Honourable Council and the Honourable House of Representatives of the State of Massachusetts-Bay, in New-England at Boston, May 26, 1779. Being the Anniversary for the Election of the Honorable Council* (Boston: T. and J. Fleet, 1779), pp. 22-25, and many others.

27. Alexander Hamilton, *The Papers of Alexander Hamilton*, Harold C. Syrett, editor (New York: Columbia University Press, 1961), Vol. I, p. 86, from "The Farmer Refuted," February 23, 1775.
28. James Otis, *A Vindication of the Conduct of the House of Representatives of the Province on the Massachusetts-Bay: Most Particularly in the Last Session of the General Assembly* (Boston: Edes & Gill, 1762), p. 20n.
29. Thomas Jefferson, *The Writings of Thomas Jefferson*, Andrew A. Lipscomb, editor (Washington, D.C.: The Thomas Jefferson Memorial Association, 1904), Vol. XV, p. 462, to James Madison on August 30, 1823.
30. Donald S. Lutz, *The Origins of American Constitutionalism* (Baton Rouge: Louisiana State University Press, 1988), p. 143.
31. Donald S. Lutz, *The Origins of American Constitutionalism* (Baton Rouge: Louisiana State University Press, 1988), p. 143.

32. John Locke, *Two Treatises of Government* (London: A. Bettesworth, 1728), Book II, pp. 206-207, Ch. VIII, §95.
33. William Findley, *Observations on "The Two Sons of Oil"* (Pittsburgh: Patterson and Hopkins 1812), p. 35.
34. John Locke, *Two Treatises of Government* (London: A. Bettesworth, 1728), Book II, p. 233, Ch. XI, §135.
35. John Locke, *Two Treatises of Government* (London: A. Bettesworth, 1728), Book II, p. 234, Ch. XI, §135 n., quoting Hooker's Eccl. Pol. 1. iii, sect. 9. (Return)
36. See, for example, John Locke, *The Works of John Locke* (London: T. Davison, 1824), Vol. V, p. 10, "A Letter Concerning Toleration"; John Locke, *Two Treatises of Government* (London: A. Bettesworth, 1728), Book II, pp. 146, 188, 199, 232-233, passim; etc.
37. Samuel Adams, *The Writings of Samuel Adams*, Harry Alonzo Cushing, editor (New York: G. P. Putnam's Sons, 1906), Vol. II, p. 351, from "The Rights Of The Colonists, A List of Violations Of Rights and A Letter Of Correspondence, Adopted by the Town of Boston, November 20, 1772," originally published in the Boston Record Commissioners' Report, Vol. XVIII, pp. 94-108.
38. John Locke, *Two Treatises of Government* (London: A. Bettesworth, 1728), Book II, p. 231,Ch. XI, §134.
39. Alexander Hamilton, John Jay, and James Madison, *The Federalist, or the New Constitution Written in 1788* (Philadelphia: Benjamin Warner, 1818), p. 281, Federalist #51 by Alexander Hamilton.
40. Alexander Hamilton, John Jay, and James Madison, *The Federalist, or the New Constitution Written in 1788* (Philadelphia: Benjamin Warner, 1818), p. 420, Federalist #78 by Alexander Hamilton.
41. John Locke, *Two Treatises of Government* (London: A. Bettesworth, 1728), Book II, p. 271, Ch. XVI, § 192.
42. John Quincy Adams, *The Jubilee of the Constitution. A Discourse Delivered at the Request of the New York Historical Society, in the City of New York, on Tuesday, the 30th of April, 1839; Being the Fiftieth Anniversary of the Inauguration of George Washington as President of the United States, on Thursday, the 30th of April, 1789* (New York: Samuel Colman, 1839), p. 40.
43. John Locke, *Two Treatises of Government* (London: A. Bettesworth, 1728), passim.

44. John Adams, *The Works of John Adams*, Charles Francis Adams, editor (Boston: Little, Brown and Company, 1856), Vol. X, pp. 45-46, to Thomas Jefferson on June 28, 1813.
45. See, for example, Richard Watson, *Theological Institutes: Or a View of the Evidences, Doctrines, Morals, and Institutions of Christianity* (New York: Carlton and Porter, 1857), Vol. I, p. 5, where Watson includes John Locke as a theologian.
46. See, for example, *Concise Oxford Dictionary of World Religions*, John Bowker, editor (Oxford: Oxford University Press, 2000), p. 151; Franklin L. Baumer, *Religion and the Use of Skepticism* (New York: Harcourt, Brace, & Company), pp. 57-59; James A. Herrick, *The Radical Rhetoric of the English Deists: The Discourse of Skepticism, 1680-1750* (Columbia, SC: University of South Carolina Press, 1997), p. 15; Kerry S. Walters, *Rational Infidels: The American Deists* (Durango, CO: Longwood Academic, 1992), pp. 24, 210; Kerry S. Walters, *The American Deists: Voices of Reason and Dissent in the Early Republic* (Lawrence: University Press of Kansas, 1992), pp. 6-7; John W. Yolton, *John Locke and the Way of Ideas* (Oxford: Oxford University Press, 1956), pp. 25, 115.
47. Jack M. Balkin, "Tradition, Betrayal, and the Politics of Deconstruction—Part II," Yale University, 1998 (at: http://www.yale.edu/lawweb/jbalkin/articles/trad2.htm). (Return)
48. Kyle-Anne Shiver, "Deconstructing Obama," AmericanThinker.com, July 28, 2008 (at: http://www.americanthinker.com/2008/07/deconstructing_obama.html).
49. Richard Price, *Observations on the Importance of the American Revolution and the Means of Making it a Benefit to the World* (Boston: True and Weston, 1818), p. 24.
50. Noah Webster, *An American Dictionary of the English Language* (New York: S. Converse, 1828), s.v. "infidel."
51. James Wilson, *The Works of the Honourable James Wilson*, Bird Wilson, editor (Philadelphia: Lorenzo Press, 1804), Vol. I, pp. 67-68, "Of the General Principles of Law and Obligation."
52. Thomas Jefferson, *The Works of Thomas Jefferson*, Paul Leicester Ford, editor (New York: G. P. Putnam's Sons, 1904), Vol. II, pp. 253-254, "Notes on Religion," October, 1776.

Charles de Secondat, Baron de la Brède et de Montesquieu (1689-1755)

Charles Louis de Secondat was born in Bordeaux, France, in 1689 to a wealthy family. Despite his family's wealth, de Secondat was placed in the care of a poor family during his childhood. He later went to college and studied science and history, eventually becoming a lawyer in the local government. De Secondat's father died in 1713 and he was placed under the care of his uncle, Baron de Montesquieu. The Baron died in 1716 and left de Secondat his fortune, his office as president of the Bordeaux Parliament, and his title of Baron de Montesquieu.

Later he was a member of the Bordeaux and French Academies of Science and studied the laws and customs and governments of the countries of Europe. He gained fame in 1721 with his *Persian Letters*, which criticized the lifestyle and liberties of the wealthy French as well as the church. However, Montesquieu's book *On the Spirit of Laws*, published in 1748, was his most famous work. It outlined his ideas on how government would best work.

Montesquieu believed that all things were made up of rules or laws that never changed. He set out to study these laws scientifically with the hope that knowledge of the laws of government would reduce the problems of society and improve human life. According to Montesquieu, there were three types of government: a monarchy (ruled by a king or queen), a republic (ruled by an elected leader), and a despotism (ruled by a dictator). Montesquieu believed that a government that was elected by the people was the best form of government. He did, however, believe that the success of a democracy—a government in which the people have the power—depended upon maintaining the right balance of power.

Montesquieu argued that the best government would be one in which power was balanced among three groups of officials. He thought England—which divided power between the king (who enforced laws), Parliament (which made laws), and the judges of the English courts (who interpreted laws)—was a good model of this. Montesquieu called the idea of dividing government power into three branches the "separation of powers." He thought it most important to create separate branches of government with equal but different powers. That way, the government would avoid placing too much power with one individual or group of individuals. He wrote, "When the [law making] and [law enforcement] powers are united in the same person . . . there can be no liberty." According to Montesquieu, each branch of government could limit the power of the other two branches. Therefore, no branch of the government could threaten the freedom of the people. His ideas about separation of powers became the basis for the United States Constitution.[1]

Note

1 www.rjgeib.com/thoughts/montesquieu/montesquieu.html

Ezra Stiles

Ezra Stiles (November 29, 1727—May 12, 1795) rarely makes even an obscure footnote in most American history texts, yet he was probably the most broadly learned man on the continent during the era of American independence. His book, *The United States Elevated to Glory and Honor*, is a showcase of his tremendous gifts, energy, and enthusiasm. Stiles considered America as a parallel to—perhaps even an extension of—God's covenant promises from deep in the Old Testament.

He begins with the text, Deuteronomy 26:19: "And to make thee high above all nations which he hath made, in praise, and in name, and in honor; and that thou mayest be a holy people unto the Lord thy God."

With God's covenant as the foundation, Stiles refers to "God's American Israel." To this he added that obedience to God was required for national happiness and prosperity (Deut. 29:10, 14; 30:9, 19). Conversely, national disobedience would lead to "the judicial chastisement of apostasy." Based on these ideas, Stiles ordered his message to the state house according to two heads: (1) On what basis could America expect God's blessings, and (2) that dominion and civil polity will remain imperfect unless "the true religion" is diffused among the people.

In other words, civil government is not an end in itself, but rather should be, along with the people themselves, a servant of God. This newly typeset and thoroughly annotated edition adds historical context and illumination through dozens of explanatory footnotes as well as an Introduction by Joel McDurmon.

Ezra Stiles was an American academic and educator, a Congregationalist minister, theologian and author. He was president of Yale College (1778-1795).[1]

Born the son of the Rev. Isaac Stiles in North Haven, Connecticut, Ezra Stiles graduated from Yale in 1746. He studied theology and was ordained in 1749, tutoring at Yale from that year until 1755. Resigning from the ministry, he studied law and practiced at New Haven from 1753 to 1755, when he returned to the ministry for 22 years.

The Ezra Stiles House in Newport is on the National Historic Register. With arrival of British troops in Newport in late 1776, Stiles left Newport and became pastor of the Congregational Church at Portsmouth, New Hampshire from 1777 until 1778, when he became president of Yale until his death. Stiles owned at least one slave, named "Newport," whom he freed on June 9, 1778.[2]

Note

1, Wikipedia, americanvision.com

Stiles quotes:

—"All the forms of civil polity have been tried by mankind, except one, and that seems to have been reserved in Providence to be realized in America."
—"Besides a happy policy as to civil government, it is necessary to institute a system of law and jurisprudence founded in justice, equity, and public right."
—"But after the spirit of conquest had changed the first governments, all the succeeding ones have, in general, proved one continued series of

injustice, which has reigned in all countries for almost four thousand years."
—"It gives me pleasure to find that public liberty is effectually secured in each and all the policies of the United States, though somewhat differently modeled."
—"Let the grand errand into America never be forgotten."
—"The constitutions of Maryland and New York are founded in higher wisdom."
—"The greater part of the governments on earth may be termed monarchical aristocracies, or hereditary dominions independent of the people."
—"The Lord shall have made his American Israel high above all nations which he hath made."—"The right of conscience and private judgment is unalienable, and it is truly the interest of all mankind to unite themselves into one body for the liberty, free exercise, and unmolested enjoyment of this right."[1]

Note

1. Brainy Quote

George Whitefield (1714-1770)

George Whitefield was born on December 16, 1714, in Gloucester, England. The youngest of seven children, he was born in the Bell Inn where his father, Thomas, was a wine merchant and innkeeper. His father died when George was two and his widowed mother Elizabeth struggled to provide for her family. Because he thought he would never make much use of his education, at about age 15 George persuaded his mother to let him leave school and work in the inn. However, sitting up late at night, George became a diligent student of the Bible. A visit to his mother by an Oxford student who worked his way through college encouraged George to pursue a university education. He returned to grammar school to finish his preparation to enter Oxford, losing only about one year of school.

In 1732 at age 17, George entered Pembroke College at Oxford. He was gradually drawn into a group called the "Holy Club" where he met

John and Charles Wesley. Charles Wesley loaned him the book, *The Life of God in the Soul of Man*. The reading of this book, after a long and painful struggle which even affected him physically, finally resulted in George's conversion in 1735. He said many years later: "I know the place . . . Whenever I go to Oxford, I cannot help running to the spot where Jesus Christ first revealed himself to me and gave me the new birth."

Forced to leave school because of poor health, George returned home for nine months of recuperation. Far from idle, his activity attracted the attention of the bishop of Gloucester, who ordained Whitefield as a deacon, and later as a priest, in the Church of England. Whitefield finished his degree at Oxford and on June 20, 1736 and Bishop Benson ordained him. The Bishop, placing his hands upon George's head, resulted in George's later declaration that "My heart was melted down and I offered my whole spirit, soul, and body to the service of God's sanctuary."

Whitefield was an astounding preacher from the beginning. Though he was slender in build, he stormed in the pulpit as if he were a giant. Within a year it was said that "his voice startled England like a trumpet blast." At a time when London had a population of less than 700,000, he could hold spellbound 20,000 people at a time at Moorfields and Kennington Common. For thirty-four years his preaching resounded throughout England and America. In his preaching ministry he crossed the Atlantic thirteen times and became known as the 'apostle of the British empire.' He was a firm Calvinist in his theology yet unrivaled as an aggressive evangelist.

Though a clergyman of the Church of England, he cooperated with and had a profound impact on people and churches of many traditions, including Presbyterians, Congregationalists, and Baptists. Whitefield, along with the Wesleys, inspired the movement that became known as the Methodists. Whitefield preached more than 18,000 sermons in his lifetime, an average of 500 a year or ten a week. Many of them were given over and over again. Fewer than 90 have survived in any form.[1]

Benjamin Franklin became good friends with Whitefield and had some interesting comments about their friendship:

"In 1739 arrived among us from England the Rev. Mr. Whitefield, who had made himself remarkable there as an itinerant Preacher. He was at first permitted to preach in some of our Churches, but the Clergy taking a Dislike to him, soon refus'd him their Pulpits and he was oblig'd to preach in the Fields. (During his second visit to America, 1739-1740, many Anglican churches excluded Whitefield but most Presbyterian churches welcomed him. Preaching in the fields was his custom in England.) The Multitudes of all Sects and Denominations that attended his Sermons were enormous and it a matter of Speculation to me who was one of the Number, to observe the extraordinary Influence of his Oratory on his hearers, and how much they admir'd and respected him . . . He had a loud and clear Voice, and articulated his Words and Sentences so perfectly that he might be heard and understood at a great Distance, especially as his Auditors, however numerous, observ'd the most exact Silence. He preached one Evening from the Top of the Court House Steps, which are in the Middle of Market Street, and on the West Side of Second Street which crosses it at right angles. Both streets were filled with his Hearers to a considerable Distance. Being among the hindmost in Market Street, I had the Curiosity to learn how far he could be heard, by retiring backwards down the Street towards the River, and I found his Voice distinct until I came near Front Street, when some Noise in that Street, obscur'd it. Imagining then a Semicircle, of which my Distance should be the Radius, and that it were filled with Auditors, to each of whom I allow'd two square feet, I computed that he might well be heard by more than Thirty Thousand. This reconcil'd me to the Newspaper accounts of his having preach'd to 25,000 People in the Fields, and to the ancient Histories of Generals haranguing whole Armies, of which I had sometimes doubted."[2]

This is certainly not a complete list of the people who had an impact or, at least an influence on the birth of our nation. Next we will take an in-depth look at some of our Founding Fathers.

The term *deist* pops up frequently in studying this era, and I would like to insert this comment about it by Robert Royal, president of the Faith and Reason Institute. He writes that "a significant minority of the founders and the other colonists had been influenced by a moderate deism of the British sort that also retained strong elements of Christianity. Few, however, were deists properly speaking; most were out-and-out Christians."[3]

Notes

1. *Dictionary of the Christian Church* (1997), 1737-38.
2. Joyce E. Chaplin, *Benjamin Franklin's Autobiography* (W. W. Norton & Company, Inc., 2012), 99, 100, 102.
3. Robert Royal, *The God that Did Not Fail: How Religion Built and Sustains the West* (New York: Encounter Books, 2006), 73

CHAPTER 7

Major Leaders

George Washington, Father of Our Country

George Washington is just one of the great Christian men who fought for freedom and liberty and who has been caught up in the onslaught of propaganda which started close to a hundred years ago to *deny* that this country was founded on biblical principles by Christian men. One example is a book, *Washington and Religion,* written by Paul Boller, which declared that Washington, despite the fact that he was raised in the Anglican Church, was at best only a nominal Christian, and that he found religion to be useful for keeping the lower classes in order. Boller further opined that Washington did not seriously believe the tenets of the faith and had little interest in religion.

Many have followed Boller's lead since at least the 1960s. Some of the descriptions of George Washington have been "a lukewarm Episcopalian"[1], a "warm Deist,"[2] "not a deeply religious man,"[3] "not particularly ardent in his faith,"[4] "one who avoided as was the Deist custom, the word of God."[5] In contrast to this, we will find Washington referring to himself as "ardent," "fervent," "pious," and "devout." There are over one hundred different prayers composed and written by Washington himself, in his own words, in his writings. His passions flared in a letter when his church vestry considered not honoring his purchase of a family pew in his local church. He described himself as one of the deepest men of faith of his day when he confessed to a clergyman, "No man has a more perfect Reliance on the alwise, and powerful dispensations of the supreme Being than I have, nor thinks his aid more necessary."[6]

Rather than avoid the word *God* on the very first national Thanksgiving under the US Constitution, he said, "It is the duty of all Nations to acknowledge the Providence of Almighty God, to obey his will, to be grateful for his benefits, and humbly to implore his protection and favor." He never once used the word *Deist* in his many writings, but he frequently mentioned religion, Christianity, and the Gospel. He spoke of Christ as "the Author of our blessed Religion." He encouraged missionaries who were seeking to "Christianize" the "aboriginals." He took an oath in a private letter to Robert Stewart on April 27, 1763, "On my honor and the faith of a Christian." He wrote of "the blessed religion revealed in the Word of God" and encouraged seekers to learn "the religion of Jesus Christ." He even said to his soldiers, "To the distinguished Character of a Patriot, it should be our highest Glory to add the more distinguished Character of Christian."

There has been some confusion and even some argument between congregations as to who could claim his allegiance. It seems most reliable that he was a real eighteenth-century Anglican. He continually exhibited that he was an orthodox, Trinity believer and believer in Jesus Christ as the Savior of the Bible who died for sinners and was raised from the grave to life.

Over the years, educators have joined with nonbelievers to try and remove any heroic character from the roles of Christians and add them to the growing list of "dead white guys." In fact, the *Washington Times* reported, "George Washington, Thomas Jefferson, and Benjamin Franklin are not included in the revised version of the New Jersey Department of Education history standards, a move some critics view as political correctness at its worst."[7]

This kind of approach to history is evident in various venues, such as a Washington College poll, taken a couple years after his presidency. It said that more Americans had a higher respect for Bill Clinton's job performance as the nation's forty-second president than they did George Washington's."[8] This is shocking!

It was obvious that Washington prayed regularly and often. His literacy in biblical language and his prayers showed that he used the 1662 *Book of Common Prayer* from the Church of England. This was a very strict guide for Christian worship and is considered to be more theologically sound than most books and materials today. This letter, which he wrote on January 20, 1799, to a longtime friend, Reverend Bryan Fairfax, tells a lot about his faith. Lord Fairfax had been the pastor of Washington's church in Alexandria, Virginia:

> The favourable sentiments which others, you say, have been pleased to express respecting me, cannot but be pleasing to a mind who always walked on a straight line, and endeavoured as far as human frailties, and perhaps strong passions, would enable him, to discharge the relative duties to his Maker and fellowmen, without seeking any indirect or left-handed attempts to acquire popularity.[9]

Along the lines the he mentioned in that letter, he openly spoke of his own "fervent prayer" to soldiers. Here is the concluding line from the December 5, 1775, letter to Benedict Arnold: "Give him all the Assistance in your Power, to finish the glorious Work you have begun. That the almighty may preserve and prosper you in it, is the sincere and fervent Prayer of, Dear Sir, Your Humble & Obedient Servant, George Washington."[10]

He also often expressed his own deep faith in God's Providence with such heartfelt language as this letter written on May 13, 1776, to another close friend and minister from Boston, Reverend William Gordon. In referring to God's "many other signal Interpositions of Providence," he declares that they "must serve to inspire every reflecting Mind with Confidence." And then he describes himself with these striking words of spiritual commitment: "No Man has more perfect Reliance on the all-wise, and powerful dispensations of the Supreme Being than I have nor thinks his aid more necessary."[11]

It is not well known, but in Washington's youth and much of his adult life, Virginia had followed the practice of the Church of England and had an established church—the Anglican Church. And by law, everyone was required to attend services and tithe. All colonists were included. In 1786, due primarily to the efforts of Thomas Jefferson and James Madison, the Act for Establishing Religious Liberty became law.

One of the main arguments made by Jefferson was that almighty God has made the mind free and that any punishments that men mete out against religious opinion deemed to be false are a departure from "the plan of the holy author of our religion, who being lord both of body and mind, yet chose not to propagate it by coercions on either, as was in his Almighty power to do, but to exalt it by its influence on reason alone."[12]

Jefferson basically argued that because Jesus Christ could have forced men to believe in him, but did not, and instead gave us the personal responsibility to believe, then who are we as mere men to punish others for their religious opinions, no matter how wrong these opinions may be? Secularists prefer to interpret Jefferson's argument here as a plea for unbelief. Far from it! He uses the example of Christ to argue for religious freedom. In fact, religious liberty in America springs from two great Christian clergymen who prepared the way for our liberty. They were two of our original colonists—Roger Williams and William Penn.

Since he used the word *Providence* so often, one might ask if there is something that would define what Washington means by the word. I believe the answer is found in this letter to the Hebrew congregation of Savannah, Georgia:

> May the same wonder-working Deity, who long since delivering the Hebrews from their Egyptian Oppressors planted them in the promised land—whose Providential Agency has lately been conspicuous in establishing these United States as an independent nation—still continue to water them with the dews of Heaven and to make the inhabitants of every denomination participate in the temporal and spiritual blessings of that people whose God is Jehovah.[13]

The significance of the letter is that it confirms that when George Washington referred to Providence, he was thinking in terms of the God of the Bible. By saying the same God who delivered the ancient Hebrews in the exodus from Egypt was the same God who delivered America, and by calling him the "Providential Agency," Washington is giving us his translation of the term Providence. For him, Providence is the work of Jehovah, the God of the Bible.

After Virginia disestablished the Anglican Church, men and women were free to make their own choices, they weren't required by law to attend a particular church. Washington continued to worship regularly and did so until his death.

Notes

1. Joseph J. Ellis, *His Excellency* (New York: Alfred K. Knopf, 2004), 67
2. Franklin Steiner, *The Religious Beliefs of our Presidents from Washington to FDR* (New York: Prometheus Books, 1995), 43.
3. Willard Sterne Randall, *George Washington, A Life* (New York: Henry Holt and Co., 1997), 91.
4. Douglas Southall Freeman, *George Washington, A Biography,* 7 Vols. (New York: Charles Scribners Sons, 1948), 66.
5. James T. Flesner, *Washington: The Indispensible Man* (New York: Signet, 1984), 44.
6. *Writings of George Washington*, vol. 37, 5-13-1776.
7. Ellen Sorokin, "No Founding Fathers, That's Our New History," *Washington Times* (January 28, 2002).
8. Brit Hume, "The Political Grapevine," *Fox News* (February 22, 2005).
9. *Writings of George Washington,* vol. 37, 1-20-1799.
10. Ibid., vol. 4, 12-5-1775.
11. Ibid., vol. 37, 5-13-1776.
12. Bruce Fronen, ed., *The American Republic: Primary Source* (Indianapolis: Liberty Fund, 2002), 330. Thomas Jefferson, "A Bill for Establishing Religious Freedom," 1786.
13. G.W. Parke Curtis, *Reflections of Washington*, 300-305

Thomas Jefferson—Champion of Liberty

Thomas Jefferson was born on April 13, 1743, at Shadwell, Albemarle County, Virginia. He died peacefully on July 4, 1826, at Monticello, on the fiftieth anniversary of the signing of the Declaration of Independence (age eighty-three). He lived a long and eventful life.

At age nine, Tom, as he was called by his family, was placed under the care of the Reverend William Douglas, an Anglican minister from Scotland who served as his tutor. He learned quickly, learning six languages, including Latin, French, and Greek, and later adding Spanish, Italian, and Anglo-Saxon.

At fourteen, he moved back to the farm where he was born. It was a happy time until his father, Peter, died at the young age of forty-nine. This was a heart-breaking event as young Tom loved and admired his father dearly. He later wrote about the trials and tribulations he endured after the loss of his father as a teenager:

> When I recollect that at fourteen years of age the whole care and direction of myself was thrown on myself entirely, without a relation or friend qualified to advise or guide me, and recollect the various sorts of bad company with which I associated from time to time, I am astonished I did not turn off with some of them and become as worthless to society as they were.[1]

A provision in his father's will, however, assured that his young mind was influenced by more noble influences and helped mold his character into the citizen and leader he turned out to be. After he became an adult, he was known to make a statement concerning how he would have chosen between "the classical education" which his father had made provision for and the estate left to him. He always said he would have chosen the education.

With his father gone and his mother living some distance away, Jefferson was faced with having to make choices that could make or break him as far as his future character was concerned. He eventually developed a method that proved to be quite mature in making good choices. He explained:

> I had the good fortune to become acquainted very early with some characters of very high standing, and to feel the incessant wish that I could ever become what they were. Under temptations and difficulties I would ask myself, what would Dr. Small, Mr. Wythe, [or] Peyton Randolph do in this situation? I am certain that this mode of deciding on my conduct tended more to correctness than any reasoning powers I possessed.[2]

Most of the "characters of very high standing," as he called them, had become friends with him at the College of William and Mary in Williamsburg, Virginia, while he did his advanced studies in January, 1760. He and the residents of this high society and cultural center were mutually impressed with each other. Jefferson had a statuesque physique, almost his full height of six feet, two and one half inches compared to the average man's height at the time of about five feet, six inches. He had a hunger for learning, and his quick advances and accomplishments set him above the crowd.

This statement, made by one his contemporaries sums up the impression he made:

> He was a fresh, bright, healthy-looking youth, with large feet and hands, red hair, freckled skin . . . hazel-gray eyes, prominent cheekbones, and a heavy chin. His form "was as straight as a gun barrel, sinewy and alert," and he cultivated his strength "by familiarity with saddle, gun, canoe and minuet." He early showed . . . perfect self-reliance, and had a strong propensity for mathematics and mechanics.[3]

He jumped right into his studies and often spent fifteen hours a day satisfying his great thirst for knowledge. John Page, his friend and classmate, who would become a Congressman and then Governor of

Virginia, said that Jefferson "could tear himself away from his dearest friends to fly to his studies."[4]

Not long after his arrival at William and Mary, he developed a friendship with one of his instructors, and it was a boon to his exceptional intellectual progress. He said:

> It was my great fortune, and what probably fixed the destinies of my life, that Dr. William Small of Scotland was then professor of mathematics, a man profound in most of the useful branches of science, with a happy talent of communication, correct and gentlemanly manners, and an enlarged and liberal mind. He, most happily for me, became soon attached to me, and made me his daily companion when not engaged in the school, and from his conversation I got my first views of the expansion of science and the system of things in which we are placed.[5]

After his second year at William and Mary, Jefferson graduated. He went straight into the study of law under George Wythe, who was also there in Williamsburg, and for the next five years, he worked and studied in Wythe's law firm. In his zeal for learning, he devoured books in a self-learning frenzy. He studied law, languages, mathematics, philosophy, chemistry, anatomy, zoology, botany, religion, politics, history, literature, rhetoric, and virtually every subject you could name. He was continuously writing down quotations and observations in his voluminous notebooks. Jefferson called this pattern of activity "a time of life when I was bold in the pursuit of knowledge, never fearing to follow truth and reason to whatever results they led."[6] This activity was preparing him for the future when he would be remembered as one of the eminent American statesmen.

George Wythe, who would become a member of Congress and a signer of the Declaration of Independence, was a huge influence on Jefferson, which led him to refer to Wythe at times as his second father. Jefferson paid this tribute to him: "No man ever left behind him a character more venerated than George Wythe. His nature was of the purest tint, his integrity inflexible, and his justice exact; as warm patriotism and devoted as he was to liberty and natural and equal rights of man, he might truly be called the Cato of his country."[7] It is certainly easy to see the image of Wythe's teaching in his student's own everlasting devotion to "liberty and the natural and equal rights of man."

Looking back over this hectic time in his life some fifty years later, Jefferson wrote this letter to his grandson Thomas Jefferson Randolph:

> From the circumstances of my position I was often thrown into the society of horse racers, card players, fox hunters, scientific and professional men, and of dignified men; and many a time I have asked myself in the enthusiastic moment of the death of a fox, the victory of a favorite horse, the issue of a question eloquently argued at the bar or in the great council of the nation, well, which of these kinds of reputations should I prefer? That of a horse jockey? a fox hunter? an orator? Or the honest advocate of my country's rights? Be assured, my dear Jefferson, that these little returns into ourselves, this self-catechizing habit, is not trifling nor useless, but leads to the prudent selection and steady pursuit of what is right.[8]

One of Jefferson's grandsons met an older gentleman, who stated that he had been present during some of Jefferson's legal arguments in Williamsburg. The boy, out of curiosity, asked the man about his grandfather's performance in the courtroom. "Well," said the gentleman, "it is hard to tell, because he always took the right side."[9] His reputation grew rapidly with his successes, and he became quite well-known and sought after for legal matters.

It wasn't long after the tension began to build between the colonies and Great Britain that Jefferson was drawn into the fray. He was asked to be the contact person in the negotiations with the King and his court. He reached a point of frustration in August of 1775 and wrote this letter to his grandson John Randolph:

> In an earlier part of this contest our petitions told him [George III] that from our King there was but one appeal. The admonition was despised, and that appeal forced on us. To undo his empire, he has but one truth more to learn—that after colonies have drawn the sword there is but one step more they can take. That step now is pressed upon us by the measures adopted, as if they were afraid we would not take it.
>
> Believe me, dear sir, there is not in the British Empire a man who cordially loves a union with Great Britain more than I do. But by the God that made me, I will cease to exist before I yield to a connection on such terms as the British Parliament proposes; and in this I think I speak the sentiments of America.[9]

As the situation grew more desperate, the continental Congress debated on separation from Great Britain and finally decided to do so. They considered a declaration, and after a debate between John Adams and Jefferson that ended with Adams stating that Jefferson could write "ten times better" than he could, Jefferson began working on the Declaration of Independence.

There is another debate that I would like to enter into at this point. You remember that it was Jefferson and James Madison who produced the Act for the Establishment of Religious Liberty in Virginia. This was for the purpose of giving everyone the right to worship in whatever manner they chose, without there being a government-based church or denomination that one was required to be a part of.

There has been an ongoing argument about this for a considerable period of time now. Some want to say that Jefferson stated that there should be a wall built between religion and government, denying any religious activity on government property or any government official making any statement concerning God or anything to do with God. All of this is supposedly based on a statement by Thomas Jefferson. My response to that is *ridiculous*!

The statement was extracted from a letter written by Jefferson, not from any official document. The letter was written to:

> Messrs. Nehemiah Dodge and others, a Committee of the Danbury Baptist Association, in the State of Connecticut,
>
> Gentlemen,
> The affectionate sentiments of esteem and approbation which you are so good as to express towards me, on behalf of the Danbury Baptist Association, give me the highest satisfaction. My duties dictate a faithful and zealous pursuit of the interest of my constituents, and in proportion as they are persuaded of my fidelity to these duties, the discharge of them becomes more and more pleasing.
>
> Believing with you that religion is a matter which lies solely between man and his God, that he owes account to none other for his faith or his worship, that the legislative powers of government reach actions only, and not opinions, I contemplate with solemn reverence that act of the whole American people which declared that their legislature should "make no law respecting the establishment of religion, or prohibiting the free exercise thereof," thus building a wall between church and State. Adhering to the expression of the supreme will of the nation in behalf of the rights of conscience, I shall see with sincere satisfaction the progress of those sentiments which tend to restore to man all his natural rights, convinced he has no natural right in opposition to his social duties.
>
> I reciprocate your kind prayers for the protection and blessing of the common Father and Creator of man, and tender you for yourselves and your religious association, assurances of my high respect and esteem.

Note

> Writings of Thomas Jefferson, (Library of America, 1984) 510

You will notice that Jefferson makes it quite clear that our constitution guarantees our right to freely exercise our religion. That means anytime, anywhere. It states that the government may not establish a religion of its own, but it doesn't restrict us, as citizens, from establishing a religion, and it doesn't say that when we do, we have to do it in private. Nowhere in the Constitution does it say that we cannot pray, sing religious songs, or speak to each other about the subject.

There have been judgments made by the courts, restricting religious activity on "public property." You know what? Public property means that it is owned by the taxpaying citizens, and only some special circumstance should allow any person, acting in an "official position" to demand that you vacate the premises. (We will revisit this topic several more times.)

Let's take a look at what Jefferson's own beliefs were, based on his own words and deeds. He is just one of several men of his time who have been labeled as being a Deist. He has denied this. In a letter to John Adams on April 11, 1823, he was discussing religion, which he did quite often with Adams. When the subject of "Atheist" came up in the letter, he said, "An Atheist, . . . I can never be."

On another occasion in 1807, he said this about religious freedom being the best support of good government: "Among the most inestimable of our blessings . . . is that of liberty to worship our Creator in the way we think most agreeable to his will; a liberty deemed in other countries incompatible with good government, and yet proved by our experience to be its best support."[10]

Another aspect of this debate that I find intriguing is what has been called "The Jefferson Bible." Jefferson took the New Testament and pulled out of the gospels of Matthew, Mark, Luke, and John a collection of sayings and deeds of Jesus Christ.

What he called it was *The Life and Morals of Jesus of Nazareth.* The detractors want to say he wasn't really a Christian because he purposely left out all the miracles in the Gospels. I have a copy, and I find it interesting that there are several entries that describe Jesus healing from one to several people and another where he gave the twelve disciples power over unclean spirits. There is also the subject of the letter that Jefferson wrote to Charles Thomson, where he states:

> I, too, have made a wee-little book from the same materials (gospels), which I call the Philosophy of Jesus; it is a paradigm of his doctrines, made by cutting the texts out of the book, and arranging them on the pages of a blank book, in a certain order of time or subject. A more beautiful or precious morsel of ethics I have never seen; it is a document in proof that *I am a real Christian,* . . . very different from the Platonists, who call *me* infidel and *themselves* Christians and preachers of the gospel, while they draw all their characteristic dogmas from what its author never said nor saw.[11]

Notes

1. Thomas Jefferson Randolph, *The Writings of Thomas Jefferson* (New York: Library of America, 1983), 1193-97. Thomas Jefferson to Thomas Jefferson Randolph, November 24, 1808.
2. Ibid.
3. Curtis, *The True Thomas Jefferson* (1901), 24.
4. Thomas Jefferson Randolph, *The Domestic Life of Thomas Jefferson* (1871), 31.
5. Malone, *Jefferson the Virginian* (1948), 58.
6. Randolph, *The Writings of Thomas Jefferson*, 1321-29.
7. Albert Ellery Bergh, ed., *The Writings of Thomas Jefferson* (Washington: The Thomas Jefferson Memorial Association, 1907), vol. 10:321. Thomas Jefferson to John Anderson, August 31, 1820.
8. Randolph, *The Writings of Thomas Jefferson*, 1193-97.
9. Thomas JeffersonRandolph, *The Domestic Life of Thomas Jefferson* (1871), 40.

10. Bergh, *The Writings of Thomas Jefferson*, vol. 16:291.
11. Randolph, *The Writings of Thomas Jefferson*, 1172-77. Thomas Jefferson to Charles Thomson, January 9, 1816.

Benjamin Franklin: Inventor, Statesman

Benjamin Franklin was born January 17, 1705, to Josiah and Abiah Folger Franklin. From 1714 to 1716 he attended Boston Grammar School (one year) and George Brownell's English school (one year). He was withdrawn when his father could no longer afford the school fees. He was home schooled, and in 1718 apprenticed to his brother James, a printer in Boston, where his love of writing was born.

His autobiography is the most obvious evidence of Franklin's desire to shape and record his life in very practical ways. Born a son of a Boston artisan, his father made candles and bars of soap from animal fat. Little Benjamin couldn't look forward to an inheritance and faced the certainty of having to make his own way in life. But he had an ambition bigger than just getting by. He wanted to be famous.

In those times, the only ways to become famous were through the deeds of a warrior or the written word. He thoughtfully considered both. He loved reading in Plutarch's *Lives* about the ancient heroes of the wars. His uncle, who was also named Benjamin Franklin, had warned him of the dangers of the soldier's life, and his father would not let him become a sailor. But when they placed him in the care of his brother, the printer, they opened the door to his writing, which he started under the alias "Silence Dogood." He read as many of the self-help and self-improvement books that were available as he could, including Daniel Defoe's *Essay upon Projects* (1697) and Thomas Tryon's *Way to Health* (1691).

Franklin had been trained as a printer to compose and publish only those writings that he expected to have an audience. He also wanted to help others, as the works that he had read had helped him. By the time he started his memoirs in 1771, he was one of the most famous colonists of his day. By 1784, when he began his writing again, he was the most recognizable American of the era.

The key to Franklin's fame was his work in natural science, especially the experiments that described the first convincing theory of electricity. Most children remember seeing pictures of him out on the cloudy day with his kite and a key tied to the string. He had been modestly successful prior to these experiments and was the wealthiest member of his extended family, which consisted mostly of artisans in skilled trades and some farmers. The rest were sailors and whalers.

It was only after Franklin published his *Experiments and Observations on Electricity* in 1751 that his career and reputation began to accelerate. He used that work to explain electricity in a convincing manner for the first time. Franklin was quickly recognized as the best experimenter of his time. Having been, for the most part, self-educated, he had followed the highly respected tradition of Robert Boyle and Isaac Newton to investigate the workings of nature.

In 1752 he received honorary degrees from Harvard and Yale and was awarded the Copley Medal of the Royal Society of London, Britain's premier scientific organization. More honors followed, as well as political positions—colonial agent based in London, American commissioner based in Paris—these would not have gone to a chandler's son and retired printer.[1]

Let's look now at some excerpts from some of Franklin's letters:

In 1771, while staying at the rural estate of the Bishop of St. Asaph I England, Franklin wrote to his son:

> And therefore in many Cases it would not be quite absurd if a Man were to thank God for his Vanity among the other Comforts of Life. And now I speak of thanking God, I desire with all Humility to acknowledge, that I owe the mention'd happiness of my past Life in his kind Providence, which led me to the Means I us'd and gave them Success. My Belief of This, induces me to hope, tho' I must not presume, that the same Goodness will still be exercis'd towards in continuing that Happiness, or in enabling me to bear a fatal Reverso, which I may

> experience as others have done. The Complexion of my future Fortune being known to him only: and in whose Power it is to bless to us even our Afflictions.[2]

"From a Child I was fond of Reading, and all the little Money that came into my Hands was ever laid out in Books . . . My Father's little Library consisted of Books in polemic Divinity, most of which I read, and have since often regretted, that a time when I had such a Thirst for Knowledge, more proper Books had not fallen in my Way, since it was now resolv'd I should not be a Clergyman."[3]

"I was never without some religious Principles; I never doubted, for instance, the Existence of the Deity, that he made the world, and govern'd it by his Providence; that the most acceptable Service of God was the doing good to Man; that our Souls are immortal; and that all Crime will be punished and Virtue rewarded either here or hereafter."[4]

In writing to Dr. Ezra Stiles, President of Yale College, Franklin wrote:

> You desire to know something of my religion. Here is my creed. I believe in one God, the Creator of the universe. That he governs it by his Providence. That he ought to be worshipped. That the most acceptable service we render to him is in doing good to his other children. That the soul of man is immortal, and will be treated with justice in another life respecting its conduct in this. These I take to be the fundamental points in all sound religion. As to Jesus of Nazareth, my opinion of whom you particularly desire, I think the system of morals, and his religion, as he left them to us, is the best the world ever saw, or is likely to see. I apprehend it has received various corrupting changes; and I have, with most of the present dissenters in England, some doubt as to his divinity, though it is a question I do not dogmatize upon, having never studied it, and think it needless to busy myself with now, when

> I soon will have an opportunity of knowing the truth, with less trouble. I see no harm, however, in its being believed, if that belief has the good consequence, as probably it has, of making his doctrines more respected and observed, especially as I do not perceive that the Supreme takes it amiss, by distinguishing the believers in his government of the world with any peculiar marks of his displeasure. I shall only add, respecting myself, that, having experienced the goodness of that Being in conducting me prosperously through a long life, I have no doubt in its continuance in the next, though without the smallest conceit of meriting such goodness.[5]

In writing to the Rev. George Whitefield, whom we mentioned before, Franklin makes these comments:

> For my own part, when I am employed in serving others, I do not look upon myself as conferring favors, but as paying debts. In my travels, and since my settlement, I have received much kindness from men to whom I shall never have an opportunity of making the least direct return, and numberless mercies from God, who is infinitely above being benefited by our services. These kindnesses from men I can, therefore, only return to their fellow-men; and I can only show my gratitude to God, by a readiness to help his other children and my brethren; for I do not think that thanks and compliments, though repeated weekly, can discharge our real obligation to each other, and much less to our Creator.
>
> . . . Even the mixed imperfect pleasures we enjoy in this world are rather from God's goodness than our merit: how much more so the happiness of heaven!
>
> The worship of God is a duty; the hearing and reading may be useful; but if men rest in hearing and praying—as too many do—it is as if the tree should

> value itself on being watered and putting forth leaves, though it never produced any fruit.
>
> Your good Master thought less of these outward appearances than many of his modern disciples. He preferred the doers of the word to the hearers; the son that seemingly refused to obey his father and yet performed his commands, to him that professed his readiness but neglected the work; the heretical but charitable Samaritan, to the uncharitable and orthodox priest and sanctified Levite; and those who gave food to the hungry. drink to the thirsty, and raiment to the naked, entertainment to the stranger, and never heard of his name, he declares, shall, in the last day, be accepted, when those who cry, Lord, Lord, who value themselves on their faith, though great enough to perform miracles, but having neglected good works, shall be rejected.[6]

I think we have left little doubt about this man's love and acknowledgment of almighty God and his reverence for him in all he says and does.

Notes

1. Joyce E. Chaplin, ed., *Benjamin Franklin's Autobiography* (Harvard University, New York: W. W. Norton & Co., 2012), xvii-xix.
2. Ibid., 9-10.
3. Ibid., 17.
4. Ibid., 77.
5. Benjamin F. Morris, *The Christian Life and Character of the Civil Institutions of the United States* (Powder Springs, GA: American Vision, Inc., 2007), 157-58.
6. Ibid., 158-60.

John Adams

John Adams was born October 30, in the North Precinct of Braintree, Massachusetts, the first child john Adams, Sr., a farmer, deacon, and shoemaker, and Susanna Boylston Adams. His father, who was born in 1691, was a great-grandson of Henry Adams, who immigrated to Massachusetts from Somerset in 1638. His mother was born in Brookline in 1705 and was the granddaughter of Thomas Boylston, who emigrated from London in 1656.

Adams was taught to read at home and later attended schools in Braintree. He later described himself as an indifferent student who wished to be a farmer like his father, despite his father's intention that he attend Harvard and become a minister. He later transferred to Joseph Marsh's school in Braintree where he thrived and dedicated himself to studying Latin, in keeping with traditional preparation for college. He did, in fact, enroll at Harvard and was listed as fourteenth out of the twenty-five students based on "dignity of family."

He was tutored in Latin by the Rev. Joseph Mayhew and studied mathematics and natural philosophy, including astronomy and meteorology with Professor John Winthrop. He graduated in 1755 with his BA and began to teach in Worcester, Massachusetts in order to support himself, while deciding whether to "study Divinity, Law or Physick."

He wrote to his classmate and cousin Nathan Webb saying, "At College gay, gorgeous, prospects danc'd before my Eyes, and Hope, sanguine Hope, invigorated my Body, and exhilerated my soul. But now Hope has left me, my organs rust and my Faculty's decay." He decried the "Frigid performances" of local ministers, the disciples of "Frigid John Calvin." He read Milton, Virgil, Voltaire, and Bolingbroke.[1]

The entry in Adams's diary, dated February 16, 1756, said this:

> A most beautiful morning. We have the most moderate Winter that ever was known in this country. For a long time together we have had serene and temperate Weather and all the Roads perfectly settled and smooth like Summer.—The Church of Rome has made it an Article of Faith that no man can be saved out of their Church, and all other religious

> Sects approach to this dreadful opinion in proportion to their Ignorance, and the Influence of ignorant or wicked Priests. Still reading the Independent Whigg. Oh! that I could wear out of my mind every mean and base affectation, conquer my natural Pride and Self Conceit, expect no more defference from my fellows than I deserve, acquire that meekness, and humility, which are the sure marks and Characters of a great and generous Soul, and subdue every unworthy Passion and treat all men as I wish to be treated by all. How happy should I then be, in the favour and good will of all honest men, and a sure prospect of a happy immortality![2]

During the period August 1—October 18, 1761 he wrote:

> The English Constitution is founded, tis bottomed and grounded on the Knowledge and good sense of the People. The very Ground for our Liberties, is the freedom of Elections. Every Man has in Politicks as well as religion, a Right to think and speak and Act for himself. No man, either King or Subject, Clergymen or Layman has any right to dictate to me the Person I shall choose for my Legislator and Ruler. I must judge for myself, but how can I judge, how can any Man judge, unless his Mind has been opened and enlarged by Reading. A Man who can read, will find in his Bible, in the common sermon Books that common People have by them and even in the Almanack and News Pages, Rules and observations, that will enlarge his Range of Thought, and will enable him the better to judge who has and who has not that Integrity of Heart, and that Compass of Knowledge and Understanding, which form the Statesman.[3]

The following is the first portion of "A Dissertation on the Canon and Feudal Law No. II" that Adams wrote. It appeared in the *Boston Gazette* on August 19, 1765:

> Thus accomplished were the first Planters of these Colonies. It may be thought polite and fashionable, by many modern fine Gentlemen perhaps, to deride the Characters of these Persons, as enthusiastical, superstitious, and republican: But such ridicule is found in nothing but foppery and affectation, and is grosly injurious and false. Religious to some degree of enthusiasm it may be admitted they were, but this can be no peculiar derogation from their character, not only of England, but of Christendom. Had this however, otherwise, their enthusiasm, considering the principles in which it was founded, and the ends to which it was directed, far from being a reproach to them, was greatly to their honour: for I believe it will be found universally true, that no great enterprise, for the honour or happiness of mankind, was ever achieved, without a large mixture of infirmity. Whatever imperfections may be justly ascribed to them, which however are as few, as any mortals have discovered their judgment in framing their policy, was founded in wise, humane and benevolent principles; It was founded in revelation, and in reason too; It was consistent with the principles, of the best, and greatest, and wisest legislators of antiquity.[4]

Here are some quotes by Benjamin F. Morris concerning Adams:

> "His faith and soul clung to the Christian religion as the hope of himself and his country."
>
> Quoting Jefferson he says, "Jefferson said of Adams that 'a man more perfectly honest never came from the hands of the Creator.'"
>
> Quoting Adams, he said, "The Christian religion, as I understand it, is the brightness of the glory and the express portrait of the character of the eternal, self-existent, independent, benevolent, all-powerful,

> and all-merciful Creator, Preserver and Father of the universe, the first good, the first perfect, and the first fair. It will last as long as the world. Neither savage nor civilized man, without revelation, could have discovered or invented it."
>
> "Religion and virtue are the only foundations, not only of republicanism and of all free governments, but of social felicity under all governments and in all the combinations of human society. Science, liberty, and religion are the choicest blessings of humanity; without their joint influence no society can be great, flourishing or happy."[5]

On February 4, 1789, Presidential electors met in their states and voted for two candidates for the first president of the United States. George Washington received the votes of all sixty-nine electors and was elected president, while John Adams received thirty-four votes and was elected vice president. He subsequently succeeded Washington after his two terms and was elected to be the second president of our country.

Notes

1. *John Adams, Revolutionary Writings 1755-1775*, Gordon Wood, ed. (New York: Literary Classics of the United States, Inc., 2011), 651-52.
2. Ibid., 5-6.
3. Ibid., 64-65.
4. Ibid., 118.
5. Benjamin F. Morris, *The Christian Life and Character of the Civil Institutions of the United States* (Powder Springs: GA: American Vision, Inc., 2007), 147.

James Madison

Like his close friend Thomas Jefferson, James Madison came from a prosperous family of Virginia planters, received an excellent education, and quickly found himself drawn into the debates over independence. In 1776, he became a delegate to the revolutionary Virginia Convention, where he worked closely with Thomas Jefferson to push through religious freedom statutes, among other liberal measures. The youngest member of the Continental Congress, Madison was small in stature. His soft spoken, shy demeanor was a foil for his brilliant persistence in advocating his political agenda. Madison emerged as a respected leader of the congress, known for his hard work and careful preparation.

Believing that the Articles of Confederation rendered the new republic subject to foreign attack and domestic turmoil, James Madison helped set the wheels in motion for a national convention to draft the young nation's Constitution. Madison led the Virginia delegation to the Philadelphia meeting, which began on May 14, 1787, and supported the cry for General Washington to chair the meeting. Madison's "Virginia Plan" became the blueprint for the Constitution that finally emerged, eventually earning him the revered title, "Father of the Constitution." Having fathered the document, Madison worked hard to ensure its ratification. Along with Alexander Hamilton and John Jay, he published the Federalist Papers, a series of articles arguing for a strong central government subject to an extensive system of checks and balances. He then forged twelve proposed constitutional amendments, which Congress sent to the states in 1789. The states ratified ten of them by 1791.

The First Amendment combined several rights—speech, press, assembly and religion—into one fundamental law that guaranteed freedom of expression in these different areas. Although religious speech was included, the focus was on political speech. In fact the Founders certainly had no intention of ignoring religion, nor did they embrace or even discuss separation of church and state, this phrase that we hear so often now. It is not found anywhere in the Constitution or the Bill of Rights. It is, in fact, a fabrication. As stated before, the closest thing you will find to this is a statement made by Thomas Jefferson in a letter he once wrote. There is nothing in the workings of government except for some judicial judgments that have been made by judges who used that misconception in their rulings.

Madison had long been a champion of religious liberty. He attended the College of New Jersey, which later became Princeton, and studied under the Reverend John Witherspoon. In May, 1776, when Virginia lawmakers wrote the state's new constitution, Madison changed George Mason's phrase that stated "all men should enjoy the fullest toleration" of religion to "all men are entitled to the full and free exercise of religion."

By this Madison rejected the notion that the exercise of faith originated with government, while at the same time indicating that he expected a continual and ongoing practice of religious worship. He resisted attempts to insert the name of Jesus Christ into the Virginia Bill for Religious Liberty, not because he was an unbeliever, but because he argued that "better proof of reverence for that holy name would be not to profane it by making it a topic of legislative discussion."

Later in life Madison wrote, "Belief in a God All Powerful wise and good, is so essential to the moral order of the World and the happiness of man, that arguments to enforce it cannot be drawn from too many sources." He also considered the widespread agreement within the Constitutional Convention "a miracle" and wrote, "It is impossible for the man of pious reflection not to perceive in (the convention) a finger of that Almighty hand."[1]

Religious, and especially Christian, influences in the Constitution and the Bill of Rights were so predominant that as late as the mid-twentieth century, the chairman of the Sesquicentennial Commission on the Constitution answered negatively when asked if an atheist could become president. "I maintain that the spirit of the Constitution forbids it. The Constitution prescribes an oath of affirmation . . . [that] in its essence is a covenant with the people which the President pledges himself to keep with the help of almighty God."[2]

Modern interpretations of the Constitution that prohibit displays of crosses in the name of religious freedom would rightly have been shouted down by the Founders, who intended no such separation.

Notes

1. Robert A. Rutland, ed., *The Papers of James Madison* (Chicago: University of Chicago Press, 1962), 10:208. W. Cleon Skousen, *The Making of America* (Washington, D.C.: The National Center for Constitutional Studies, 1985), 5.
2. Sol Bloom, *The Story of the Constitution* (Washington, D.C.: U.S. Sesquicentennial Commission, 1937), 43.

John Leland

This man was not widely known during his lifetime, but I believe he needs to be mentioned. I had never heard of him until I found a faded old book in a box of discarded books in our church library. This book, entitled *The John Leland Story*, by Don M. Fearheily, was published in 1964. He states that it is a story, and that it is not presented as a historical document. It does; however, bring out a colorful description of the concerns of the people about the connection, or friction, that might develop with regards to the church and the governing body of the new nation.

The story he tells is that of a group of church leaders, including John Leland who was a Baptist minister, meeting in 1788 to discuss their concerns. The twenty men made up the Baptist General Committee. Their main concern was that certain churches might find favor with the government, as had happened in the Mother Country. They had already seen the Episcopal Church incorporate and maintain ownership of great tracts of land it had been given by the Crown. Through a powerful fight by some of the men in this group they were able to see the principal provisions of the Act of Corporation repealed. They only wanted fair and balanced treatment of all church organizations.

John Leland had come up with ten suggestions for provisions to grant certain individual rights and protections, and he later met with James Madison to discuss them. It makes for an interesting story and puts a colorful light on what is presumed to be the beginning of the Bill of Rights that are the first ten amendments to the US Constitution. Let me present to you some additional information about the little-known John Leland.

John Leland (1754-1841) was a Baptist minister who lived and worked in the state of Massachusetts. Leland was committed to separation of church and state and helped Madison win the Virginia battles for religious freedom. In addition, he helped lead the fight to ratify the Constitution in Massachusetts. His writings under the name Jack Nips in *The Yankee Spy* was an effort to gain support for separation of church and state in Massachusetts.

Here are some examples of his writings:[1]

"Let it suffice on this head to say, that it is not possible in the nature of things to establish religion by human laws without perverting the design of civil law and oppressing the people" (from *The Yankee Spy*, Boston, 1794).

"To read in the New Testament, that the Lord has ordained that those that preach the gospel shall live by its institutions and precepts, sounds very harmonical; but to read in a state constitution, that the legislature shall require men to maintain teachers of piety, religion and morality, sounds very discordant" (from *The Yankee Spy,* John Leland writing under the pen name of Jack Nips, Boston, 1794).

"To say that religion cannot stand without a state establishment is not only contrary to fact (as has been proved already) but is a contradiction in phrase. Religion must have stood a time before any law could have been made about it; and if it did stand almost three hundred years without law it can still stand without it" (from *The Connecticut Dissenters Strong Box*, Number One, New London 1802).

"If government can answer for individuals at the day of judgment, let men be controlled by it in religious matters; otherwise let men be free" (from *The Connecticut Dissenters Strong Box*, Number One, New London 1802.

"[A]nd the reason why public worship is enjoined (required) by authority, and private worship is omitted, is only to pave the way for some religious establishment by human law, and force taxes from the people to support avaricious priests" (Boston, 1794).

"What leads legislators into this error, is confounding sins and crimes together—making no difference between moral evil and state rebellion: not considering that a man may be infected with moral evil, and yet be guilty of no crime, punishable by law. If a man worships one God, three Gods, twenty Gods, or no God—if he pays adoration one day in a week, seven days or no day—wherein does he injure the life, liberty or property of another? Let any or all these actions be supposed to be religious evils of an enormous size, yet they are not crimes to be punished by laws of state, which extend no further, in justice, than to punish the man who works ill to his neighbor" (Boston, 1784).

"In a well regulated state it will be the business of the legislature to prevent sectaries of different denominations from molesting and disturbing each other; to ordain that no part of the community shall be permitted to perplex and harass the other for any supposed heresy, but that each individual shall be allowed to have and enjoy, profess and maintain his own system of religion, provided it does not issue in overt acts of treason against the state undermining the peace and order of society (from *The Yankee Spy*, John Leland writing under the pen name of Jack Nips, Boston, 1794).

You have to admire this man's tenacious efforts to see that all men have the right to worship as they are led without interference from other groups or the government. *That is religious freedom!*

Notes

1. Charles Hyneman and Donald Lutz, *Political Writing During the Founding Era: 1760-1805* (1983) 123-125

CHAPTER 8

The Character of Our Founders

There were so many exceptional people involved in the birth and formation of this country that I felt it would be unfair not to at least offer a capsulized narrative of who and what they were. These people showed how important it was to risk everything, including their lives, to form and defend this country.

James Otis

Otis was one of the Massachusetts founders and was among the first and foremost champions of freedom. He was educated by Rev. Jonathan Russell, minister of his parish, and in this Christian school caught the indomitable spirit of resistance to despotism. "Otis," said John Adams, "is a flame of fire,"—referring to a speech he made in Boston, in 1761, against the oppression of the British Government. "With a promptitude of classical allusions, a depth of research, a rapid summary of historical events and dates, a profusion of legal authorities, a prophetic glance of his eyes into futurity, and a rapid torrent of impetuous eloquence, he hurried all before him. American independence was then and there born. The seeds of patriot, and heroes to defend the vigorous youth were there and then sown. In fifteen years—i.e. in 1776—he grew up to manhood and declared himself free."

"There can be," said Otis, "no prescriptions old enough to supersede the law of nature, and the grant of Almighty God, who has given all men a right to be free. Government springs from the necessities of our nature, and has an everlasting foundation in the unchangeable will of God. The first principle and great end of government being to provide for the best good of all the people, this can be done only by a supreme legislature and executive, ultimately in the people, or the whole community, where God has placed it.

"The right of every man to his life, his liberty, no created being can rightfully contest. They are rights derived from the Author of nature—inherent, inalienable, and indefeasible by any law, compacts, contracts, covenants, or stipulations which man can devise. God made all men naturally equal."

Joseph Warren

Warren was known for his virtues and for his intense patriotism. He became a martyr to liberty at Bunker Hill, the 17th of June, 1775. He combined in a remarkable degree the qualities requisite for excellence in civil pursuits, with a strong taste for the military. He was educated at Cambridge University, and had in high perfection the gift of eloquence. His fine accomplishments as an orator, a patriot, and a professional and literary man were crowned with the virtues of religion. Jared Sparks, a historian and educator of the time, said of Warren, "There is hardly one whose example exercised a more inspiring and elevating influence upon his countrymen and the world than that of the brave, blooming, generous, self-devoted martyr of Bunker Hill. Such a character is the noblest spectacle which the moral world affords. It is declared by a poet to be a spectacle worthy of the gods. The friends of liberty, from all countries and throughout all time, as they kneel upon the spot that was moistened by the blood of Warren, will find their better feelings strengthened by the influence of the place, and will gather from it a virtue in some degree allied to his own."

On the morning of the battle of Bunker Hill, at a meeting of the Committee of Safety, Elbridge Gerry earnestly requested him not to expose his person. "I am aware of the danger," replied Warren; "but I should die with shame if I were to remain at home in safety while my friends and fellow-citizens are shedding their blood and hazarding their lives in the cause." "Your ardent temper," replied Gerry, "will carry you forward into the midst of peril, and you will probably fall." "I know that I may fall," replied Warren; "but where is the man who does not think it glorious and beautiful to die for his country?"

"*Dulce et decorum est pro patria mori.*"

"In the private walks of life," said an orator who pronounced a eulogy on Warren in Boston, April 8, 1776, at the reinterment of his remains, "he was a pattern for mankind. In public life, the sole object of his ambition was to acquire the conscience of virtuous enterprises: *amor patrioe* was the spring of his actions, and *mens conscia recti* as his guide. And on this security he was, on every occasion, ready to sacrifice his health, his interest, and his ease to the calls of his country. When the liberties of his country were attacked, he appeared an early champion in the contest; and though his knowledge and abilities would have insured riches and preferment (could he have stooped to prostitution), yet he nobly withstood the fascinating charm, tossed fortune back her plume, and pursued the inflexible purpose of his soul in guiltless competence. The greatness of his soul shone even in the moment of death. In fine, to complete the great character, like Harrington he wrote, like Cicero he spoke, and like Wolfe he died. The name and the virtues of Warren shall remain immortal."

In an oration delivered in Boston, March 5, 1772, Warren, after discussing the principles of liberty, closes as follows—

"If you with united zeal and fortitude oppose the torrent of oppression; if you feel the true fire of patriotism burning in your breasts; if you from your souls despise the most gaudy dress that slavery can wear; if you really prefer the lonely cottage (whilst blest with liberty) to gilded palaces surrounded with the ensigns of slavery—you may have the fullest assurances that tyranny, with her whole accursed train, will hide their hideous heads in confusion, shame, and despair. If you perform your part, you must have the strongest confidence that The Same Almighty Being who protected your venerable and pious forefathers, who enabled them to turn a barren wilderness into a fruitful field, who so often made bare his arm for their salvation, will be still mindful of you, their offspring.

"May this Almighty Being graciously preside in all our councils. May he direct us to such measures as he himself will approve and be pleased to bless. May we ever be a people favored of God. May our land be a land of liberty, the seat of virtue, the asylum of the oppressed, a name and a praise in the whole earth, until the last shock of time shall bury the empires of the world in one common undistinguished ruin."

Samuel Adams

Benjamin Morris called Samuel Adams a true Christian statesman and hero, wise, ardent, fearless, and influential. Adams was "a member of the church, and in a rigid community was an example of morals and the scrupulous observance of every ordinance. Evening and morning his house was a house of prayer; and no one more revered the Christian Sabbath." He was among the foremost patriots of the Revolution, and one of the signers of the Declaration of Independence. After that act had been passed, he stood on the steps of the Continental State-House, on the first of August, 1776, in Philadelphia, and, before thousands of patriots, delivered an oration, in which are the following passages—

"The time at which this attempt on our liberties was made, when we were ripened into maturity, had acquired a knowledge of war, and were free from intestine enemies—the gradual advances of our oppressors, enabling us to prepare for our defence—the unusual fertility of our lands—the success which at first attends our feeble arms, producing unanimity among our friends and reducing our internal foes to acquiescence—these are strong and palpable assurances that Providence is yet gracious unto our Zion, that it will turn away our captivity.

"These are instances of, I would say, an almost astonishing providence in our favor; so that we may truly say that it is not our arm that has saved us. The hand of Heaven appears to have led us on to be, perhaps, humble instruments and means in the great providential dispensation which is completing. Brethren and fellow-countrymen, if it was ever granted to mortals to trace the designs of Providence and interpret its manifestations in favor of its cause, we may, with humility of soul, cry out, 'Not unto us, not unto us, but to thy name be the praise.'

"My countrymen, from the day on which an accommodation takes place between England and America on any other terms than as independent states, I shall date the ruin of this country. We are now, to the astonishment of the world, three millions of souls united in one common cause. This day we are called on to give a glorious example of what the wisest and best of men were rejoiced to view only in speculation. This day presents the world with the most August spectacle that its annals ever unfolded—millions of freemen voluntarily and deliberately forming themselves into a society for the common defence and common happiness. Immortal spirits of Hampden, Locke, and Sidney! Will it not add to your benevolent joys to behold your posterity rising to the dignity of men, and evincing to the world the reality and expediency of your systems, and in the actual enjoyment of that equal liberty which you were happy, when on earth, in delineating and recommending to mankind!"

Patrick Henry

This passionate and eloquent orator of liberty and the Revolution, was a profound believer in the divinity of Christianity, and declared its necessity to nations and governments as well as to the salvation and happiness of the soul. In April, 1775, he uttered the following sentiments—

"He had no doubt that the God who, in former ages, had hardened Pharaoh's heart, that he might show his power and glory in the redemption of his chosen people, for similar purposes had permitted the flagrant outrages which had occurred throughout the continent. It was for them now to determine whether they were worthy of divine interference—whether they would accept the high boon now held out to them by Heaven;—that, if they would, though it might lead them through a sea of blood, they were to remember that the same God whose power divided the Red Sea for the deliverance of Israel still reigned in all his glory, unchanged and unchangeable—was still the enemy of the oppressor and the friend of the oppressed—that he would cover them from their enemies by a pillar of cloud by day, and guide them through the night by a pillar of fire."

In an impassioned burst of patriotism, he exclaimed, "We must fight. I repeat it, sir, we must fight. An appeal to arms and the God of hosts is all that is left us. Nor shall we fight our battles alone. That God who presides over the destinies of nations will raise up friends for us."

In reference to resolutions against the scheme of taxing the colonies, passed by the Virginia legislature in 1765, he stated, "Whether they will prove a blessing or a curse will depend on the use which our people make of the blessings which a gracious God hath bestowed on us. If they are wise, they will be great and happy. If they are of a contrary character, they will be miserable. Righteousness alone can exalt them as a nation." Reader, whoever thou art, remember this, and in thy sphere practise virtue thyself, and encourage it in others.

"He was," says Wirt, his biographer, "a sincere Christian. His favorite religious works were Doddridge's *Rise and Progress of Religion in the Soul*, Butler's *Analogy of Religion Natural and Revealed*, and Jenyn's *Views of the Internal Evidences of the Christian Religion*." "Here," said he to a friend (holding up the Bible), "is a book worth more than all other books that were ever printed." His last will bears this testimony, to his children and his countrymen, to the truth and importance of religion—"I have now disposed of all my worldly property to my family: there is one thing more I wish I could give them, and that is the Christian religion. If they had this, and I had not given them one shilling, they would be rich; and if they had it not, and I had given them all the world, they would be poor."

John Hancock

The son of a clergyman of Braintree, Massachusetts, was distinguished for his patriotism, piety, and benevolence. His great wealth and eminent talents were consecrated to his country. He was President of the Congress of 1776, and his name, in a bold, broad hand, stands first on the Declaration of Independence. Early in the struggle for independence and freedom, he inspired his patriot companions with such stirring Christian words as these—

"I have the most animating confidence that the present noble struggle for liberty will terminate gloriously for America. And let us play the men for our God, and for the cities of our God: while we are using the means in our power, let us humbly commit our righteous cause to the great Lord of the Universe, who loveth righteousness and hateth iniquity. And, having secured the approbation of our hearts by a faithful and unwearied discharge of our duty to our country, let us joyfully leave our concerns in the hands of Him who raiseth up and putteth down the empires and kingdoms of the earth as he pleaseth, and, with cheerful submission to his sovereign will, devoutly say, 'Although the fig tree shall not blossom, neither shall fruit be in the vines; the labor of the olive shall fail, and the field shall yield no meat; the flock shall be cut off from the fold, and there shall be no herd in the stall: yet we will rejoice in the Lord, we will joy in the God of our salvation.'"

Robert Treat Paine

A signer of the Declaration of Independence, had studied prayerfully and thoroughly the whole range of theology before he entered upon the study of law. He was for a short time chaplain in the army, and preached occasionally in Boston. "He was a decided, firm believer in the Christian revelation, and was fully convinced of its divine origin. He received it as a system of moral truth and righteousness given by God for the instruction, consolation, and happiness of man. His intellectual, moral, and religious character was strongly marked with integrity."

Elbridge Gerry

Also a signer of the Declaration of Independence, and Vice-President of the United States, was a statesman who recognized the providence of God in human affairs, and had faith in the divinity of Christianity. In a letter to Samuel Adams, December 13, 1775, he says, "History can hardly produce such a series of events as has taken place in favor of American opposition. The hand of Heaven seems to have directed every occurrence. Had such an event as lately occurred at Essex happened to Cromwell, he would have published it as a miracle in his favor, and excited his soldiers to enthusiasm and bravery." "It is the duty of every citizen," he said, "though he had but one day to live, to devote that day to the service of his country."

"May that Omnipotent Being," (in addressing the Senate in 1814,) "who with infinite wisdom and justice presides over the destinies of nations, confirm the heroic patriotism which has glowed in the breasts of the national rulers, and convince the enemy that, whilst a disposition to peace on honorable and equitable terms will ever prevail in their public councils, one spirit, animated by the love of country, will inspire every department of the national government."

Matthew Thornton

A native of Ireland, was distinguished in the cause of liberty. He was a signer of the Declaration of Independence, and the disciple and friend of Washington. "No man was more deeply impressed with a belief in the existence and bounties of an overruling Providence—which he strongly manifested by a practical application of the strongest and wisest injunctions of the Christian religion. A believer in the divine mission of our Savior, he followed the great principles of his doctrines."

William Ellery

An ardent patriot, active and influential in Congress, and a signer of the Declaration of Independence, was a Christian statesman. "He studied the Scriptures with reverence and diligence; feeling their value, seeking for the truth, and aiming at the obedience they require." He had firm faith in the justice and goodness of God. In the most gloomy periods of the Revolution, he always ended his cheering addresses by saying, "Let us be hopeful and trusting; for 'the Lord reigneth.'"

Roger Sherman

Sherman was a wise legislator, an ardent and incorruptible patriot, and a ripe Christian statesman. He had the unbounded confidence of Congress, and was on the committee to draft the Declaration of Independence. In Congress he advocated the Christian duty and propriety of appointing days of fasting and prayer and thanksgiving to Almighty God, and was the author of several of those eminently Christian state papers. He had great influence in imbuing the public and legislative transactions of the country with a scriptural sense of the need of God's presence and blessing. Washington esteemed and revered him as an eminent Christian and as a wise statesman. Adams said, "He was one of the soundest and strongest pillars of the Revolution."

In early youth he made a public profession of religion, and for more than a half-century he defended its doctrines and illustrated its virtues. He applied Christian principles to every department of society, and considered all governments sadly defective that were not based on the moral teachings and principles of the Bible.

At his funeral it was said by his pastor, Jonathan Edwards, Jun., D.D., that, "whether we consider him as a politician or a Christian, he was a great and good man. The words of David concerning Abner may with great truth be applied on this occasion—'Know ye not that there is a great man fallen this day in Israel?' He ever adorned the profession of Christianity which he made in youth, was distinguished through life for public usefulness, and died in prospect of a blessed immortality."

The predominant traits in Mr. Sherman's character were his practical wisdom and his strong common sense. Mr. Jefferson, on one occasion, when pointing out the various members of Congress to a friend, said—"That is Mr. Sherman, of Connecticut, a man who never said a foolish thing in his life." He possessed a singular power of penetrating into the characters and motives of men, while the rectitude and integrity of his own nature enabled him to acquire an extraordinary influence. "Though a man naturally of strong passions, he obtained a complete control over them, by means of his deep religious spirit, and became habitually calm, sedate, and self-possessed."

Richard Stockton

Stockton was a true patriot, a ripe statesman, an eloquent orator, a profound jurist, and an honor to the Christian Church. He signed the Declaration of Independence, and aided greatly in our struggle for freedom. His will attests his views of the truth and importance of the Christian religion, in these words—

"As my children will have frequent occasion of perusing this instrument, and may be particularly impressed with the last words of their father, I think proper here not only to subscribe to my entire belief in the great leading doctrines of the Christian religion, such as the being of a God, and the universal defection and depravity of human nature, the divinity of the Person and the completeness of the redemption purchased by the blessed Saviour, the necessity of the operations of the Divine Spirit, of divine faith accompanied with an habitual virtuous life, and the universality of the Divine Providence, but also, in the bowels of a father's affection, to charge and exhort them to remember that the fear of the Lord is the beginning of wisdom."

John Witherspoon

Witherspoon was a prominent Christian patriot, and a learned minister of the gospel. He was from Scotland, the land of learning and of liberty, and a descendant of John Knox, the Reformer. His great learning attracted the attention of the friends of education, and he was called to the presidency of Princeton College. Soon after his arrival the scenes of the Revolution opened, and the college was suspended. "Under his auspices," says Dr. Rogers, a contemporary, "have been formed a large proportion of the clergy of the Presbyterian Church, and to his instructions America owes many of her most distinguished patriots and legislators. In the civil councils of his adopted country he shone with equal lustre, and his talents as a legislator and senator showed the extent and the variety of the powers of his mind. His distinguished abilities pointed him out to the citizens of New Jersey as one of the most proper delegates to the convention which formed their republican Constitution. In this assembly he appeared to all the professors of law as profound a civilian as he had before been known to be a philosopher and divine. Early in the year 1776 he was sent, as a representative of the people of New Jersey, to the Congress of the United States. He was seven years a member of that illustrious body, which, under Providence, in the face of innumerable difficulties and dangers, led us on to the establishment of our independence.He was one of the signers of the Declaration of Independence. While he was thus engaged in serving his country in the character of a civilian, he did not lay aside his ministry."

He advocated the cause of the country, with admirable simplicity, by his pen; exalting it in the pulpit by associating the interests of civil and religious liberty, and zealously co-operating in its active vindication in Congress. He was an eminent Christian statesman, as well as a pious and learned divine. "If the pulpit of America," says Headley, "had given only this one man to the Revolution, it would deserve to be held in everlasting remembrance for the service it rendered the country."

A sermon which Dr. Witherspoon preached at Princeton, on the 17th of May, 1776, being the general fast appointed by the Congress through the United Colonies, entitled "The Dominion of Providence over the Passions of Men," was rich in profound thought, and eloquent and just in its views of civil and religious liberty. His object in the discourse was to show that public calamities and commotions, the ambition of mistaken princes, and the passions and wickedness of men, are under the dominion of God, and will be overruled for the advancement and establishment of religion and liberty.

The passage on which he based this noble discourse was, "Surely the wrath of man shall praise thee: the remainder of wrath shalt thou restrain."—(Psalm 76: 10.)

The following extracts are given—

"There is no part of Divine Providence in which a greater beauty and majesty appears, than when the Almighty Ruler turns the councils of wicked men into confusion, and makes them militate against themselves." This he illustrates by many marked events in sacred and profane history. And, applying the doctrine of the discourse to the condition of the colonies struggling for liberty, he says, "You may perceive what ground there is to give praise to God for his favors already bestowed on us respecting the public cause. It would be a criminal inattention not to observe the singular interposition of

Providence hitherto in behalf of the American colonies. How many discoveries have been made of the designs of the enemy in Britain and among ourselves, in a manner as unexpected to us as to them, and in such season as to prevent their effect! What surprising success has attended our encounters in almost every instance! Has not the boasted discipline of regular and veteran soldiers been turned into confusion and dismay before the new and maiden courage of freemen in defence of their property and rights? In what great mercy has blood been spared on the side of this injured country! Some important victories have been gained in the South, with so little loss that enemies will probably think it dissembled. The signal advantage we have gained by the evacuation of Boston, and the shameful flight of the army and navy of Britain, was brought on without the loss of a man. To all this we may add, that the counsels of our enemies have been visibly confounded, so that I believe I may say with truth that there is hardly any step which they have taken but it has operated strongly against themselves, and been more in our favor than if they had followed a contrary course.

"While we give praise to God, the supreme disposer of all events, for his interposition in our behalf, let us guard against the dangerous error of trusting in or boasting of an arm of flesh. I could earnestly wish that, while our arms are crowned with success, we might content ourselves with a modest ascription of it to the power of the Highest. The Holy Scriptures in general, and the truths of the glorious gospel in particular, and the whole course of Providence, seem intended to abase the pride of man and lay the vain-glorious in the dust. The truth is, that through the whole frame of nature and the whole system of human life, that which promises most performs the least. The flowers of finest colors seldom have the sweetest fragrance.

"The trees of greatest growth or fairest form are seldom of the greatest value or duration. Deep waters run with the least noise. Men who think most are seldom talkative. And I think it holds as much in war as in any thing, that every boaster is a coward. I look upon ostentation and confidence to be a sort of outrage upon Providence; and when it becomes general and infuses itself into the spirit of a people, it is the forerunner of destruction.

"From what has been said you may learn what encouragement you have to put your trust in God, and hope for his assistance in the present important conflict. He is the Lord of Hosts, great in might and strong in battle. Whoever has his countenance and approbation shall have the best at last. If your cause is just, you may look with confidence to the Lord and entreat him to plead it as his own. I would neither have you to trust in an arm of flesh, nor to sit with folded hands and expect that miracles shall be wrought in your defence. In opposition to it, I would exhort as Joab did the host of Israel, who in this instance spoke like a prudent general and a pious man—'Be of good courage, and let us behave ourselves valiantly for our people, and for the cities of our God; and the Lord do that which is good in his sight.'" (2 Sam. 10:12)

"He is the best friend to American liberty who is the most sincere and active in promoting true and undefiled religion, and who sets himself with the greatest firmness to bear down profanity and immorality of every kind. Whoever is an avowed enemy to God, I scruple not to call him an enemy to his country. It is your duty in this important and critical season to exert yourselves, everyone in his proper sphere, to stem the tide of prevailing vice, to promote the knowledge of God, the reverence of his name and worship, and obedience to his laws. Your duty to God, to your country, to your families, and to yourselves, is the same.

"True religion is nothing else but an inward temper and outward conduct suited to your state and circumstances in Providence at any time. And as peace with God and conformity to him add to the sweetness of created comforts while we possess them, so in times of difficulty and trial it is the man of piety and inward principle that we may expect to find the uncorrupted patriot, the useful citizen, and the invincible soldier. God grant that in America true religion and civil liberty may be inseparable, and that the unjust attempts to destroy the one may in the issue tend to the support and establishment of both."

In affixing his name to the Declaration of Independence, he rose in that illustrious body of men and uttered the following thrilling words—

"Mr. President—That noble instrument on your table, which insures immortality to its author, should be subscribed this very morning by every pen in the House. He who will not respond to its accents, and strain every nerve to carry into effect its provisions, is unworthy the name of freeman. Although these gray hairs must descend into the sepulchre, I would infinitely rather they should descend thither by the hand of the executioner, than desert at this crisis the sacred cause of my country."

The appeal was electric. Every member rose and affixed his name to that immortal declaration.

George Mason

Part of the Virginia group, Mason was one of the purest and ablest of the men who conducted the important events of the Revolution to a fortunate and triumphant issue. He was a man endowed by nature with a vigorous understanding, which had been well cultivated by a liberal education. In temperament he was like the younger Cato, constitutionally stern, firm, and honest. His profound legal learning and his political views and public duties, as well as his private life and character, were all under the guidance of virtue and religion, which gave him an illustrious and influential position in the cause of liberty and independence.

"He was among the earliest and most distinguished of all the champions of freedom and an independent constitutional government; and no man exerted a greater influence on the fortunes of the country. He was a member of the Convention of Virginia which, on the 15th of May, 1776, declared that State independent, and formed a State constitution; and to him belongs the honor of having drafted the first declaration of rights ever adopted in America. It was made a part of the Constitution of Virginia, where it yet remains. In this declaration of Mason's, man seems to stand erect in all the majesty of his nature—to assert the inalienable rights and equality with which he has been endowed by his Creator, and to declare the fundamental principles by which all rulers should be governed and on which all governments should rest. Several of the fundamental articles are listed below:

"1. That all men are created equally free and independent, and have certain inherent natural rights, of which they cannot, by any compact, deprive or divest their posterity; among which are the enjoyment of life and liberty, with the means of acquiring and procuring property and pursuing and obtaining happiness and safety.

"2. That all power is by God and nature vested in, and consequently derived from, the people; that magistrates are their trustees and servants, and at all times amenable to them.

"3. That government is, or ought to be, instituted for the common benefit, protection, and security of the people, nation, or community.

"15. That no free government, or the blessings of liberty, can be insured to any people, but by a firm adherence to justice, moderation, temperance, frugality, and virtue, and by frequent recurrence to fundamental principles.

"16. That religion, or the duty which we owe to our Creator, and the manner of discharging it, can be directed only by reason and conviction, not by force and violence, and, therefore, that all men should enjoy the fullest toleration in the exercise of religion, according to the dictates of conscience, unpunished and unrestrained by the magistrate; unless under color of religion any man disturb the peace or the safety of society; and that it is the mutual duty of all to practise Christian forbearance, love, and charity towards each."

"If I can only live to see," said Mason, "the American Union firmly fixed, and free government well established in our Western world, and can leave to my children but a crust of bread and liberty, I shall die satisfied, and say, with the Psalmist, 'Lord, now lettest thou thy servant depart in peace.'"

The following extract from Mr. Mason's last will and testament attests to his passionate patriotism and presents his view of public life—

"I recommend it to my sons, from my own experience in life, to prefer the happiness of independence and a private station to the troubles and vexatious of public business; but, if their own inclinations or the necessity of the times should engage them in public affairs,

I charge them, on a father's blessing, never to let the motives of private interest or ambition induce them to betray, nor the terrors of poverty and disgrace, or the fear of danger and death, deter them from asserting, the liberty of their country, and endeavoring to transmit to their posterity those sacred rights to which themselves were born."

This great man, whose soul was ever inflamed with liberty, and whose masterly intellect illuminated the grand era of the Revolution with its clear and steady light, died in a ripe old age, chastened and sanctified by providential afflictions in his family, leaving a legacy of glory and virtue to his country.

Gouverneur Morris

A resident of New York, Morris was an eminent statesman of the Revolution, and he exerted a prominent influence in the formation of our republican institutions. He was for many years in Congress and an ambassador to France. During the terrific reign of atheism in that country, he drew up a constitution for France, one article of which read as follows—

"Religion is the solid basis of good morals: therefore education should teach the precepts of religion and the duties of man towards God. These duties are—internally, love and adoration; externally, devotion and obedience: therefore provision should be made for maintaining divine worship as well as education. But each has a right to entire liberty as to religious opinions, for religion is the relation between God and man: therefore it is not within the reach of human authority."

"The education of young citizens," another article declared, "ought to form them to good manners, to accustom them to labor, to inspire them with a love of order, and to impress them with respect for lawful authority."

To a nobleman of France, Mr. Morris wrote, in June, 1792, "I believe that religion is the only solid basis of morals, and that morals are the only possible support of free governments."

In 1816, Mr. Morris was elected the first president of the New York Historical Society. In his inaugural address he presented his views of Christianity as follows—

"The reflection and experience of many years have led me to consider the holy writings not only as most authentic and instructive in themselves, but as the clue to all other history. They tell us what man is, and they alone tell us what he is. All of private and of public life is there displayed. From the same pure fountain of wisdom we learn that vice destroys freedom, that arbitrary power is founded on public immorality, and that misconduct in those who rule a republic, the necessary consequence of general licentiousness, so disgusts and degrades that, dead to generous sentiment, they become willing slaves.

"There must be religion. When that ligament is torn, society is disjointed, and its members perish. The nation is exposed to foreign violence and domestic convulsion. Vicious rulers, chosen by a vicious people, turn back the current of corruption to its source. Placed in a situation where they can exercise authority for their own emolument, they betray their trust. They take bribes. They sell statutes and decrees. They sell honor and office. They sell conscience. They sell their country. By this vile practice they become odious and contemptable.

"The most important of all lessons from the Scriptures is the denunciation of the rulers of every state that rejects the precepts of religion. Those nations are doomed to death who bury in the corruption of criminal desire the awful sense of an existing God, cast off the consoling hope of immortality, and seek refuge from despair in the dreariness of annihilation. Terrible, irrevocable doom—loudly pronounced, repeatedly, strongly exemplified in the sacred writings, and fully confirmed by the long record of time! It is the clue which leads through the intricacies of universal history. It is the principle of all sound political science.

"Hail! Columbia! Child of science, parent of useful arts, dear country, hail! Be it thine to ameliorate the condition of man. Too many thrones have been reared by arms, cemented by blood, and reduced again to dust by sanguinary conflict of arms. Let mankind enjoy at last the consolatory spectacle of thy throne, built of industry on the basis of peace, and sheltered under the wings of justice. May it be secured by a pious obedience to the divine will, which prescribes the moral orbit of the empire with the same precision that his wisdom and power have displayed in the wheeling millions of planets round millions of suns, through the vastness of infinite space."

Charles Cotesworth Pinckney

Pinckney was a distinguished Revolutionary officer of South Carolina, and among the most brilliant lawyers of his age. His eminent abilities and virtues induced Washington to proffer him several of the highest places of trust in the Government—Judge of the Supreme Court, Secretary of War, and Secretary of State—all of which he declined because of private considerations. He was a member of the convention which framed the Constitution of the United States. He was profoundly read in legal learning, and in his practice liberal and benevolent, never taking a fee from the widow and orphan. His great talents and attainments were sanctified and directed by the Christian religion, and his character adorned by its virtues. He had practical faith in the divinity of the Bible and its essential need for a republican government, and for more than fifteen years before his death he acted as President of the Bible Society in Charleston, an office to which he was elected with unanimity by Christians of every sect.

Benjamin Rush

Benjamin Rush was an eminent physician and philanthropist and one of the immortal men who signed the Declaration of Independence. He was as eminent a Christian as he was distinguished for his influence in the councils of the country. John Adams declared him to be "one of the greatest and best of Christians." He delighted in acts of Christian charities, and "esteemed the poor his best patients; for God," said he, "is their paymaster." He was an earnest advocate of introducing and reading the Bible daily as a common school book in all public schools and in every seminary of learning. He wrote as follows on this important subject—

The Bible as a School-Book

"Before I state my arguments in favor of teaching children to read by means of the Bible, I shall assume the five following propositions—

"I. That Christianity is the only true and perfect religion, and that in proportion as mankind adopt its principles and obey its precepts, they will be wise and happy.

"II. That a better knowledge of this religion is to be acquired by reading the Bible than in any other way.

"III. That the Bible contains more knowledge necessary to man in his present state than any other book in the world.

"IV. That knowledge is most durable, and religious instruction most useful, when imparted in early life.

"V. That the Bible, when not read in schools, is seldom read in any subsequent period of life.

"My arguments in favor of the use of the Bible as a schoolbook are founded, first, in the constitution of the human mind. The memory is the first faculty which opens in the minds of children. Of how much consequence, then, must it be to impress it with the great truths of Christianity before it is preoccupied with less interesting subjects! There is also a peculiar aptitude in the minds of children for religious knowledge. I have constantly found them, in the first six or seven years of their lives, more inquisitive upon religious subjects than upon any others; and an ingenious instructor of youth has informed me that he has found young children more capable of receiving just ideas upon the most difficult tenets of religion than upon the most simple branches of human knowledge.

"There is a wonderful property in the memory, which enables it, in old age, to recover the knowledge it had acquired in early life, after it had been apparently forgotten for forty or fifty years. Of how much consequence, then, must it be to fill the mind with that species of knowledge, in childhood and youth, which, when recalled in the decline of life, will support the soul under the infirmities of age and smooth the avenues of approaching death! The Bible is the only book which is capable of affording this support to old age; and it is for this reason that we find it resorted to with so much diligence and pleasure by such old people as have read it in early life. I can recollect many instances of this kind, in persons who discovered no attachment to the Bible in the meridian of their lives, who have, notwithstanding, spent the evening of them in reading no other book.

"My second argument in favor of the use of the Bible in schools, is founded upon an implied command of God, and upon the practice of several of the wisest nations of the world. In the sixth chapter of Deuteronomy we find the following words, which are directly to my purpose—'And thou shalt love the Lord thy God with all thine heart, and with all thy soul, and with all thy might. And these words which I command thee this day shall be in thine heart: and thou shalt teach them diligently unto thy children, and shalt talk of them when thou sittest in thine house, and when thou walkest by the way, and when thou liest down, and when thou risest up.'

"I have heard it proposed that a portion of the Bible should be read every day by the master, as a means of instructing children in it. But this is a poor substitute for obliging children to read it as a school-book; for by this means we insensibly engrave, as it were, its contents upon their minds; and it has been remarked that children instructed in this way in the Scriptures seldom forget any part of them. They have the same advantage over those persons who have only heard the Scriptures read by a master, that a man who has worked with the tools of a mechanical employment for several years has over the man who has only stood a few hours in the workshop and seen the same business carried on by other people."

Dr. Rush was an active friend of every philanthropic and Christian reform. He was an earnest advocate of temperance and wielded his pen powerfully in its defence. In an address to the people of the United States, in 1787, Dr. Rush said—

"There is nothing more common than to confound the terms of the American Revolution with those of the late American War. The

American War is over; but this is far from being the case with the American Revolution. On the contrary, nothing but the first act of the great drama is closed. It remains yet to establish and perfect our new forms of government, and to prepare the principles, morals, and manners of our citizens for these forms of government, after they are established and brought to perfection.

"To conform the principles, morals, and manners of our citizens to our republican forms of government, it is absolutely necessary that knowledge of every kind should be disseminated through every part of the United States.

"For this purpose let Congress found a federal university. In this university let everything connected with government—such as history, the law of nature and nations, the civil law, the municipal laws of our country, and the principles of commerce—be taught by competent professors. Let masters be employed likewise to teach gunnery, fortification, and everything connected with defensive and offensive war. Above all, let a professor of, what is called in the European universities, economy, be established in this federal seminary. His business should be to unfold the principles and practice of agriculture and manufactures of all kinds; and, to make his lectures more extensively useful, Congress should support a travelling correspondent for him, who should visit all the nations of Europe, and transmit to him, from time to time, all the discoveries and improvements that are made in agriculture and manufactures.

"Let every man exert himself in promoting virtue and knowledge in our country, and we shall soon become good republicans. Every man in a republic is public property. His time and talents, his youth and manhood, his old age, nay, more, his life, his all, belong to his country."

Fisher Ames

Ames was a distinguished lawyer, a pure patriot, a fascinating orator, and an eminent Christian statesman. He was active and influential in giving form and direction to the civil government of the United States.

As a representative in the legislature of Massachusetts, he advocated the adoption of the Federal Constitution and for eight years, the whole of Washington's administration, was a member of Congress from that State. His character as a patriot rests on the highest grounds. He loved his country with equal purity and fervor. This affection was the spring of all his efforts to promote her welfare. he sought the glory of being a benefactor to a great people he justly valued. In the character of Mr. Ames the circle of the virtues seemed to be complete, and each virtue in its proper place.

"The objects of religion presented themselves with a strong interest to his mind. The relation of the world to its Author, and of this life to a retributory scene in another, could not be contemplated by him without the greatest solemnity. The religious sense was, in his view, essential in the constitution of man. He placed a full reliance on the divine origin of Christianity. He felt it his duty and interest to inquire, and discovered on the side of faith a fullness of evidence little short of demonstration. At about thirty-five he made a public profession of his belief in the Christian religion, and was a regular attendant to its services. In regard to articles of belief, his conviction was confined to those leading principles about which Christians have little diversity of opinion.

"He loved to view religion on the practical side, as designed to operate by a few simple and grand truths on the affections, actions, and habits of men. He cherished the sentiment and experience of religion, careful to ascertain the genuineness and value of impressions and feelings by their moral tendency. His conversation and behavior evinced the sincerity of his religious impressions. No levity on these subjects ever escaped his lips; but his manner of recurring to them in conversation indicated reverence and feeling. The sublime, the affecting character of Christ he never mentioned without emotion."

This distinguished orator, in all his writings and speeches, imbued them with the pure and lofty sentiments of religion. In an article, written in 1801 for a periodical in Boston, on the subject of books for children, he speaks of the Bible, as adapted to the tender years and opening minds of children—

"Why, then, should not the Bible regain the place it once held as a school-book? Its morals are pure, its examples captivating and noble. The reverence for the sacred book, that is thus early impressed, lasts long, and probably, if not impressed in infancy, never takes firm hold of the mind. One consideration more is important. In no book is there so good English, so pure, and so elegant; and by teaching all the same book, they will speak alike, and the Bible will justly remain the standard of language as well as of faith."

Robert Morris

Morris was the great financier of the Revolution, a signer of the Declaration of Independence, and a member of the convention that framed the Constitution of the United States. It may be truly said of him, as it was of the Roman Curtius, that he sacrificed himself for the safety of the commonwealth. He was a great and good man. "The Americans owed, and still owe, as much acknowledgment to the financial operations of Robert Morris as to the negotiations of Benjamin Franklin, or even to the arms of George Washington."

Alexander Hamilton

Hamilton was the intimate friend and companion of Washington. He was a statesman of the highest order and had pre-eminent influence in forming the national Constitution and the present government. He was educated by Rev. Hugh Knox, a Presbyterian minister, to whom Hamilton was greatly attached. The fervent piety of this gentleman gave a strong religious bias to his feelings. When Hamilton was appointed aid-de-camp and secretary to Washington, Knox wrote him as follows—

"We rejoice in your good character and advancement, which is indeed the only just reward of merit. May you still live to deserve more and more of America, and justify the choice and merit the approbation of the great and good Washington, a name dear to the friends of the liberties of mankind! Mark this: you must be the annalist and biographer, as well as the aid-de-camp, of General Washington, and the historiographer of the American war. I believe, few men will be so well qualified to write the history of the present glorious struggle. God only knows how it will terminate. But, however that will be, it will be an interesting story."

"Hamilton was stamped by the Divine hand with the impress of genius. He had indeed a mind of immense grasp and unlimited original resources." He uttered such views of moral government as follows—

"The Supreme Intelligence who rules the world has constituted an eternal law, which is obligatory upon all mankind, prior to any human institution whatever. He gave existence to man, together with the means of preserving and beautifying that existence, and invested him with an inviolable right to pursue liberty and personal safety. Natural liberty is the gift of the Creator to the whole human race. Civil liberty is only natural liberty modified and secured by the sanctions of civil society. It is not dependent on human caprice, but it is conformable to the constitution of man, as well as necessary to the well-being of society. The sacred rights of mankind are not to be rummaged for among old parchments or musty records. They are written, as with a sunbeam, in the whole volume of human nature, by the hand of Divinity itself, and can never be erased or obscured by human power. This is what is called the law of nature, which, being coeval with mankind and dictated by God himself, is, of course, superior in obligation to any other. No human laws are of any validity if contrary to this. It is binding over all the globe, in all countries, and at all times."

In reference to the death of Washington, Hamilton said, "If virtue can secure happiness in another world, he is happy. This seal is now upon his glory. It is no longer in jeopardy by the fickleness of fortune."

"It is difficult," says Fisher Ames, speaking of Hamilton, after his death, "in the midst of such varied excellences, to say in what particular the effect of his greatness was most manifest. No man more promptly discerned truth; no man more clearly displayed it: it was not merely made visible; it seemed to come bright with illumination from his lips. He thirsted only for that fame which virtue would not blush to confer, nor time to convey to the end of his course. Alas! The great man who was at all times the ornament of our country is withdrawn to a purer and more tranquil region. May Heaven, the guardian of our liberty, grant that our country may be fruitful of Hamiltons and faithful to their glory."

Charles Carroll

Carroll was the last survivor of the signers of the Declaration of Independence, was a member of the Roman Catholic Church, and was distinguished in his Christian patriotism and virtues. Lord Brougham says, "He was among the foremost to sign the celebrated Declaration of Independence. As he set his hand to the instrument, someone said, 'There go some millions of property;' but, as there were many of the same name, he was told he might get clear. 'They will never know which to take.' 'Not so,' he replied, and instantly added—'of Carrollton.' He was universally respected for his patriotism and virtues. He had talents and acquirements which enabled him effectually to help the cause he espoused. His knowledge was various, and his eloquence was of a high order. It was like his character, mild and pleasant—like his deportment, correct and faultless."

In the year 1826, after all save one of the band of patriots whose signatures are on the Declaration of Independence had descended to the tomb, and the venerable Carroll alone remained among the living, the government of the city of New York deputed a committee to wait on the illustrious survivor, and obtain from him, for deposit in a public hall of the city, a copy of the Declaration of 1776, graced and authenticated anew with his sign-manual. The aged patriot yielded to the request, and affixed with his own hand to a copy of the instrument the grateful, solemn, and pious supplementary declaration which follows—

"Grateful to Almighty God for the blessings which, through Jesus Christ our Lord, he has conferred on my beloved country in her emancipation, and in permitting me, under circumstances of mercy, to live to the age of eighty-nine years, and to survive the fiftieth year of American Independence, adopted by Congress on the 4th of July, 1776, which I originally subscribed on the 2nd day of August of the same year, and of which I am now the last surviving signer, I do hereby recommend

to the present and future generations the principles of that important document as the best inheritance their ancestors could bequeath to them, and pray that the civil and religious liberties they have secured to my country may be perpetuated to remotest posterity and extended to the whole family of man." Chas. Carroll, of Carrollton
August 2, 1826

Charles Thomson

Thomson was the Secretary of the Continental Congress, a Quaker by birth and education, and a man of distinguished virtue and integrity of character. He possessed in an eminent degree the confidence of Congress, and was the active and steadfast friend of the Christian religion. His selection as secretary has a historic interest and singularity. The Continental Congress first sat in the building then called Carpenter's Hall, up the court of that name in Chestnut Street. On the morning of the day that they first convened, their future secretary, Charles Thomson, who resided at that time in the Northern Liberties, and who afterwards so materially assisted to launch our first-rate republic, had ridden into the city and alighted in Chestnut Street. He was immediately accosted by a messenger from Congress; they desired to speak with him. He followed the messenger, and, entering the building, he said he was struck with awe upon viewing the aspects of so many great and good men impressed with the weight and responsibility of their situation, on the perilous edge of which they then were advancing. He walked up the aisle, and, bowing to the president, desired to know their pleasure. "Congress requests your services, sir, as their secretary." He took his seat at the desk, and never looked back until the vessel was securely anchored in the haven of independence.

John Jay

John Jay was a Christian legislator, statesman, and judge. He exerted a large and active influence in the Revolution, and in founding and administering the civil government of the United States. In private and public life he was an eminent Christian. His recognition of God and belief in the Christian religion were striking elements of his character.

"Whoever," said he, "compares our present with our former constitution will find abundant reasons to rejoice in the exchange, and readily admit that all the calamities incident to this war will be amply compensated by the many blessings flowing from this revolution.

"We should always remember that the many remarkable and unexpected means and events by which our wants have been supplied and our enemies repelled or restrained are such strong and striking proofs of the interposition of Heaven, that our having been hitherto delivered from the threatened bondage of Britain ought to be forever ascribed to its true cause (the favor of God), and, instead of swelling our breasts with arrogant ideas of our prowess and importance, kindle in them a flame of gratitude and piety which may consume all remains of vice and irreligion."

During a most gloomy period of the Revolution, when New York was in the hands of the British, and Washington was retreating through New Jersey, with an almost naked army, and the country desponding, John Jay animated his countrymen with such stirring words as the following—

"Under the auspices of divine Providence your forefathers removed to the wilds and wilderness of America. By their industry they made it a fruitful, and by their virtues a happy, country; and we should still have enjoyed the blessings of peace and plenty, if we had not forgotten the source from which these blessings flowed, and permitted our country to be contaminated by the many shameful vices which have prevailed among us. It is a well-known fact that no virtuous people were ever oppressed, and it is also true that a scourge was never wanting to those of an opposite character. Even the Jews, those favorites of Heaven, met with the frowns whenever they forgot the smiles of their benevolent Creator. They for their wickedness were permitted to be scourged; and we for our wickedness are scourged by tyrants as cruel and implacable as theirs. If we turn from our sins, God will turn from his anger. Then will our arms be crowned with success, and the pride and power of our enemies, like the pride and arrogance of Nebuchadnezzar, will vanish away.

"Let a general reformation of manners take place; let universal charity, public spirit, and private virtue be inculcated, encouraged, and practised. Unite in preparing for a vigorous defence of your country as if all depended on you. And when you have done all these things, then rely on the good providence of Almighty God for success, in full confidence that without his blessing all our efforts will inevitably fail.

"Rouse, then, brave citizens! Do your duty like men, and be persuaded that Divine Providence will not let this Western World be involved in the horrors of slavery. Consider that from the earliest ages of the world religious liberty and reason have been bending their course towards the setting sun. The holy gospels are yet to be preached to these western regions; and we have the highest reason to believe that the Almighty will not suffer slavery and the gospel to go hand in hand. It cannot, it will not be."

In September, 1777, Jay, as Chief-Justice of the Supreme Court of New York, delivered a charge to the Grand Jury of Ulster county, on the political condition of the country. It was given at a time when the Assembly and Senate were convening, and the whole system of government, established by the Constitution of New York, about being put in motion. The grand inquest was composed of the most respectable characters in the county. In that charge are found the following Christian passages—

"Gentlemen—It affords me very sensible pleasure to congratulate you on the dawn of that free, mild, and equal government which now begins to rise and break from amidst those clouds of anarchy, confusion, and licentiousness which the arbitrary and violent domination of the King of Great Britain had spread throughout this and the other American States. This is one of those signal instances in which Divine Providence has made the tyranny of princes instrumental in breaking the chains of their subjects, and rendering the most inhuman designs productive of the best consequences to those against whom they were intended—a revolution which, in the whole course of its rise and progress, is distinguished by so many marks of the divine favor and interposition that no doubt can remain of its being finally accomplished.

"It was begun, and has been supported, in a manner so singular and, I may say, miraculous, that when future ages shall read its history they will be tempted to consider great part of it as fabulous. Will it not appear extraordinary that thirteen colonies, divided by a variety of governments and manners, should immediately become one people, and, though without funds, without magazines, without disciplined troops, in the face of their enemies, unanimously determine to be free, and, undaunted by the power of Great Britain, refer their cause to the justice of the Almighty, and resolve to repel force by force—thereby presenting to the world an illustrious example of magnanimity and virtue scarcely to be paralleled? However incredible these things may in future appear, we know them to be true, and we should always remember that the many remarkable and unexpected means and events by which our wants have been supplied and our enemies repelled or restrained are such strong and striking proofs of the interposition of Heaven, that our having been hitherto delivered from the threatened bondage of Britain ought, like the emancipation of the Jews from Egyptian servitude, to be forever ascribed to its true Cause, and, instead of swelling our breasts with arrogant ideas of our own prowess and importance, kindle in them a flame of gratitude and piety which may consume all remains of vice and irreligion.

"The Americans are the first people whom Heaven has favored with an opportunity of deliberating upon and choosing the forms of government under which they should live. While you possess wisdom to discern and virtue to appoint men of worth and abilities to fill the offices of the state, you will be happy at home and respected abroad. Your life, your liberties, your property, will be at the disposal only of your Creator and yourselves.

"Security under our Constitution is given to the rights of conscience and private judgment. They are by nature subject to no control but that of Deity, and in that free situation they are now left. Every man is permitted to consider, to adore, and to worship his Creator in the manner most agreeable to his conscience. No opinions are dictated, no rules of faith are prescribed, no preference given to one sect to the prejudice of others. The Constitution, however, has wisely declared that the 'liberty of conscience, thereby granted, shall not be so construed as to excuse acts of licentiousness or justify practices inconsistent with the peace or safety of the state.' In a word, the convention by whom that Constitution was formed were of opinion that the gospel of Christ, like the ark of God, would not fall, though unsupported by the arm of flesh; and happy would it be for mankind if that opinion prevailed more generally.

"But let it be remembered that whatever marks of wisdom, experience, and patriotism there may be in the Constitution, yet, like the beautiful symmetry, the just proportions, and elegant forms of our first parents before their Maker breathed into them the breath of life, it is yet to be animated, and, till then, may indeed excite admiration, but will be of no use. From the people it must receive its spirit, and by them be quickened.

"Let virtue, honor, the love of liberty and science, be and remain the soul of the Constitution, and it will become the source of great and extreme happiness to this and future generations. Vice, ignorance, and want of vigilance will be the only enemies that can destroy it. Against these provide, and of these be forever jealous. Every citizen ought diligently to read and study the Constitution of his country, and teach the rising generation to be free."

"Providence," said he, "has given to our people the choice of their rulers, and it is the duty, as well as the privilege and interest, of a Christian nation to select and prefer Christians for their rulers."

Mr. Jay, from 1822 till his death in 1827, was President of the Bible Society, and at each annual meeting delivered an address. He demonstrated the divinity of the Bible, showed its relations and results to civil government and human society, and urged its universal circulation as the means to illumine and regenerate the world.

He was an active and devout member of the Episcopal Church, but eminently liberal and charitable in his Christian views. His life was a beautiful exhibition of Christian faith, and his public career a noble illustration of the value of Christianity in forming the character and acts of a Christian statesman. Webster said of this eminent Christian jurist, that "when the ermine fell on him it touched nothing less pure than itself."

He was eminently a man of prayer, and drew up a form, full of spirituality and of Christian truths, as an extract will show—

"Enable me, merciful Father, to understand thy holy gospels, and to distinguish the doctrines thereof from erroneous expositions of them; and bless me with that fear of offending thee, which is the beginning of wisdom. Let thy Holy Spirit purify and unite me to my Saviour forever; and enable me to cleave unto him as unto my very life, as indeed he is. Perfect and confirm my faith, my trust, my hope of salvation in him, and in him only.

"Give me grace to love and obey, and be thankful unto thee, with all my heart, with all my soul, with all my mind, and with all my strength, and to worship and to serve thee in humility of spirit, and in truth. Give me grace also to love my neighbor as myself, and wisely and diligently to do the duties incumbent on me according to thy holy will, and not from worldly consideration. Condescend, merciful Father, to grant, as far as proper, these imperfect petitions, these inadequate thanksgivings, and to pardon whatever of sin hath mingled in them, for the sake of Jesus Christ, our blessed Lord and Saviour, unto whom, with thee and the blessed Spirit, even one God, be rendered all honor and glory, now and forever."

In his dying hour, he was asked if he had any farewell counsels to leave his children. His reply was, "They have the Book."

Elias Boudinot

Boudinot played a prominent part in the period of the Revolution, and was an able and active member of the Continental Congress. He was a brilliant lawyer, an upright judge, a wise legislator, and a true Christian statesman. His Christian feelings found a voice concerning the propriety of observing the memory of American independence—

"The history of the world, as well sacred as profane, bears witness to the use and importance of setting apart a day as a memorial of great events, whether of a religious or a political nature. No sooner had the great Creator of the heavens and the earth finished his almighty work, and pronounced all very good, but he set apart (not as anniversary, or one day in a year, but) one day in seven, for the commemoration of his inimitable power in producing all things out of nothing.

"The deliverance of the children of Israel from a state of bondage to an unreasonable tyrant was perpetuated by eating the paschal lamb, and enjoining it to their posterity as an annual festival forever, with a 'remember this day, in which ye came out of Egypt, out of the house of bondage.'

"The resurrection of the Saviour of mankind is commemorated by keeping the first day of the week, not only as a certain memorial of his first coming in a state of humiliation, but the positive evidence of his future coming in glory.

"Let us, my friends and fellow-citizens, unite all our endeavors this day to remember with reverential gratitude to our Supreme Benefactor all the wonderful things he has done for us, in a miraculous deliverance from a second Egypt—another house of bondage. 'And thou shalt show thy son, on this day, saying, This day is kept as a day of joy and gladness, because of the great things the Lord has done for us, when we were delivered from the threatening power of an invading foe. And it shall be a sign unto thee upon thine hand, be in thy mouth; for with a strong hand hast thou been delivered from thine enemies. Thou shalt therefore keep this ordinance, in its season, from year to year forever.'

"Who knows but the country for which we have fought and bled may hereafter become a theater of greater events than have yet been known to mankind? May these invigorating prospects lead us to the exercise of every virtue, religious, moral, and political. And may these great principles, in the end, become instrumental in bringing about that happy state of the world when from every human breast, joined by the grand chorus of the skies, shall arise, with the profoundest reverence, that divinely celestial anthem of universal praise, 'Glory to God in the highest; peace on earth; good will towards men.'"

In 1816, Mr. Boudinot was elected the first President of the American Bible Society: In accepting, he said, "I am not ashamed to confess that I accept the appointment of President of the American Bible Society as the greatest honor that could be conferred on me this side of the grave." He served, also, from 1812 till his death in 1821, as a member of the American Board of Commissioners for Foreign Missions. His great wealth was consecrated to objects of Christian benevolence. He gave a liberal sum to the New Jersey Bible Society, to purchase spectacles for the aged poor to enable them to read the Bible.

James Monroe

James Monroe was an active patriot and statesman of Revolutionary and later modern times, taking a leading part in the political affairs of the nation. He was twice elected President. He has left but little in reference to his views on the subject of religion. The following sentences occur in his messages—

"I enter on the trust with my fervent prayers to the Almighty, that he will he graciously pleased to continue to us that protection which he has already so conspicuously displayed in our favor."

"The fruits of the earth have been unusually abundant, commerce has flourished, the revenue has exceeded the most favorable anticipations, and peace and amity are preserved with foreign nations on conditions just and honorable to our country. For these inestimable blessings we cannot be too grateful to that Providence which watches over the destinies of nations."

"When we view the great blessings with which our country has been favored, those which we now enjoy, and the means which we possess of handing them down unimpaired to our latest posterity, our attention is irresistibly drawn to the source from whence they flow. Let us, then, unite in offering our most grateful acknowledgment for these blessings to the Divine Author of all good."

William Henry Drayton

From South Carolina, Drayton was an eminent jurist and statesman, who devoted his great learning and abilities to achieve our independence and to form our free institutions. In April, 1776, he presented, in an official paper, the following sentiments—

"I think it my duty to declare, in the awful seat of justice and before Almighty God, that, in my opinion, the Americans can have no safety but by the Divine favor, their own virtue, and their being so prudent as not to leave it in the power of British rulers to injure them. The Almighty created America to be independent of Britain: let us beware of the impiety of being backward to act as instruments in the Almighty's hand, now extended to accomplish his purpose, and by the completion of which alone America can be secure against the craft and insidious designs of her enemies, who think her prosperity and power already by far too great. In a word, our piety and political safety are so blended, that to refuse our labors in this divine work is to refuse to be a great, a free, a pious, and a happy people! And now, having left the important alternative, political happiness or wretchedness, under God, in a great degree in your hands, I pray the Supreme Arbiter of the affairs of men so to direct your judgment as that you may act agreeably to what seems to be his will, revealed in his miraculous works in behalf of America bleeding at the altar of liberty."

Major-General Nathanael Greene

During the revolutionary war, Greene was eminently distinguished in the military service of his country, and was the confidential companion of Washington. He was as eminent for his virtues as for his patriotism and devotion to his country. Alexander Hamilton, in a eulogium on him, pronounced July 4, 1789, before the Society of Cincinnati, stated—

"The name of Greene will at once awaken in your minds the image of whatever is noble and estimable in human nature. As a man, the virtues of Greene are admitted; as a patriot, he held a place in the foremost rank; as a statesman, he is praised; as a soldier, he is admired.

"But where, alas! is now this consummate general, this brave soldier, this discerning statesman, this steady patriot, this virtuous citizen, this amiable man? Why could not so many talents, so many virtues, so many bright and useful qualities shield him from a premature grave? It is not for us to scan, but to submit to, the dispensations of Heaven."

"He was a great and good man," was the comprehensive eulogy passed upon him by Washington, when he heard the news of General Greene's death. "Thus," says Washington, "some of the pillars of the Revolution fall. Others are mouldering by insensible degrees. May our country never want props to support the glorious fabric."

Henry Knox

Knox was a Major-general in the American army during the Revolutionary War, was the right hand of Washington, and one whose resources for the emergencies of the war were infinite. His parents were of Scottish descent, and educated him in that piety which has ever distinguished the people of that country. He possessed a taste for literary pursuits, which he retained through life; and this, in union with his fine military genius and personal qualities, constituted him an accomplished gentleman and an able officer in the army and in the War Department, to which he was appointed by Congress before the adoption of the Constitution, and, after the government was organized, by Washington to the same office.

"The amiable virtues of the citizen and the man were as conspicuous in the character of General Knox as the more brilliant and commanding talents of the hero and statesman. The afflicted and destitute were sure to share of his compassion and charity. 'His heart was made of tenderness.' Mildness ever beamed in his countenance; 'on his tongue were the words of kindness. The poor he never oppressed; the most obscure citizen could never complain of injustice at his hands.'

"To these amiable qualities and moral excellencies of General Knox we may justly add his prevailing disposition to piety. With much of the manners of the world, and opposed as he was to all superstition and bigotry, he might not appear, to those ignorant of his better feelings, to possess religion and devout affections. He was a firm believer in the natural and moral attributes of the Deity and his overruling and all-prevailing providence."

Gilbert Mothier Lafayette

This man deserves an eminent place among American heroes, as the champion of freedom and the friend of humanity. His chivalrous and heroic devotion in the American cause constitutes a romantic chapter in the history of the Revolution. He was a member of the Catholic Church, a friend of Christianity.

His sentiments and life were of a high moral tone. His inspirations of liberty, his just and rational views of the rights of all men, and his devotion to humanity and a Christian civilization, entitle Lafayette to be enrolled among the Christian champions of freedom. In reference to American slavery he said that if he had supposed he was fighting to perpetuate the system, he never would have unsheathed his sword for American liberty in our Revolutionary struggle.

John Quincy Adams, in his eulogy on Lafayette, prepared at the request of Congress, in 1834, says, "The self-devotion of Lafayette in the cause of America was twofold. First, to the maintaining of a bold and seemingly desperate struggle against oppression and for national existence. Secondly and chiefly, to the principles of their declaration, which then first unfurled before his eyes the consecrated standard of human rights.

"To the moral principle of political action, the sacrifices of no other man were comparable to his. Youth, health, fortune, the favor of the king, the enjoyment of ease and pleasure, even the choicest blessings of domestic felicity—he gave them all for toil and danger in a distant land, and an almost hopeless cause; but it was the cause of justice, and of the rights of human kind."

Mr. Clarkson, of England, describes Lafayette "as a man who desired the happiness of the human race in consistence with strict subservience to the cause of truth and the honor of God." At the close of the

Revolution, Congress appointed a committee to receive and, in the name of Congress, to take leave of Lafayette, and to express to him their grateful and admiring sense of his services.

A memorable sentence of his reply is as follows—

"May this immense temple of freedom ever stand a lesson to oppressors, an example to the oppressed, a sanctuary for the rights of mankind! And may these happy United States attain that complete splendor and prosperity which will illustrate the blessings of their Government, and for ages to come rejoice the departed souls of its founders."

William Livingston

Livingston was a Christian lawyer of New York, and afterwards distinguished as a Christian statesman and Governor of New Jersey. In the earliest conflicts of the Revolution he said—

"Courage, Americans! Liberty, religion, and science are on the wing to these shores. The finger of God points out a mighty empire to your sons. The savages of the wilderness were never expelled to make room for idolaters and slaves. The land we possess is the gift of Heaven to our fathers, and Divine Providence seems to have decreed it to our latest posterity. So legible is this munificent and celestial deed in past events, that we need not be discouraged by the bickerings between us and the parent country. The angry cloud will soon be dispersed, and America advance to felicity and glory with redoubled activity and vigor. The day dawns in which the foundation of this mighty empire is to be laid by the establishment of a regular American Constitution.

"Let us, both by precept and example, encourage a spirit of economy, industry, and patriotism, and that public integrity which cannot fail to exalt a nation—setting our faces at the same time like a flint against that dissoluteness of manners and political corruption which will ever be the reproach of any people. May the foundation of our infant state be laid in virtue and the fear of God, and the superstructure will rise gloriously and endure for ages. Then we may humbly expect the blessing of the Most High, who divides to nations their inheritance and separates the sons of Adam. While we are applauded by the whole world for demolishing, the old fabric, rotten and ruinous as it was, let us unitedly strive to approve ourselves master-builders, by giving beauty, strength, and stability to the new.

"May we, in all our deliberations and proceedings, be influenced by the great Arbiter of the fate of nations, by whom empires rise and fall, and who will not always suffer the sceptre of the wicked to rest on the lot of the righteous, but in due time avenge an injured people on their unfeeling oppressor and his bloody instruments."

Governor Livingston, in 1778, published the following views on the liberty of conscience in matters of religion—

"If in our estimate of things we ought to be regulated by their importance, doubtless every encroachment upon religion, of all things the most important, ought to be considered as the greatest imposition, and the unmolested exercise of it a proportionate blessing . . .

"The laws of England, indeed, do not peremptorily inhibit a man from worshipping God according to the dictates of his own conscience, nor positively constrain him to violate it, by conforming to the religion of the state. But they punish him for doing the former, or, what amounts to the same thing, for omitting the latter, and, consequently, punish him for his religion. For what are the civil disqualifications and the privation of certain privileges he thereby incurs, but so many punishments? And what else is the punishment from worshipping God according to the dictates of his own conscience, nor positively constrain him to violate it, by conforming to the religion of the state. But they punish him for doing the former, or, what amounts to the same thing, for omitting the latter, and, consequently, punish him for his religion."

Francis Marion, The "Swamp Fox"

Francis Marion (1732-1795) was a brigadier general in the South Carolina Militia during the Revolutionary War. He became known as the "Swamp Fox" because he set up his base of operations in a swamp. "Marion's Brigade" was a volunteer force that could assemble at a moment's notice, hit British and Loyalist units and garrisons, and then disappear into the swamps. He is considered one of the fathers of modern guerilla warfare.

While the British occupied most of the southern colonies, large scale resistance was impossible. Marion and his patriot unit was a powerful force in the south, as Nathaniel Greene later wrote in praise: "Surrounded on every side with a superior force, hunted from every quarter with superior troops, you have found means to elude their attempts and keep alive the aspiring hopes of an oppressed militia."

After the war, Marion served in the state senate of South Carolina for several terms. He stated: "Who can doubt that God created us to be happy, and thereto made us to love one another? It is plainly written as the Gospel. The heart is sometimes so embittered that nothing but divine love can sweeten it, so engaged that devotion can only becalm it, and so broken down that it takes all the forces of heavenly hope to raise it. In short, the religion of Jesus Christ is the only sure and controlling power over sin."

Note

At this point I want to acknowledge and thank the Reverend Benjamin F. Morris, long since deceased, for the devotion and hard work that he put into the research and writing of the original work in 1864 that most of this chapter has come from. He was determined to show what kind of people had dreamed of, worked for, and built this country. The theme of his character descriptions of these great forefathers of ours was to exhibit what kept them forging ahead with the divine plan they felt obliged to follow. I urge any who read this and want more to go to www.AmericanVision.org to secure your own copy of this republished work.

1. Benjamin F. Morris, *The Christian Life and Character of the Civil Institutions of the United States* (Powder Springs, GA: American Vision, Inc., 2007).

CHAPTER 9

The Framework of the New Nation

We have looked at the people who worked so hard to build a new nation in this new world. Now we will look at the document that is the backbone of the nation and what makes it different from all others.

The Constitution of the United States has been the supreme law of the nation since it was adopted on September 17, 1787, by the Constitutional Convention in Philadelphia, Pennsylvania. George Washington was chosen to serve as president of the convention by the fifty-five delegates who represented twelve states. The delegates drafted the document and sent it to Congress for approval. It was then sent to the states for ratification in the name of "the People." All thirteen states had ratified the Constitution by May 29, 1790. The first US Congress also ratified ten amendments, which became known as the Bill of Rights. Seventeen more amendments have been added since. It is the oldest federal constitution of any existing nation and occupies the central place in United States law and political culture.

The Constitution provides the framework for the organization of the United States government, outlining the three main branches of government. The legislature branch is embodied in the bicameral Congress. The executive branch is headed by the President. The judicial branch is headed by the Supreme Court. The Constitution carefully outlines the limits of delegated powers each branch may exercise. It also reserves numerous rights for the individual states, and thus establishes the United States federal system of government.

Our Founders wrote, "We the people of the United States" in the preamble of the Constitution, designating that the power to govern belongs to the people who have created the government to protect their rights and promote their welfare. The preamble established the fact that the federal government has no authority outside of the limited powers given to the three government branches that follow in the preamble, as amended. It is imperative, therefore, that we know those specific delegated powers.

Much has been made of the Constitution's silence on the subject of God or any Christian designation. The consensus of the Framers was that religious matters were best left to the individual citizens and their respective state governments, and relationships between religion and civil government were already defined in most state constitutions in the founding era. For the federal government to enter into matters regarding religion would have been to encroach upon or usurp state jurisdiction.

Reactions from the Delegates

James Madison had several comments following the convention:

"The great objects which presented themselves [to the Constitutional Convention] . . . formed a task more difficult than can well be conceived by those who were not concerned in the execution of it. Adding to these considerations the natural diversity of human opinions on all new and complicated subjects, it is impossible to consider the degree of concord which ultimately prevailed as less than a miracle."[1]

"Is it not the glory of the people of America that, while they have paid a decent regard to the opinions of former times and other nations, they have not suffered a blind veneration for antiquity, for custom, or for names to overrule the suggestions of their own good sense, the knowledge of their own situation, and the lessons of their own experience? To this manly spirit posterity will be indebted for the possession, and the world for the example, of the numerous innovations displayed on the American theater in favor of private rights and public happiness . . . Happily for America, and we trust for the whole human race, [the founders of the nation] pursued a new and more noble course. They accomplished a revolution which has no parallel in the annals of human society. They reared the fabric of governments which have no model on the face of the globe. They formed the design of a great confederacy, which it is incumbent on their successors to improve and perpetuate."[2]

"The real wonder is that so many difficulties should have been summoned [in the federal convention], and surmounted with a unanimity almost as unprecedented as it must have been unexpected. It is impossible for any man of candor to reflect on this circumstance without partaking of the astonishment. It is impossible for the man of pious reflection not to perceive in it a finger of that Almighty hand which has been so frequently and signally extended to our relief in the critical stages of the revolution."[3]

James Wilson made these observations:

"Governments, in general, have been the results of force, of fraud, and accident. After a period of six thousand years has elapsed since the creation, the United States exhibits to the world the first instance, as far as we can learn, of a nation, unattacked by external force, unconvulsed by domestic insurrection, assembling voluntarily, deliberating fully, and deciding calmly concerning that system of government under which they would wish that they and their posterity should live."[4]

"I can well recollect, though I believe I cannot convey to others, the impression which, on many occasions, was made by the difficulties which surrounded and pressed the [federal] convention. The great undertaking sometimes seemed to be at a stand; at other times, its motion seemed to be retrograde. At the conclusion, however, of our work, many of the members expressed their astonishment at the success of which it terminated."[5]

Benjamin Rush opined:

"Doctor Rush then proceeded to consider the origin of the proposed [Constitution], and fairly deduced it [was] from heaven, asserting that he as much believed the hand of God was employed in this work as that God had divided the Red Sea to give a passage to the children of Israel, or had fulminated the Ten Commandments from Mount Sinai."[6]

John Adams made these comments:

"[The Constitution] is . . . the greatest single effort of national deliberation that the world has ever seen." "I first saw the Constitution of the United States in a foreign country . . . I read it with great satisfaction, as the result of good heads prompted by good hearts, as an experiment better adapted to the genius, character, situation, and relations of this nation and country than any which had ever been proposed . . . . I have repeatedly laid myself under the most serious obligations to support the Constitution . . . What other form of government, indeed, can so well deserve our esteem and love?"[7]

Benjamin Franklin confessed:

"I have so much faith in the general government of the world by Providence that I can hardly conceive a transaction of such momentous importance [as the framing of the Constitution] . . . should be suffered to pass without being in some degree influenced, guided, and governed by that omnipotent, omnipresent, and beneficent Ruler in whom all inferior spirits live and move and have their being."[8]

Charles Pinckney made this statement:

"When the general convention met, no citizen of the United States could expect less from it than I did, so many jarring interests and prejudices to reconcile! The variety of pressing dangers at our doors, even during the war, were barely sufficient to force us to act in concert and necessarily give way at times to each other. But when the great work was done and published, I was not only most agreeably disappointed, but struck with amazement. Nothing less than a superintending hand of Providence that so miraculously carried us through the war . . . could have brought it about.[9]

George Washington had these comments:

"It appears to me . . . little short of a miracle that the delegates from so many states (which states . . . are also different from each other in their manners, circumstances, and prejudices) should unite in forming a system of national government so little liable to well-founded objections."[10]

"[The adoption of the Constitution] will demonstrate as visibly the finger of Providence as any possible event in the course of human affairs can ever designate it."[11]

"The Constitution . . . approaches nearer to perfection than any government hitherto instituted among men."[12]

"This Constitution is really, in its formation, a government of the people . . . No government before introduced among mankind ever contained so many checks and such efficacious restraints to prevent it from degenerating into any species of oppression . . . The balances arising from the distribution of the legislative, executive, and judicial powers are the best that have [ever] been instituted."[13]

And Thomas Jefferson made these comments about the Constitution:

"The example of changing a constitution by assembling the wise men of the state, instead of assembling armies, will be worth as much to the world as the former examples we had given them. The constitution, too, which was the result of our deliberation is unquestionably the wisest ever yet presented to men."[14]

"May you and your contemporaries . . . preserve inviolate [the] Constitution, which, cherished in all its charity and purity, will prove in the end a blessing to all the nations of the earth."[15]

Notes

1. William T. Hutchinson, William M. E. Rachal, and Robert A. Rutland, eds., *The Papers of James Madison,* 15 vols. by 1985 (Chicago and Charlottesville: University of Chicago Press and University Press of Virginia, 1962), 10:207-8. To Thomas Jefferson, October 24, 1787.
2. Alexander Hamilton, James Madison, and John Jay, *The Federalist Papers* (New York: Mentor Books, 1961), 104-5. No. 14 (November 30, 1787).
3. *The Federalist Papers*, 230-31. No. 37 (January 11, 1788).
4. Jonathan Elliot, ed., *The Debates of the Several State Conventions on the Adoption of the Federal Constitution,* 2d ed. rev., 5 vols. (Philadelphia: J. B. Lippincott, 1907), 2:422. Remarks in Pennsylvania ratifying convention, November 26, 1787.
5. Ibid., 426.
6. Max Farrand, ed., *The Records of the Federal Convention of 1787*, rev. ed., 4 vols. (New Haven, Conn.: Yale University Press, 1937), 3:168. Notes of remarks in Pennsylvania ratifying convention, December 12, 1787.
7. C. R. King, ed., *The Life and Correspondence of Rufus King*, 6 vols. (New York: G.T Putnam's sons,1894-1900), 1:320-21.
8. Albert Henry Smyth, ed., *The Writings of Benjamin Franklin*, 10 vols. (New York: Macmillan Company, 1905-7), 9:702-3. To the editor of the Federal Gazette, 1788.
9. Farrand, *The Records of the Federal Convention of* 1787, 3:301. Letter to the *State Gazette of South Carolina*, May 2, 1788.
10. John C. Fitzpatrick, ed., *The Writings of George Washington*, 39 vols. (Washington: U.S. Government Printing Office, 1931-44), 29:409. To the Marquis de Lafayette, February 7, 1788.
11. Ibid., 29:507. To Lafayette, May 28, 1788.
12. Ibid., 30:73. To Sir Edward Newenham, August 29, 1788.
13. Ibid., 30:299. Proposed address to Congress (never delivered), April?, 1789.
14. Albert Ellery Bergh, ed., *The Writings of Thomas Jefferson*, 20 vols. (Washington: Thomas Jefferson Memorial Association, 1907), 7:322. To David Humphreys, March 18, 1789.
15. Ibid., 15:352. To Philip N. Nicholas, December 11, 1821.

Religious Developments

While the government was being born, the religious developments were moving rapidly also. The American religious experience had developed several characteristics that separated it from any of the European churches. Americans de-emphasized the clergy. Not only did states such as Virginia refuse to fund the salaries of ministers, which had been more common in the old country, but the Calvinist/Puritan tradition that each man read, and interpret, the Bible for himself meant that the clergy's authority had already diminished. Second, Americans were at once both evangelically active and liturgically lax. What mattered was salvation and "right" living, not the form or structure of the religion. Ceremonies and practices differed wildly, even within denominations. And most importantly, as with America's new government itself, the nation's religion made the person's individual salvation the central theme. All of this affected the separation of the American churches from their European ancestors and also fostered sects and divisions within the Christian community.

The word we hear in this country today is tolerance. In America, during this early period, the dominant church groups were not so much tolerant to the Jews, Muslims, Buddhists, and others, it was more of indifference. They were such a small minority that no one made an issue of it.

Someone once opined that "the essential difference between the American Revolution and the French Revolution was that the American Revolution was a religious event, whereas the French revolution was an anti-religious event."[1]

John Adams made a similar point when he stated, "Revolution was in the mind and hearts of the people; and change in their religious sentiments of their duties and obligations."[2] As a result of this situation, America, while not attaching itself to any specific variant of Christianity, took on a mind-set that the nation would adopt an unofficial, generic Christianity that fit well with republicanism. Alexis de Tocqueville provided a virtual road map for the future direction of the fledgling country as he observed that the United States had developed a spirit of religion and a spirit of freedom that "were intimately united, and that they reigned in common over the same country."

"Americans," he stated, viewed religion as "indispensable to the maintenance of the republican institutions," because it facilitated free institutions. Certain fundamentals seemed to be unanimously agreed: posting of the Ten Commandments in public places was appropriate; prayers in virtually all official and public functions were expected; America was particularly blessed because of her trust in God; and even when individuals in civic life did not ascribe to a specific faith, they were expected to act like "good Christians" and conduct themselves as would a believer.[3]

Politicians like Washington walked a fine line between maintaining the secularist form and yet supplying the necessary spiritual substance. In part, this explains why so many of the early writings and speeches of the Founders were both timeless and uplifting. Their message of spiritual virtue, cloaked in republican processes of civic duty, reflected a sense of providential mission for the young country.

With no state boundaries to stop them, religious doctrines found themselves in a competition every bit as sharp as Adam Smith's "invisible hand" of the market. Most communities built a church as one of their first civic acts, and traveling preachers visited all the backwoods and communities, church or no church. Ministers such as Lyman Beecher (1775-1863) exemplified the new breed of traveling evangelist. He was a New Haven Presbyterian who later would become president of Cincinnati Theological Seminary. He was well known for his essay against dueling after Alexander Hamilton's death in 1803.

There was one serious development that came from all the new ministers and the congregations that grew around them. New doctrines and sects appeared, breeding regional differences and sectarianism. Each new division weakened the formerly held consensus about what constituted accepted doctrines of Christianity.

Especially in education, the divisions threatened to undermine the Christian basis that had formed this young country. Other dangerous splits in doctrine appeared as to the proper relationship with Indians. Eleazar Wheelock (1711-79), who was a Congregationalist and key influence in the Awakening movement, founded a school for Indians that became Dartmouth College in 1769. In order to offer education to the Indians, segregated schools had to be set up similar to Wheelock's. He, of course, was not the first religious leader to establish a school.

Religious groups of all denominations and doctrines had accounted for the majority of quality education, particularly in the higher levels. To name a few: Brown University, in Rhode Island (1764), was established by the Baptists; Princeton, in New Jersey, by the Revivalist Presbyterians (1746), which later became a theological institute (1812); Yale, in New Haven, Connecticut, by the Congregationalists (1701); William and Mary, in Virginia, by the Anglicans (1693); and Georgetown College in Washington, D.C. (then Maryland), by the Jesuit father John Carroll (1789); and others.

Sadly, the fact that so many of these schools and colleges presently have a very liberal outlook is nothing new. The process began many years ago. Rather than reinforcing the existing orthodoxy of the day, colleges soon produced heretics—or at least, liberals who shared very few of their founders' doctrinal views. For example, Harvard University, founded to enforce Puritanism in 1636 by the Reverend John Harvard, with its original motto, *Veritas, Christo et Ecclesiae* (Truth, Christ and the Church), and its logo with two books facing up and one facing downward to represent the hidden knowledge of God, were ditched when the school slipped into the hands of liberal groups in 1707.

The new motto, simply *Veritas*, and its symbol of all three books facing up aptly illustrated the dominance of a Unitarian elite that dominated the school, including such notable as John Quincy Adams and Henry Wadsworth Longfellow. By focusing on a rationalistic Enlightenment approach to salvation in which virtually all men were saved—not to mention the presumption that all knowledge could be known—the Unitarians (who denied the Trinity, hence the term "Unitarian," from unity, or one) had opposed the Great Awakening of the 1740s. Henry Ware, at Harvard, and later Willard Ellery Channing, whose 1819 sermon, "Unitarian Christianity" established the basis for the sect, challenged by the Congregational and Puritan precepts from 1805-25. At that point the American Unitarian Association was formed, but much earlier it had exerted such a powerful influence in Boston that in 1785 King's Chapel removed all references to the trinity from the prayer books.[4]

The Unitarians were not the only ones developing unorthodox viewpoints in their doctrines. Many sects strained at the limits of what was accepted or tolerated under even the broadest definitions of Christianity. [*And I thought this was a modern phenomenon!*] The people still maintained a general consensus on what constituted morality and ethics. As a consequence, a subtle and yet profound shift began in which the religious populace in America just avoided theological issues and attempted to form a set of moral assumptions or accepted norms under which even the Jews and other non-Christians could fit in.

Thomas Jefferson's objection to state funding of a particular religion focused on the use of tax money for clerical salaries. The result of this controversy led to pressure to eliminate any sectarian doctrine from public school and hence clashes with state governments over which concepts were actually denominational and which were generically Christian. Church-state separation spilled over into debates about the applicability of charters and incorporation laws for churches. Charters always contained elements of favoritism, but in trying to avoid granting a charter to any particular church, the state denied religious organizations the same rights accorded to hospitals and railroads.

Even in Virginia, where "separation of church and state" began, the reluctance to issue religious charters endowed churches with special characteristics that were not applied to other corporations. In trying to keep religion and politics apart, Virginia lawmakers unintentionally "wrapped religion and politics, church and state ever more closely together."[5]

The bright side of the matter was that anyone who was dissatisfied with a state's religion could move west. That dynamic would later propel the Methodists to Oregon and the Mormons to Utah. Meanwhile, the call of the frontier was irrepressible for reasons entirely unrelated to heaven and completely oriented toward the future homes of the brave colonists. Every year more adventurers and traders headed west, to that irresistible "call of the wild."

Notes

1. Paul Johnson, *A History of the American People* (New York: Harper Collins, 1997), 179.
2. Ibid., 166; Johnson, "God and the Americans," *Commentary* (January1995): 25-45.
3. Alexis de Tocqueville, *Democracy in America*, vol. 1 (New York: Vintage, 1935), 316, 319.
4. Edward L. Queen II, Stephen R. Prothero, *The Encyclopedia of American Religious History* (New York: Facts on File and Proseworks, 1996), 682-86.
5. Thomas Buckley, "After Disestablishment: Thomas Jefferson's Wall," *Journal of Southern History* (1995): 445-800, quotation on 479-80.

CHAPTER 10

Birth of the United States Congress

The colonies all had a conviction of a need for religion as the only true basis of civil government. They had been taught in the faith and practice of the Protestant religion, and when the time came for them to institute governments for themselves, they were prepared to found them and operate them according to the religion of the Bible.

Edmund Burke was a member of the British Parliament, but was sympathetic to the colonists in their struggle to form an independent nation. Speaking to Parliament he said:

> The people of the colonies, are descendants of Englishmen. England is a nation which still, I hope, respects and formerly adored, freedom. The colonists went from you when this part of your character was most predominant; and they took this bias and direction the moment they parted from your hands. They are, therefore, not only devoted to liberty, but liberty according to British ideas and on British principles. Their governments are popular in a high degree. If anything were wanting to this necessary operation of the form of government, RELIGION would have given it a complete effect. Religion—always a principle of energy to this new people—is no way

> worn out or impaired; and their mode of professing is also one main cause of this free spirit. The people are Protestants, and of that kind which is most adverse to all implicit submission of mind and opinion. This is a persuasion, sir, not only favorable to liberty, but built upon it. The dissenting interests have sprung up in direct opposition to all the ordinary powers of the world, and could justify that opposition only on a strong claim to natural liberty.
>
> All Protestantism, even the most cold and passive, is a sort of dissent. But the religion most prevalent in our Northern colonies is a refinement on the spirit of the principle of resistance: it is the dissidence of dissent, and the *protestantism of the Protestant religion.* This religion, under a variety of denominations, agreeing in nothing but in the communion of the spirit of liberty, is predominant in most of the Northern Provinces.
>
> The colonists left England when this spirit was high, and in the emigrants was highest of all; and even the stream of foreigners which has been constantly flowing into these colonies has, for the greater part, composed of dissenters of their own countries, and have brought with them a temper and a character far from alien to that of the people with whom they mixed. A fierce spirit of liberty has grown up; it has grown up with the growth of your people, and increased with the increase of their population and wealth—a spirit that, unhappily, meeting with an excess of power in England, which, however lawful, is not reconcilable to any idea of liberty, much less with theirs, has kindled this flame which is ready to consume us.

This thorough education of the colonists in the Protestant school of Christianity, from their earliest history down to the Revolution, prepared the statesmen who instituted our forms of government to found them on the principles of Christianity. This policy respected the will of the people, as well as the views and convictions of the men who framed our free institutions.

Bishop McIlvaine said:

> That some religion . . . and that the Christian religion, is recognized as the religion of this nation and government, and as such is interwoven in its laws, and has a legal preference, though not "establishment" in technical language, over whatever else has the name of religion, and especially over all forms of infidelity, all must admit. We are thankful that our system of government, our common law, and administration of justice, were instituted by men having the wisdom to see how entirely the liberties and interests of the nation are dependent on the teaching and keeping of the truths and institutions of Christianity.

Daniel Webster said:

> There is nothing we look for with more certainty than this principle, that Christianity is a part of the law of the land. Everything declares this. The generations which have gone before speak to it from the tomb. We feel it. All, proclaim that Christianity, general, tolerant Christianity, independent of sects and parties, that Christianity which the sword and the fagot are unknown, is the law of the land.

The statesmen of the Continental Congress, in their deliberations, officially recognized the Christian religion, and incorporated its principles into their legislative acts. That body of great men is who Webster spoke about. He describes the first Congress this way:

> No doubt the assembly of the first Continental Congress may be regarded as the era at which the union of these States commenced. This event took place in Philadelphia, the city distinguished by the

great civil events of our early history, on the 5th of September, 1774, on which day the first Continental Congress assembled. Delegates were present from New Hampshire, Massachusetts, Rhode Island, Connecticut, New York, New Jersey, Pennsylvania, Delaware, Maryland, Virginia, North Carolina, South Carolina, and Georgia.

Let this day be ever remembered! It saw assembled from the several colonies those great men whose names have come down to us and will descend to all posterity. Their proceedings are remarkable for simplicity, dignity and unequaled ability. At that day, probably, there could have been convened on no part of the globe an equal number of men possessing greater talents and ability, and animated by a higher and more patriotic motive. They were men full of the spirit of the occasion, imbued deeply with the general sentiment of the country, of large comprehension, of long foresight, and of few words. They made no speeches for ostentation; they sat with closed doors, and their great maxim was, "*faire sans dire.*"They knew the history of the past, they were alive to all the difficulties and all the duties of the present, and they acted from the first as if the future were all open before them. In such a constellation it would be insidious to point out the bright particular stars. Let me only say—what none can consider injustice to others—that George Washington was one of the number.

This first Congress, for the ability which it manifested, the principles which it proclaimed, and the characters which composed it, makes an illustrious chapter in American history. Its members should be regarded not only individually, but in a group; they should be viewed as living pictures, exhibiting young America as it then was, and when the seeds of its public destiny were beginning to start into life, well described by

> our early motto as being full of energy and prospered by Heaven—"Non sine Diis animosus infans" (translates—"the courageous child was aided by the gods") . . . .
>
> For myself, I love to travel back in imagination, to place myself in the midst of this assembly, this union of greatness and patriotism, and to contemplate, as if I had witnessed, its profound deliberations, and its masterly exhibitions both of the rights and wrongs of the country.

The proceedings of the Assembly were introduced by religious observances and devout supplications to the throne of grace, for the inspiration of wisdom and the spirit of good counsels.

The first act of the first session of the Continental Congress was to pass the following resolution:

> *Tuesday, September* 6, 1774,—*Resolved,* That the rev. Mr. Duche' be desired to open Congress to-morrow morning with prayer, at Carpenter's Hall, at nine o'clock.
>
> *Wednesday, September* 7, 1774, A.M.—Agreeable to the resolve yesterday, the meeting was opened with prayer by Rev. Mr. Duche'.

John Adams wrote to his wife, Abigail, describing the scene:

> "When the Congress met, Mr. Cushing first made a motion that it should be opened with a prayer. It was opposed by one or two, because we were so divided in religious sentiments—some were Episcopalians, some Quakers, some Anabaptists, some Presbyterians, and some Congregationalists—that we could not agree in the same act of worship. Mr. Samuel Adams rose and said, 'he was no bigot, and could hear a prayer

> from a gentleman of piety and virtue, who was at the same time a friend to his country. He was a stranger in Philadelphia, but had heard that Mr. Duche' deserved that character, and therefore he moved that Mr. Duche', an Episcopalian clergyman, might be desired to read prayers to the Congress to-morrow morning.' The motion was seconded and passed in the affirmative. Mr. Randolph, our President, waited on Mr. Duche', and received for answer if his health would permit he certainly would. Accordingly, next morning he appeared, with his clerk and his pontifical, and read the collect for the seventh day of September, which was the thirty-first Psalm. You must remember that this was the first morning after we heard the horrible rumor of the cannonade of Boston. I never saw a greater effort produced upon an audience. It seemed as if Heaven had ordained that Psalm to be read on that morning. It has had an excellent effect upon everybody here.
>
> "After this," Adams said, "Mr. Duche', unexpectedly to everybody, struck out into an extemporaneous prayer, which filled the bosom of every man present. I must confess I never heard a better prayer, or one so well pronounced. Episcopalian as he is, Dr. Cooper himself never prayed with such fervor, such ardor, such earnestness and pathos, and in language so elegant and sublime, for America, for the Province of Massachusetts, and especially the town of Boston."

Adams entered this in his diary, September 7, 1774, the same scene:

> Went to Congress again; heard Mr. Duche' read prayers; the collect for the 7th of the month was most admirably adapted—though this was accidental, or, rather, providential. A prayer which he gave us of his own composition, was as pertinent, as affectionate, as sublime, as devout, as I ever heard offered up to Heaven. He filled every bosom present.

After this buildup from Adams, I must share this prayer as it was taken from Thatcher's "Military Biography" dated December, 1777:

> O Lord our heavenly Father, high and mighty King of kings and Lord of lords, who dost from thy throne behold all the dwellers on earth, and reignest with power supreme and uncontrolled over all the kingdoms, empires and governments; look down in mercy, we beseech thee, on these American States who have fled to thee from the rod of the oppressor, and thrown themselves on thy gracious protection, desiring to be henceforth dependent only on thee; to thee they have appealed for the righteousness of their cause; to thee do they now look up for that countenance and support which thou alone canst give; take them, therefore, heavenly father, under thy nurturing care; give them wisdom in council, and valor in the field; defeat the malicious designs of our cruel adversaries; convince them of the unrighteousness of their cause, and if they still persist in the sanguinary purposes, oh, let the voice of thine own unerring justice, sounding in their hearts, constrain them to drop the weapons of war from their unnerved hands in the day of the battle. Be thou present, O God of wisdom, and direct the councils of this honorable assembly; enable them to settle things on the best and surest foundation, that the scene of blood be speedily closed, that order, harmony and peace may be effectually restored, and truth and justice, religion and piety, prevail and flourish among the people. Preserve the health of their bodies and the vigor of their minds; shower down on them and the *millions* they here represent, such temporal blessings as thou seest expedient for them in this world and crown them with everlasting glory in the world to come. All this we ask in the name and through the merits of Jesus Christ, thy Son, our Saviour. Amen!

One observer gave this description of the scene:

> Here we have a minister, bound to forms, finding extemporaneous words to suit the occasion, where the Quaker, the Presbyterian, the Episcopalian, and the Rationalist—some kneeling, some standing, but all praying, and looking to Heaven for wisdom and counsel in this hour of doubt, anxiety, and responsibility. Adams and Sherman, the Puritans, standing erect—Thomson, the Quaker, finding the movement of the Spirit in the words of a consecrated priest—with Washington, Henry, and other Episcopalians, kneeling, according to their creed, and all invoking wisdom from above, would make a touching and instructive picture. Its moral would be, that the greatest of minds, in moments of difficulty and danger, acknowledge their dependence upon God, and feel the necessity of elevating and purifying their hearts by prayer; and that the differences of sect, the distinctions of form, all vanish when emergency presses upon the consciences of men and forces them to a sincere and open avowel of their convictions.

The Bible was an important point of discussion and consequent action early in the workings of Congress. Actual legislation concerning the Bible was some of the earliest on record. The fact is this focus showed the faith of the statesmen of that period and their feeling for the divinity of this precious book and their purpose to place it at the cornerstone of our republican institutions.

The beginnings of the Revolution cut off the supply of "books printed in London." Bibles were in short supply, so Dr. Patrick Allison, one of the chaplains to Congress, and others, brought the subject to Congress and asked for the printing of an edition of the Scriptures. On September 11, 1777, the subject was voted on by the Congress. The Committee of Commerce was directed to order twenty thousand copies of the Bible.

Note

All quotes were taken from Benjamin F. Morris, *The Christian Life and Character of the Civil Institutions of the United States* (Powder Springs, GA: American Vision, Inc., 2007).

CHAPTER 11

All Those Rights

The Founders of this country did not believe that human rights were given or granted by kings, emperors, potentates, or any other earthly or governmental authority. They believed that basic rights came from our Creator God. That being the case, these rights were sacred. The influential John Locke put it this way:

> The state of Nature has a law of Nature to govern it, which . . . teaches all mankind who will but consult it, that being all equal and independent, no one ought to harm another in his life, health, liberty, or possessions; for men being all the workmanship of one omnipotent and infinitely wise maker; all the servants of one sovereign master, sent into the world by His order and about His business; they are His property . . . And being furnished with like faculties, sharing all in one community of Nature, there cannot be supposed any such subordination among us that may authorize us to destroy one another.[1]

So what makes a right "unalienable" you ask? Well, the substantive nature of those rights which are inherent in all mankind, according to William Blackstone, the English jurist are these:

> Those rights, then, which God and nature have established, and are therefore called natural rights, such as life and liberty, need not the aid of human laws to

> be more effectually invested in every man than they are; neither do they receive any additional strength when declared by the municipal laws to be inviolable. On the contrary, no human legislature has the power to abridge or destroy them, unless the owner himself commit some act that amounts to forfeiture.[2]

In other words, we may forfeit our God-given rights by our own actions or deeds, but no one else has the right to take them. *Unalienable* simply means they are inherent rights given to us by the Creator, thereby being called natural rights.

Other rights that we may have are called *vested* rights, and these come from the community, state, or country that we belong to. They are subject to change at any time. Rights to hunt or fish or drive on public roads would fall into this category. Our natural "right to life" protects us from genocide and other serious situations and conditions.

The Founders recognized a number of unalienable rights in the Declaration of Independence *among which* are life, liberty, and the pursuit of happiness. There are quite a few more that were not listed there, but most have been added to the Constitution through the first ten amendments, called the Bill of Rights, or subsequent amendments over time.

The Founders commonly discussed these natural rights, and some appeared in the states' documents. The Virginia Declaration of Rights adopted by the Virginia Assembly June 12, 1776 (before the Declaration of Independence) states:

> All men are by nature equally free and independent and have certain inherent rights of which, when they into a state of society, they cannot, by any compact, deprive or divest their posterity; namely, the enjoyment of life and liberty, with the means of acquiring or possessing property and pursuing and obtaining happiness and safety.[3]

The similar meanings of "property rights" and "pursuit of happiness" was considered when it was originally debated. John Adams stated it this way:

> All men are born free and independent, and have certain natural, essential, and unalienable rights, among which may be reckoned the right of enjoying and defending their lives and liberties; that of acquiring, possessing, and protection of property; in fine, that of seeking and obtaining their safety and happiness.[4]

The idea of natural rights was also associated with English common law. Sir William Blackstone wrote about the subject in 1765:

> And these [great natural rights] may be reduced to three principal or primary articles: the right of *personal security*; the right of *personal liberty*; and the right of *private property*; because there is no other method of compulsion, or of abridging man's natural free will, but by an infringement or diminution of one or other of these important rights, the preservation of these, inviolate, may justly be said to include the preservation of our civil immunities in their largest and most extensive sense.[5]

Some of the state constitutions offered protection of these important rights. This excerpt from the Pennsylvania document gives an example:

> Article 1, Section 1. All men are born equally free and independent, and have certain inherent and indefeasible rights, among which are those of enjoying life and liberty, of acquiring, possessing, and protecting property and reputation and of pursuing their own happiness.[6]

The French have had their own battles for freedom and human rights also. This piece shows one man's concern for self-preservation:

> We hold from God the gift which includes all others. The gift of life—physical, intellectual, and moral life.
>
> But life cannot maintain itself alone. The Creator of life has entrusted us with the responsibility of preserving, developing, and perfecting it. In order that we may accomplish this, He has provided us with a collection of marvelous faculties. And He has put us in the midst of a variety of natural resources. By the application of our faculties to these natural resources we convert them into products, and use them. The process is necessary in order that life may run its appointed course.
>
> Life, faculties, production—in other words, individuality, liberty, property—this is man. And in spite of the cunning of artful political leaders, these three gifts from God precede all human legislation, and are superior to it.
>
> Life, liberty, and property do not exist because men have made laws. On the contrary, it was the fact that life, liberty, and property existed beforehand that caused men to make laws (for the protection of them) in the first place.[7]

Sadly, unalienable rights that are endowed by God cannot be protected unless certain laws are put in place that are just as divinely given as the rights were. William Blackstone had this to say about the matter:

> He insists that the Creator is not only omnipotent . . . "but as He is also a Being of infinite *wisdom*, He has laid down only such laws as were founded in those relations of justice, that existed in the nature of things . . . These are the eternal, immutable laws of good and evil, to which the Creator Himself in all His dispensations conforms; and which he has enabled human reason to discover, so far as they are necessary for the conduct of human actions. Such, among others, are these

> principles; that we should live honestly, should hurt nobody, and should render unto everyone his due.[8]

According to Blackstone, these laws must be revealed by God:

> The doctrines thus delivered we call the revealed divine law, and they are to be found only in the Holy Scriptures. These precepts, when revealed, are found upon comparison to be really a part of the original law of nature, as they tend in all their consequences to man's felicity.[9]

As we analyze the essential elements of God's code of conduct, we find that he deigned it to promote, preserve, and protect man's unalienable rights. The Ten Commandments clearly lay out the basis for man's relationship to each other and the world. In other words, with all the natural rights come *natural duties.* We could also point out what Thomas Jefferson called "social duties." There are public duties and private duties that we all have. Public duties include our responsibility to obey the laws and rules of our society, either local or state. Our private duties come under our relation to our Creator.

Blackstone had these comments on the matter:

> Let a man therefore be ever so abandoned in his principles, or vicious in his practice, provided he keeps his wickedness to himself, and does not offend against the rules of public decency, he is out of the reach of human laws. But if he makes his vices public, though they be such as seem principally to affect himself (as drunkenness, or the like), then they become by the bad example they set, of pernicious effects to society; and therefore it is then the business of human laws to correct them . . . *Public* sobriety is a relative duty [relative to other people], and therefore enjoined by our laws; *private* sobriety is an absolute duty, which, whether it be performed or not, human tribunals can

> never know; and therefore they can never enforce it by any civil sanction.[10]

Supreme Law

Among all the laws and customs that have existed in the world, two groups of people have held that God's law was always the supreme law over all. The Anglo-Saxon people, who were the predominate group during the colonization of America, and the Israelites. Dr. Colin Rhys Lovell wrote quite a bit about this in *English Constitutional and Legal History.* For example, Dr. Lovell explains that they considered the law

> . . . *immutable.* Even the all-powerful tribal assembly had no legislative power, and this theory of legislative impotence endured for a long time in the development of the English constitution and disappeared only very gradually; even many centuries later the fiction that specific legislation was not making new law, but reinforcing ancient customs was preserved. Most of the great steps forward in the development of the English constitution have been taken with loud assertions that nothing new was being contemplated, only the old was being restored.[11]

Even when the truth was discovered that Parliament was writing new statutes, it was required that none of the new laws contradict the provisions of divine law.

John Locke was the person who established a principle our Founders adopted. It stated: "The law of Nature stands as an eternal rule to all men, legislators as well as others. The rules that they make for man's actions must . . . be comfortable to the law of Nature—i.e., to the will of God."[12]

Sir William Blackstone, in his *Commentaries on the Laws of England,* said this:

> Man, considered as a creature, must necessarily be subject to the laws of his Creator . . . This will of his Maker is called the law of nature . . . This law of nature, being coeval with mankind, and dictated by God, Himself, is of course superior in obligation to any other. It is binding over all the globe in all countries, and at all times: no human laws are of any validity, if contrary to this.[13]

How can we be sure of this maxim? The Founders of this republic were quite settled on the premises we just described.

Notes

1. John Locke, *Second Essay Concerning Civil Government*, Great Books of the Western World, vol. 35 (Chicago: Encyclopedia Britannica, Inc., 1952), 26.
2. William Blackstone, *Commentaries on the Laws of England*, (!862), 1:93.
3. Abiel Holmes, *Annals of America*, (1829), 2:432.
4. George A. Peek, Jr., ed., *The Political Writings of John Adams* (New York: Liberal Arts Press, 1954), 96.
5. Blackstone, *Commentaries on the Laws of England*, 1:219-20.
6. Quoted in Judson A. Crane, *Natural Law in the United States* (Pittsburgh: University of Pittsburgh), 6:144.
7. Frederic Bastiat, *The Law* (Irvington-on-Hudson, NY: The Foundation for Economic Education, Inc., 1974), 5-6.
8. Blackstone, *Commentaries on the Laws of England*, 1:59-60.
9. Ibid., 1:64.
10. Ibid., 1:208.
11. Colin Rhys Lovell, *English Constitutional and Legal History* (New York: Oxford University Press, 1962), 36.
12. Locke, *Second Essay Concerning Civil Government*, p. 56, par. 135.
13. Blackstone, *Commentaries on the Laws of England*, 1:54, 56, 63.

"Divine Right of Kings"?

The old adage of "divine right of kings" had been around for quite a while. At least two situations come to mind with this phrase as a backdrop. King James authorized his "King James version" of the Bible in 1611, primarily because he didn't like the Geneva Bible's discounting this premise in its commentary. Also known as the Breeches Bible, it had been printed in 1560 and again in 1599. It was the first English edition to introduce verse numeration.

The more gruesome story was that in 1683, King Charles II had Algernon Sidney beheaded for denouncing this right to rule that the British royalty had declared a "God-given right." Sidney had insisted that the right to rule actually was the people's right, not the aristocracy's. When asked "whether the supreme power be . . . in the people," Sidney had stated, "I say, that they who place the power to govern in a multitude, understand a multitude composed of freemen, who think it for their convenience to join together, and to establish such laws and rules as they oblige themselves to observe."[1]

During the same time, John Locke had fled the country and traveled to Holland where he could voice the same opinion as Sidney without fear of death or prison. Later, Locke returned to England, ironically, on the same boat as the new Queen (Mary). In 1690, he published his two famous essays on "The Original Extent" and "End of Civil Government." In the second essay, he wrote:

> In all lawful governments, the designation of the persons who are to bear rule being as natural and necessary a part of the form of government itself, and that which had its establishment ORIGINALLY FROM THE PEOPLE . . . all commonwealths, therefore, with the form of government established, have rules also to appointing and conveying the right to those who are to have any share in the public authority; and whoever gets into the exercise of any part of the power by other ways than what the laws of the community have prescribed hath no right to be obeyed, though the form

> of the commonwealth be still preserved, since he is not the person the laws have appointed, and, consequently, not the person THE PEOPLE HAVE CONSENTD TO. Nor can such a usurper, or any deriving from him, ever have a title till the PEOPLE ARE BOTH AT LIBERTY TO CONSENT, AND HAVE ACTUALLY CONSENTED, to allow and confirm in him the power he hath till then usurped.[2]

The American Founders never had a thought about this divine right of kings. They held firmly to the premise that rulers are, instead, servants of the "people" in whom all authority lies. They still held on to the Anglo-Saxon principles.

This is a subject that Dr. Lovell often wrote about. He says that the tribal council, consisting of the entire body of freemen, would meet each month to discuss their problems and seek a solution through consensus. The chief or king was only one among equals: "The chief owed his office to the tribal assembly, which selected and could also depose him. His authority was limited at every turn, and though he no doubt commanded respect, his opinion carried no more weight in the debates of the assembly than that of any freeman."[3]

Alexander Hamilton had the same understanding of this. He said, "The fabric of American empire ought to rest on the solid basis of THE CONSENT OF THE PEOPLE. The streams of national power ought to flow immediately from that pure, original fountain of all legitimate authority."[4]

The same divine right of the people to govern themselves and exercise exclusive power of sovereignty in their official affairs was expressed by the commonwealth of Massachusetts in its Proclamation of January 23, 1776:

> It is a maxim that in every government, there must exist, somewhere, a supreme, sovereign, absolute, and uncontrollable power; but this power resides always in the BODY OF THE PEOPLE; and it never was,

> or can be, delegated to one man. Or a few; the great Creator has never given to men a right to vest others with authority over them, unlimited either in duration or degree.[5]

James Madison was surprised to find that many people were frightened by the Constitution when it was presented for ratification, because they felt a federal government was being given autocratic authority. This was his response:

> The adversaries of the Constitution seem to have lost sight of the PEOPLE altogether in their reasonings on the subject; and to have viewed these different establishments not only as mutual rivals and enemies, but as uncontrolled by any common superior in their efforts to usurp the authorities of each other. These gentlemen must here be reminded of their error. They must be told that the ULTIMATE AUTHORITY, wherever the derivative may be found, RESIDES IN THE PEOPLE ALONE.[6]

But even if it is acknowledged that the *people* are divinely endowed with the sovereign power to govern, what happens if elected or appointed officials usurp the authority of the people to impose a dictatorship or some form of abusive government on them?

On that question lies the principle that the Founders based their bold Declaration of Independence!

Notes

1. Algernon Sidney, *Discourses on Government*, 3 vols. (New York: Printed for Richard Lee by Deare and Andres, 1805), 2:18.
2. John Locke, *Second Essay Concerning Civil Government*, Great Books of the Western World, vol. 35 (Chicago: Encyclopedia Britannica, Inc., 1952), pp. 70-71, par. 198.

3. Colin Rhys Lovell, *English Constitutional and Legal History* (New York: Oxford University Press, 1962), 5.
4. James Madison, Alexander Hamilton, and John Jay, *The Federalist Papers* (New York: Penguin, 1987), No. 22, p. 152.
5. Quoted by Hamilton Albert Long, *Your American Yardstick* (Philadelphia: Your Heritage Books, Inc., 1963), 167, emphasis added.
6. Madison, *Federalist Papers,* No. 46, p. 294, emphasis added.

CHAPTER 12

Why Are We Called a Republic?

Throughout history, people have come together and formed communities. They have ranged in size, shape, and definition from a village to a metropolis. And their form of government has varied greatly as well. When the colonies began to grow to the place where some sort of "central government" seemed essential, there were some differences of opinion as to what style or function would be best.

The American colonies benefited greatly from having some of the best educated men in the world to ponder this situation. Our pledge of allegiance specifies the choice that was made:

> I pledge allegiance to the flag
> Of the United States of America
> And to the *Republic*
> For which it stands . . .

When we consider the options that the Founders had to choose from, only two seem to have been discussed. Those were a *democracy* or a *republic*. Let's take a look at the pros and cons of these choices. From a theoretical viewpoint, for a democracy to function properly it must have the people's full participation. Sadly, this never works, as the people become disinterested or preoccupied and don't become involved enough to study and learn the issues and concerns that need their attention and action. The most well-known democracy was set up by the ancient Greeks who tried the mass-participation procedures in their city-states. Eventually these all were taken over by tyrants.

James Madison made this assessment of the differences between the two systems:

> Democracies have ever been spectacles of turbulence and contention; have ever been found incompatible with personal security and rights of property; and have in general been as short in their lives as they have been violent in their deaths . . . A republic, by which I mean a government in which the scheme is representation takes place, opens a different prospect and promises the cure for which we are seeking.[1]

Madison went on to say later that a growing country like America could not confine itself to the limited functions of a democracy. It would need to rely on the representative form of government that a republic would offer. He said:

> In a democracy the people meet and exercise the government in person; in a republic they assemble and administer it by their representatives and agents. A democracy, consequently, must be confined to a small spot. A republic may be extended over a large region.[2]

In order to make sure he had made his point perfectly clear, Madison made this concise definition of a republic in his writings:

> We may define a republic to be . . . a government which derives all its powers directly or indirectly from the great body of the people, and is administered by the persons holding their offices during pleasure for a limited period, or during good behavior. It is essential to such a government that it be derived from the great body of the society, not from an inconsiderable proportion of a favored class of it; otherwise a handful of tyrannical

> nobles, exercising their oppression by a delegation of their powers, might aspire to the rank of republicans and claim for their government the honorable title of republic.[3]

One of the problems we have today is that few people understand these premises when they call for and expect the functions of a democracy, which can result in what is known as "mob rule." The Founders hoped that future generations would maintain the clear distinction between a republic and a democracy.

The problem seems to have started in the early 1900s when a new movement started in the United States. Some one hundred people met in New York and founded the Intercollegiate Socialist Society (ISS). They established chapters on some sixty college and university campuses across the country. Harry Laidler and Thomas Laidler, codirectors, declared that the organization was formed in order to "throw light on the world-wide movement of industrial 'democracy' known as socialism."[4]

So what, might we ask, was their purpose? First, let us take a look at what socialism is. The term is defined by Merriam Webster online as ": any of various economic and political theories advocating collective or governmental ownership and administration of the means of production and distribution of goods." This rather destroys the idea that it is "social" democracy.

The ISS thought to put a smile on their premise by using this perky slogan: "Production for use, not profit." It did, however, catch on with a wide variety of people across the country.

We will come back to this subject later, as we have ventured far ahead of our timeline.

The Aftermath of the Revolution

As the country was gearing up to move forward, the War of 1812 began and involved more military action to resolve. We won't go into any of the details of the conflict, except to call attention to what happened just offshore in US territory in the defense of Fort Henry.

In 1814, Francis Scott Key wrote the poem, "Defense of Fort McHenry." The poem was later put to the tune of (John Stafford Smith's song) "The Anacreontic Song," modified somewhat, and retitled, "The Star Spangled Banner." Congress proclaimed "The Star Spangled Banner" the US National Anthem in 1931.

The War of 1812 is one of the forgotten wars of the United States. The war lasted for over two years and ended in a stalemate. It did, however, once and for all confirm American independence. The offensive actions of the United States failed to capture Canada. On the other hand, the British army was successfully stopped when it attempted to capture Baltimore and New Orleans. There were a number of American naval victories in which American vessels proved themselves superior to similarly sized British vessels. Here is the complete, war-inspired anthem:

The Star Spangled Banner

Oh, say, can you see, by the dawn's early light,
What so proudly we hail'd at the twilight's last gleaming?
Whose broad stripes and bright stars, thro' the perilous fight,
O'er the ramparts we watch'd, were so gallantly streaming?
And the rockets' red glare, the bombs bursting in air,
Gave proof thro' the night that our flag was still there.
O say, does that star-spangled banner yet wave
O'er the land of the free and the home of the brave?

On the shore dimly seen thro' the mists of the deep,
Where the foe's haughty host in dread silence reposes,
What is that which the breeze, o'er the towering steep,
As it fitfully blows, half conceals, half discloses?
Now it catches the gleam of the morning's first beam,
In full glory reflected, now shines on the stream:
'Tis the star-spangled banner: O, long may it wave
O'er the land of the free and the home of the brave!

And where is that band who so vauntingly swore
That the havoc of war and the battle's confusion
A home and a country should leave us no more?
Their blood has wash'd out their foul footsteps' pollution.
No refuge could save the hireling and slave
From the terror of flight or the gloom of the grave:
And the star-spangled banner in triumph doth wave
O'er the land of the free and the home of the brave.

O, thus be it ever when freemen shall stand,
Between their lov'd homes and the war's desolation;
Blest with vict'ry and peace, may the heav'n-rescued land
Praise the Pow'r that hath made and preserv'd us a nation!
Then conquer we must, when our cause is just,
And this be our motto: "In God is our trust"
And the star-spangled banner in triumph shall wave
O'er the land of the free and the home of the brave!

More Reasons for the Protection of a Republic

Thomas Jefferson was a brilliant man, and he spoke strongly against trusting in human nature for a safely run government:

> It would be a dangerous delusion were a confidence in the men of our choice to silence our fears for the safety of our rights; that confidence is everywhere the parent of despotism; free government is founded in jealousy, and not in confidence, which prescribes limited constitutions to bind down those whom we obliged to trust with power; that our Constitution has accordingly fixed the limits to which, and no farther, our confidence may go . . . In questions of power, then, let no more be said of confidence in man, but bind him down from mischief by the chains of the Constitution.[5]

George Washington was quite clear as to why these limitations were necessary. He and the other founders looked at the government as an explosive instrument of power which had to be harnessed by a restrictive Constitution. He said: "Government is not reason, it is not eloquence—it is force! Like fire, it is a dangerous servant and a fearful master."[6]

Madison also recognized the potential problem of placing power in the hands of fallible human beings who, by nature, have many attributes that can be good or evil. He knew that all men have the proclivity to harbor tendencies toward ego-maniacal behavior and self-aggrandizement. Concerning the many human frailties he stated:

> It may be a reflection on human nature that such devices [as Constitutional chains] should be necessary to control the abuses of government. But what is government itself but the greatest of all reflections on human nature? . . . If angels were to govern men, neither external nor internal controls would be necessary. [But lacking these,] in framing a government which is to be administered by men over men, the great difficulty lies in this: You must first enable the government to control the governed; and in the next place oblige it to control itself.[7]

So we see what one of the most important features of the Constitution is: to prohibit freedom abuse by those in authority. This example throws water on those who say the Constitution is obsolete just because our society is "progressing" and people's attitudes have "evolved" concerning certain ideas and ideals. The Constitution was designed to stand firm and not to change with every whim and fancy that comes along. It is to be our "rock and foundation" of a sensible society.

The Founders knew that freedoms can be silently eroding without a stabilizing force, such as this strong Constitution to hold on to. Madison added, "I believe there are more instances of the abridgement of the freedom of the people by gradual and silent encroachments of those in power, than by violent and sudden usurpations . . . This danger ought to be wisely guarded against."[8]

In his own state of Virginia, in 1785, Madison issued a stern warning:

> It is proper to take alarm at the first experience on our liberties. We hold this prudent jealousy to be the first duty of citizens and one of the noblest characteristics of the late Revolution. The Freemen of America did not wait till usurped power had strengthened itself by exercise and entangled the question in precedents. They saw all the consequences [of government abuses] in the principle, and they avoided the consequences by denying the principle [on which the abuses were based]. We revere this lesson too much . . . to forget it.[9]

Where, might we ask, are the encroachments of abusive rulers most likely to attack? Is there some particular basic right which self-aggrandizing politicians seek to destroy first? According to the Founders, the answer is yes! Mankind has so many rights that it is sometimes difficult to watch them all. But the right to own property seemed to be the most important. We will look at that next.

Origin of Our Property Rights

Our Founders carried over their strong belief in the right to own property from English common law, which held strongly to the unalienable right of possessing, developing, and deposing of property. It held that land and the products of the earth were considered a gift of God and were to be cultivated, beautified, and brought under dominion. It was backed up by this passage from the book of Psalms: "Even the heavens are the Lord's: but the earth hath he given to the children of men (Psalm 115:16 KJV).

John Locke made the point that humans originally received the earth as a gift and mankind was given the responsibility and capability to improve it. He said, "God, who had given the world to men in common, hath also given them reason to make use of it to the best advantage of life and convenience."[10] He went on to say that man received the commandment from his Creator to "subdue" the earth and "have dominion" over it (Genesis 1:28).

Of course "dominion" implies control and control requires exclusiveness, so necessarily, private rights to property became an inescapable necessity in the subduing and developing of the earth. Without private "rights" to any developed or improved property, there would be no protection from anyone just coming in and taking over and therefore benefiting from someone else's labor.

It is important to note that there are several things that can happen that would damage greatly the blessing of property rights granted by our Creator. For example: if someone did come in and take over a property, it would destroy the very incentive for any person to work and develop and improve the property. He would have lost all the time and effort he put into it. This premise of ownership by force could grow into ganglike groups taking over whole regions. And eventually, mankind would lose any motivation or desire to acquire and develop any real property.

Locke had another insight into this matter. He allowed that property is an extension of a person's life, energy, and ingenuity and for that property to be destroyed or confiscated would be, in essence, an attack on life itself. This is his opinion:

> Though the earth and all inferior creatures be common [as the gift of God] to all men, yet every man has a "property" in his own "person." This, nobody has any right to but himself. The "labour" of his body and the "work" of his hands, we may say, are properly his. Whatsoever, then, he removes out of the state that Nature hath provided and left it in, he hath mixed his labour with it, and joined to it something that is his own, and thereby makes it his property . . . .
>
> He that is nourished by the acorns he picked up under an oak, or the apples he gathered from the wood, has certainly appropriated them to himself. Nobody can deny but the nourishment is his. I ask, then, when did they begin to be his? When he digested? Or when he ate? Or when he boiled? Or when he brought them

> home or when he picked them up? And it is plain, If the first gathering made them not his, nothing else could.[11]

Locke has an answer to this powerful question:

> That labour . . . added something to them [fruit or nuts] more than Nature, the common mother of all, had done, and so they became his private right. And will anyone say he had no right to those acorns or apples he thus appropriated because he had not the consent of all mankind to make them his? . . . If such a consent as that was necessary, [the] man [would have] starved, notwithstanding the plenty God had given him . . . It is the taking any part of what is common, and removing it out of the state Nature leaves it in, which begins the property, without which the common [gift from God] is of no use . . .
>
> Thus this *law of reason* makes the deer that [property of the Indian] who hath killed it; it is allowed to be his goods who hath bestowed his labour upon it, though, before, it was the common right of everyone.[12]

Some have wanted to use the word *sacred* to describe property rights. But under the heading of common law, it simply protects ownership. Justice George Sutherland of the US Supreme Court once told the New York State Bar Association:

> It is not the right *of* property which is protected, but the right *to* property. Property, *per se*, has no rights, but the individual—the man—has three great rights, equally sacred from arbitrary interference: the right to his life, the right to his liberty, the right to his property . . . The three rights are so bound together as to be essentially one right. To give a man his life but to deny him his liberty, is to take from him all that makes his life worth living. To give him his liberty but take from him the

> property which is the fruit and badge of his liberty, is to still leave him a slave.[13]

Interestingly, Abraham Lincoln made this statement about property:

> Property is the fruit of labor. Property is desirable, is a positive good in the world. That some should be rich shows that others may become rich and hence is just encouragement to industry and enterprise. Let not him who is houseless pull down the house of another, but let him work diligently to build one for himself, thus by example assuring that his own shall be safe from violence . . . I take it that it is best for all to leave each man free to acquire property as fast as he can. Some will get wealthy. I don't believe in a law to prevent a man from getting rich; it would do more harm than good.[14]

Property rights were, according to John Adams, the most important single foundation stone solidifying human liberty and human happiness. He said, "The moment the idea is submitted into society that property is not as sacred as the laws of God, and that there is not a force of law and public justice to protect it, anarchy and tyranny commence. Property must be secured or liberty cannot exist."[15]

Throughout history there have been occasions where governments have used excessive taxation to take property from its rightful owners. And to add insult to injury, give it to others. The Founders saw this as a horrible sin. James Madison had this to say about that:

> Government is instituted to protect property of every sort . . . This being the end of government, that alone is not a just government . . . nor is property secure under it, where the property which a man has in his personal safety and personal liberty is violated by arbitrary seizures of one class of citizens for the service of the rest.[16]

Notes

1. James Madison, Alexander Hamilton, and John Jay, *The Federalist Papers* (New York: Penguin, 1987), No. 10, p. 81.
2. Ibid., No. 14, p. 100.
3. Ibid., No. 39, p. 241.
4. *The New York Times* (January 28, 1919).
5. The Kentucky Resolutions of 1798, *Annals of America,*(1829) 4:65-66.
6. Jacob M. Braude, *Lifetime Speaker's Encyclopedia,* 2 vols. (Englewood Cliffs, NJ: Prentice-Hall, Inc., 1962), 1:326.
7. Madison, *The Federalist Papers,* No. 51, p. 322.
8. Jonathon Elliot, *Debates in the State Conventions,*(1787), 3:87.
9. Rives and Fendall, "Memorial and Remonstrance," *Letters and Other Writings of James Madison,* Philadelphia: J.P. Lippincott & Co, (1865), 1:163.
10. John Locke, *Second Essay Concerning Civil Government,* Great Books of the Western World, vol. 35 (Chicago: Encyclopedia Britannica, Inc., 1952), p. 30, par. 25.
11. Ibid., pp. 30-31, par. 26-27.
12. Ibid., p. 31, par. 27-29.
13. "Principle or Expedient?" Annual Address to the New York State Bar Association (January 21, 1921), p.18.
14. *The Freeman: Ideas on Liberty,* May 1955, 7. Re-published by Foundation on Economic Education, 2008
15. Charles Francis Adams, ed., *The Works of John Adams,* 10 vols. (Boston: Little, Brown and Co., 1850-56), 6:9, 280.
16. Saul K. Padover, ed., *The Complete Madison* (New York: Harper & Bros., 1953), 267.

CHAPTER 13

Lincoln—The Emancipator

We're going to make a major leap in time here from discussing the beginnings of this country to a major period that involved a mass of the population rivaling the American Revolution and having a loss of lives that has seldom been equaled. It tore at the heartstrings and very souls of those on both sides of the conflict. And on top of it all, we had friends and neighbors and even family members fighting each other. This, of course, was the Civil War.

We won't be discussing the war, in particular, but the people involved, and especially the man who was the central figure and received both praise and condemnation from every direction. But the thing that kept him going was his faith.

Abraham Lincoln was a deeply spiritual man. He lost many loved ones during his lifetime and was seen as a very melancholy person. When he was still a young boy, his mother and sister died. As a young adult, he lost his fiancée, and as a father, he lost two sons. Walt Whitman, who spent a lot of time with him while he was president, said that he had a "deep latent sadness" in his expression.

William Herndon's biography of Lincoln, written in 1889, entitled *Herndon's Lincoln: The True Story of a Great Life*, quoted Lincoln as saying, "All that I am, or hope to be, I owe to my angel mother." He went on, "I remember her prayers. They have always followed me. They have clung to me all my life."

William J. Wolf, a theology professor at Union Theological Seminary, published a study of Lincoln's religious beliefs in 1959 entitled *The Almost Chosen People.* During the same time, Presbyterian minister Clarence MaCartney wrote *Lincoln and the Bible,* and Harlan Hoyt Horner's *The Growth of Lincoln's Faith* became a bestseller. There are many more books, and some being written now about this intriguing man.

Each writing takes a different approach, but a similar core seems to stand out. To the point, Lincoln was engrossed in the Holy Scriptures and thought of them as the "perfect moral code." He said the Bible spoke to people "in all conditions of life." It also contained "all things most desirable for man's welfare." He doused his speeches and letters with biblical references and allusions. The second inaugural address was so peppered with New Testament references that Wolf called it "one of the most astute pieces of Christian theology ever written."

Lincoln memorized much of the Bible and was quite capable of applying its teachings in everyday situations. Carl Sandburg said he knew the Bible "from cover to cover." He proved in his dealings with all people that he was indeed "honest Abe."

Lincoln was certainly a uniter, not a divider. He never actually joined a church, and he refused to endorse any particular Christian dogma or doctrine. He once told congressman Henry C. Deming, "When any church will inscribe over its altar as the sole qualification or membership the Savior's condensed statement of the substance of both law and gospel: 'Thou shalt love the Lord thy God with all thy heart and with all thy soul and with all thy mind, and love thy neighbor as thyself,' that church will I join with all my heart." That's the magnitude of Lincoln's faith. It is so straightforward that it transcends the trivialities that divide most of us. He actually believed that the Bible was to be taken in its entirety, not split up and conceptualized.

Lincoln once visited with one of his generals after his near-execution by a twelve-pound cannonball at Gettysburg. Major General Sickles asked him if he was anxious about the Battle of Gettysburg, where more than fifty thousand Union and Confederate soldiers died. Lincoln replied that he was not. When the general inquired how this could be, Lincoln hesitated before giving the following explanation:

> Well, I will tell you how it was. In the pinch of your campaign up there, when everybody seemed panic-stricken, and nobody could tell what was going to happen, oppressed by the gravity of our affairs, I went to my room one day, and locked the door, and got down on my knees before Almighty God, and prayed to Him mightily for victory at Gettysburg. I told Him that this was His war, and our cause was His cause . . . And then and there made a solemn vow to Almighty God, that if he would stand by our boys at Gettysburg, I would stand by him.

God honored his prayer, and Lincoln honored His promise. Lincoln explained to the general that soon after he prayed, "a sweet comfort crept into my soul that God Almighty had taken the whole business into his own hands and that things would go all right at Gettysburg. And that is why I had no fears about you." Indeed the battle of Gettysburg was the turning point for the Union army in the war.

Lincoln had no fear for his own life either, even though he was repeatedly warned about the plots against him. During the war, a prominent Presbyterian minister, Charles Chiniquy, visited Lincoln on several occasions to caution him about the impending danger of assassination. Lincoln simply replied, "I see no other safeguard against these murderers, but to be always ready to die, as Christ advises it. As we must all die sooner or later, it makes very little difference to me whether I die from a dagger plunged through the heart or from an inflammation of the lungs." Jesus warned us that we would have problems in this world, and he gave us the power to overcome our worries.

Lincoln relied on the Bible's answer to overcoming fear and anxiety. He opened his Bible in the presence of Father Chiniquy and read from Deuteronomy 3:23-25:

> Then I pleaded with the Lord at that time, saying: "O Lord God, You have begun to show your servant Your Greatness and Your mighty hand, for what god is there in heaven or on earth who can do anything like Your works and Your mighty deeds? I pray, let me cross over and see the good land beyond the Jordan, those pleasant mountains and Lebanon."

Lincoln felt convinced that those passages of Scripture were meant for him. After reading them aloud, he added with the gravest sincerity, "Just as the Lord heard no murmur from the lips of Moses when He told him that he had to die before crossing the Jordan for the sins of his people, so I hope and pray that he will hear no murmur from me when I fall for my nation's sake."

Lincoln understood that only by laying down his life could he find it. He also knew that only in God's presence could one find the peace needed to overcome the overwhelming sense of fear and distress that often comes from living in a war-torn world. Like David and Moses before him, he did not rely on his own understanding, but put his complete trust in God.

It is said that Lincoln became very solemn after being elected president. He felt so desperate as he boarded the train to go to Washington, D.C., he felt impelled to make a short comment from the back of the train to the crowd that had gathered. He spoke briefly in saying:

> I now leave, not knowing when, or whether ever, I may return, with a task before me greater than that which rested upon George Washington. Washington never would have succeeded except for the aid of Divine Providence, upon which all times he relied. I feel that I cannot succeed without the same Divine aid which sustained him, and on the same Almighty Being I place my reliance and support.

As he concluded, emotions ran high. *New York Times* reporter Henry Villard wrote that many in the audience were moved to tears. Some were taken aback by Lincoln's next request: "I hope you, my friends, will all pray that I receive Divine assistance." As the train pulled away, many ran after it crying out, "We will pray for you, Mr. Lincoln!" The next time the people of Springfield gathered on his behalf, they hosted his funeral.

He made several stops along the 1,094 miles to Washington—through Indiana, Ohio, and Pennsylvania, up to New York and down through Trenton and Philadelphia—at each stop stepping to the back of the train and calling out the name of God. "Without the assistance of that Supreme Being who has never forsaken us I shall surely fail," he said in Buffalo. "With my own ability I cannot succeed, with the sustenance of Divine Providence, I cannot fail," he proclaimed in Newark. Over and over, he asked for prayer. Lincoln cautioned, "Intoxicated by unbroken success, we have become too self-sufficient to feel the necessity of redeeming and preserving grace, too proud to pray to the God that made us."

In 1908, Clarence McCartney said, "If a public man were to quote the Bible today as frequently as Lincoln did during the Civil War, he would be charged with cant and hypocrisy." Lincoln once said, "In regard to this Great Book, I have but to say, it is the best gift God has given to man. All the good the Savior gave to the world was communicated through this book."

Speaking to L. E. Chittenden, the register of the treasury, Lincoln said, "I decided a long time ago that it was less difficult to believe that the Bible was what it claimed to be, than to disbelieve it." Lincoln's son Robert recalled that, "In the later years of his life, he always had a bible very near him," and it comforted him "at all times."

Early in his presidency, Lincoln appointed James Pollock as director of the Philadelphia Mint. Pollock had just been elected governor of Pennsylvania after serving in Congress for several years. However, Pollock was best known for his strong Christian faith. Pollock, along with Secretary of the Treasury Salmon P. Chase, recommended to Lincoln that the words, "In God We Trust," be inscribed on all US coins.

On March 3, 1865, Congress passed an act allowing the director of the mint—with the Secretary of the Treasury's approval—to place the motto on all gold and silver coins. This act, one of the last passed by Congress before Lincoln's death, immortalized the essence of his heart.

On another occasion, Lincoln made this statement about his beloved book, "But for [the Bible] we could not know right from wrong. All things most desirable for man's welfare, here and hereafter, are to be found portrayed in it."

In a conversation with L. E. Chittenden, Lincoln divulged his beliefs regarding the legitimacy of the Bible and its inherent value: "The character of the Bible is easily established, at least to my satisfaction. It is a good book for us to obey—it contains the Ten Commandments, the Golden rule, and many other rules which ought to be followed. No man was ever worse for living according to the directions of the Bible."

His political opponents generally found themselves on dangerous ground when they attempted to quote Scripture when refuting Lincoln. For example, when Stephen A. Douglas cited Adam and Eve as the first beneficiaries of "popular sovereignty" (a doctrine that allowed settlers of new territories to determine the status of slavery for themselves), Lincoln aptly corrected him. "God did not place good and evil before man, telling him to make his choice. On the contrary, he did tell him there was one tree, of the fruit of which he should not eat, upon pain of certain death." Then Lincoln added pointedly, "I should scarcely wish so strong a prohibition against slavery in Nebraska."

Lincoln's second Inaugural Address was a dramatic expression of his strong faith. Numerous people said that it was more of a sermon than a speech. He made fourteen references to God, four scriptural quotations, including Gen. 3:19, Ps. 19:7-9, Matt. 7:1-3, and 1 Peter 4:8, in addition to several allusions to biblical teaching. The *London Spectator* commented prophetically on this Scripture steeped masterpiece:

> We cannot read it without a renewed conviction that it is the noblest political document known to history, and should have for the nation and the statesmen he left behind him something of a sacred and almost prophetic character. Surely, none was ever written under a stronger sense of the reality of God's government. And certainly none written in a period of passionate conflict ever so completely excluded the partiality of victorious faction, and breathed so pure a strain of mingled justice and mercy.

This speech became one of Lincoln's most influential, if not commonly remembered, legacies. At a time when the nation faced its most critical crisis in history—when the very fiber of its union was threatened—the president drew timeless wisdom from the deep wells of Scripture for answers. It was also his last public address.

Abraham Lincoln held on to his faith to the end. He said, "Let us have faith that right makes might; and in that faith, let us, dare to do our duty as we understand it." Lincoln's faith was based on what he saw as truth—as the Bible so declared. In accepting the Republican nomination for Senate in 1858, he drafted a speech that his colleagues felt would certainly end his political career. In it, he begged the nation to end slavery. Against opposition, he gave the speech, telling his colleagues that he wanted to "strike home to the minds of men in order to raise them up to the peril of the times," and that if "it is decreed that I should go down because of this speech, then let me go down linked to the truth."

Abe Lincoln had an uncommon fear of God and trusted that God's purposes would ultimately prevail. He relied on God to lead him; he trusted God and placed his life in God's hands. Compared to the fate of a nation, and the role of that nation in God's sovereign plan, what value did his life have? He said:

> I know there is a God, and that He hates injustice and slavery. I see the storm coming, and I know that His hand is in it. If He has a place and a work for me,—and

> I think He has—I believe I am ready. I am nothing, but truth is everything. I know I am right because I know that liberty is right, for Christ teaches it, and Christ is God.

Honest Abe

From his own mouth—"Resolve to be honest in all events, and if in your judgment you cannot be an honest lawyer, resolve to be honest without being a lawyer."

In his 1908 biography, *The Story-Life of Lincoln*, author Wayne Whipple wrote about young Abe's year at Denton Offutt's store: "It was while he was performing the work at the store that he acquired the sobriquet, 'honest Abe'—a characterization that he never dishonored, and an abbreviation that he never outgrew." Whipple describes how this young man began finding his unique niche in society:

> He was judge, arbitrator, referee, umpire, authority, in all disputes, games of matches of man-flesh, horse-flesh, a pacificator in all quarrels; everybody's friend; the best-natured, the most sensible, the best-informed, the most modest and unassuming, the kindest, gentlest, roughest, strongest, best fellow in all New Salem and the region around about.

R. B. Rutledge, son of a New Salem tavern owner, recalled that "Mr. Lincoln's judgment was final in all that region of the country. People relied implicitly on his honesty, integrity, and impartiality." His reputation both preceded and followed him.

Lincoln did not hesitate to speak about where our direction in life should come from. He said, "Whereas, it is fit and becoming of all people, at all times, to acknowledge and revere the supreme government of God; to bow in humble submission to his chastisements; to confess and deplore their sins and transgressions, in the full conviction that the 'fear of the Lord is the beginning of wisdom.'"

On March 30, 1863, Lincoln declared a national day of prayer and fasting, claiming that the nation needed to humble itself before God:

> Intoxicated with unbroken success, we have become too self-sufficient to feel the necessity of redeeming and preserving grace, too proud to pray to the God who made us. It behooves us, then, to humble ourselves before the offended Power, to confess our national sins, and to pray for clemency and forgiveness . . . I therefore designate the 30th day of April, 1863, as a day of national humiliation, fasting, and prayer.

William Wolf, in The *Almost Chosen People*, states that Lincoln "counseled personal and national repentance" and argued "the Bible and the course of history showed the necessity for a nation to acknowledge God." He urged the people to "keep the day holy to the Lord.

"It is the duty of nations as well as of men to owe their dependence upon the overruling powers of God, to confess their sins and transgressions, in humble sorrow, yet with assured hope that genuine repentance will lead to mercy and pardon; and to recognize the sublime truth, announced in the Holy Scriptures and proven by all history, that those nations only are blessed whose God is the Lord."

He went on to say, "The awful calamity of war, which now desolates the land, may be but a punishment inflicted upon us for our presumptuous sins to the needful end of our national reformation as a whole people."

Wolf says, "When Lincoln charged the nation with its need for redemption, it was as if he had paraphrased Luther's statement that the essence of sin is the sinner's unwillingness to admit he is a sinner."

Lincoln firmly believed that God would hear and honor the humble prayers of his people. He believed that God was merciful and would graciously forgive every confessed sin.

A Southern newspaper widely publicized Lincoln's reply to a clergyman who expressed hope that the "Lord was on our side." Lincoln responded: "I am not at all concerned about that, for I know that the Lord is always on the side of right. But it is my constant anxiety and prayer that I and this nation should be on the Lord's side." Amen!

Elizabeth Keckley, who lived with the Lincolns, wrote in *Behind the Scenes* that on one troubling day, she observed the following: Lincoln entered the room where she was fitting a dress for Mary and threw himself onto the sofa, covering his face with his hands. "A complete picture of dejection," she recalled. Mary asked him where he had been, and he replied, "The War Department," "Any news," she asked. "Yes, plenty of news, but no good news. It is dark, dark everywhere," he answered. She records his consequent actions this way:

> He reached forth one of his long arms and took a small Bible from a stand near the head of the sofa, opened the pages of the Holy Book, and soon was absorbed in reading them, A quarter of an hour passed and on glancing at the sofa the face of the President seemed cheerful. The dejected look was gone, and his countenance was lighted up with new resolution and hope. The change was so marked that I could not wonder at it . . . He read with Christian eagerness, and courage and the hope he derived from the inspired pages made him a new man.

The Word of God strengthened and encouraged Lincoln. It made him a "new man" so that he was able to encourage others. He received a greater—more resilient—hope from reading the Bible, and this gave him the uncommon ability to resist discouragement regardless of the circumstances.

In *Abraham Lincoln: The Christian*, William Jackson Johnstone notes that "in referring to the Deity, Mr. Lincoln used no less than forty-nine designations. This is very significant, revealing, as it does, the breadth of his thinking and showing how full was his conception of God and his attributes." George Washington used a large number of titles and descriptions also.

An example of this appears in a reply to a letter on January 5, 1863, where Lincoln invoked the "gracious favor of the God of Nations upon the struggles our people are making for the preservation of their precious birthright of civil and religious liberty."

Lincoln gave thanks to his Father in heaven regularly. On election night, November 9, 1864, he received the applause of his supporters and delivered a speech in which he clearly acknowledged his gratitude to God:

> I am thankful to God for the approval of the people. But while deeply thankful for this mark of their confidence in me, if I know my heart, my gratitude is free from any taint of personal triumph . . . It is no pleasure for me to triumph over anyone, but I give thanks to the Almighty for the evidences of the people's resolution to stand by free government and the right of humanity.

He was certain that God is sovereign in all things. He said, "Men are flattered by being shown there has been a difference of the purposes of the Almighty and them. To deny, however, in this case, is to deny there is a God governing the world."

In a telling letter he wrote to Quaker activist Eliza Gurney in the fall of 1864, he said:

> The purposes of the Almighty are perfect, and must prevail, though we erring mortals may fail to accurately perceive them in advance. We hoped for a happy termination of this terrible war before this; but God knows best, and has ruled otherwise. We shall yet acknowledge His wisdom, and our own error therein. Meanwhile, we must work earnestly in the best light He gives us, trusting that so working still conduces

> to the great ends He ordains. Surely He intends some great good to follow this mighty convulsion.

"Lincoln's preoccupation with the issue of God's will and the providential meaning of the nation's calamitous ordeal is particularly evident throughout the last year of his life," says Douglas L. Wilson in *Lincoln's Sword.* Wilson traces the emerging theme of God's sovereignty in Lincoln's speeches as he wrestled with the ongoing war. "When the war began, three years ago, neither party, nor any man, expected it would last till now. Each looked for the end, in some way, long ere today," he stated in a speech in 1864. "Neither did anyone anticipate that domestic slavery would be much affected by the war. But here we are, the war has not ended, and slavery has been much affected . . . So is it that man proposes, and God disposes."

Nurturing the Soul

Abraham Lincoln nurtured his soul, much as he cultured his mind and his body. Always learning and striving to improve, he fed his soul by reading the Bible, by praying, and by fellowshipping with others. In *Faith and the Presidency,* historian Gary Scott Smith reports that "as an adult, Lincoln's church attendance was sporadic until 1850, when his son Eddie died at age three. From then until 1861, Lincoln worshipped regularly at the First Presbyterian Church in Springfield." After Lincoln was elected president, Smith writes, "The prairie politician rented a pew at New York Avenue Presbyterian Church in Washington and faithfully attended services there."

Lincoln was friendly with Colonel Jacques, an army veteran turned pastor and went to hear him speak one night on the words of Jesus in John 3:7, "Ye must be born again"(KJV). "I noticed that Mr. Lincoln appeared to be deeply interested in the sermon," Jacques recalled. A few days later Lincoln visited him, "impressed with my remarks," and to discuss the subject further. "I invited him in, my wife and I talked and prayed with him for hours. Now, I have seen persons converted; I have seen hundreds brought to Christ, and if ever a person was converted, Abraham Lincoln was converted that night in my house.

He never joined my church, but I will always believe that since that night, Abraham Lincoln lived and died a Christian gentleman."

- Lincoln sought counsel from the great men of faith he respected. And rather than relying solely on his personal study of the Bible, he eagerly gleaned from the expositions he heard from the pulpit. Many have remarked how intently he listened to a sermon. When Lincoln was sitting with the congregation during one of Henry Ward Beecher's sermons, one of the ushers observed: "Mr. Lincoln's body swayed forward, his lips parted, and he seemed at length entirely unconscious of his surroundings—frequently giving vent to his satisfaction, at a well-put point or illustration."

Lincoln said, "In the very responsible position in which I happen to be placed, being a humble instrument in the hands of our Heavenly Father, as I am, and as we all are, to work out his just purposes."

His willingness to yield to the sovereign purposes of God, who he was convinced had preordained the greatest good, is evident in a letter he wrote to the Quaker abolitionist Eliza Gurney:

> I have desired that all my works and acts may be according to His will, and that it might be so, I have sought His aid; but if, after endeavoring to do my best in the light which He affords me, I find my efforts fail, I must believe that for some purpose unknown to me, He wills it otherwise. If I had my way, this war would never have been commenced. If I had been allowed my way, this war would have ended before this; but we find it still continues, and we must believe that He permits it for some wise purpose of His own, mysterious and unknown to us, and though with our limited understandings we may not be able to comprehend it, yet we cannot but believe that He that made the world still governs it.

Lincoln did not necessarily feel equipped or prepared. He was a rough and unusual instrument of God to use in such a great role. But he submitted himself, willingly, and God used him effectively. "God selects his own instruments," he wrote to his friend James Gilmore, "and sometimes they are queer ones; for instance, he chose me to steer the ship through a great crisis."

He had said to his friend Joshua Speed way back in July of 1842, "Whatever He designs He will do for me yet, 'Stand still, and see the salvation of the Lord!'"

Twenty years later, in July of 1864, aware that people were growing impatient with the war, Lincoln urged the American people to ask the Holy Spirit to intervene. In one of many proclamations, he invited the people of the United States "to invoke the influence of the Holy Spirit to guide the counsels of the government with wisdom adequate to so great a national emergency." His thoughtful invocation continued as follows:

> To visit with care and consolation throughout the length and breadth of our land all those who, through the vicissitudes of marches, voyages, battles, and sieges have been brought to suffer in mind, body, or estate, and finally to lead the whole nation through the paths of repentance and submission to the Divine Will back to the perfect enjoyment of union and fraternal peace.

When we speak of a "man of the hour," we must always remember to include Abraham Lincoln.

Note

Unless otherwise noted, all quotes by Lincoln come from Thomas Freiling, *Walking with Lincoln: Spiritual Strength from America's Favorite President* (Grand Rapids, MI: Revel, division of Baker Publishing, 2009).

CHAPTER 14

The Dawn of the Twentieth Century

The United States entered the twentieth century on a roll of success, having benefitted greatly from the free-market economy that guided them into becoming the biggest and richest industrial nation of the time. This system had been built primarily on the ideas and principles touted by Adam Smith in his groundbreaking book that came out in 1776 called *The Wealth of Nations*.

Adam Smith was born in a small village in Kirkcaldy, Scotland, where his widowed mother raised him. At age fourteen, as was the usual practice, he entered the University of Glasgow on scholarship. He later attended Balliol College at Oxford, graduating with an extensive knowledge of European literature and an enduring contempt for English schools.

He returned home, and after delivering a series of well-received lectures, was made first chair of logic (1751), then chair of moral philosophy (1752), at Glasgow University. He left academia in 1764 to tutor the young duke of Buccleuch. For more than two years, they traveled throughout France and into Switzerland, an experience that brought Smith into contact with his contemporaries Voltaire, Jean-Jacques Rousseau, François Quesnay, and Anne-Robert-Jacques Turgot. With the life pension he had earned in the service of the duke, Smith retired to his birthplace of Kirkcaldy to write *The Wealth of Nations*.

It was published in 1776, the same year the American Declaration of Independence was signed.

Today Smith's reputation rests on his explanation of how rational self-interest in a free-market economy leads to economic well-being. It may surprise those who would discount Smith as an advocate of ruthless individualism that his first major work concentrates on ethics and charity.

Someone earning money by his own labor benefits himself. Unknowingly, he also benefits society, because to earn income on his labor in a competitive market, he must produce something others value. In Adam Smith's lasting imagery, "By directing that industry in such a manner as its produce may be of greatest value, he intends only his own gain, and he is in this, as in many other cases, led by an invisible hand to promote an end which was no part of his intention."

The Wealth of Nations, published as a five-book series, sought to reveal the nature and cause of a nation's prosperity. Smith saw the main cause of prosperity as increasing division of labor. Using the famous example of pins, Smith asserted that ten workers could produce 48,000 pins per day if each of eighteen specialized tasks was assigned to particular workers. Average productivity: 4,800 pins per worker per day. But absent the division of labor, a worker would be lucky to produce even one pin per day.

Adam Smith has sometimes been caricatured as someone who saw no role for government in economic life. In fact, he believed that government had an important role to play. Like most modern believers in free markets, Smith believed that the government should enforce contracts and grant patents and copyrights to encourage inventions and new ideas. He also thought that the government should provide public works, such as roads and bridges, that, he assumed, would not be worthwhile for individuals to provide. Interestingly, though, he wanted the users of such public works to pay in proportion to their use.

Smith's writings are both an inquiry into the science of economics and a policy guide for realizing the wealth of nations. Smith believed that economic development was best fostered in an environment of free competition that operated in accordance with universal "natural laws." Because Smith's was the most systematic and comprehensive study of economics up until that time, his economic thinking became the basis for classical economics. And because more of his ideas have lasted than those of any other economist, some regard Adam Smith as the alpha and the omega of economic science.

Despite the great success that the free-market economy had provided, a number of prominent business people, including wealthy industrialists and major banking institutions began looking for other methods. Some felt that the market economy needed some adjustments or refinements, while others were beginning to consider dumping it altogether. At the same time a new Populist movement, primarily involving agriculture and labor groups promoting the premise of the government getting into the business of redistribution of wealth came on the scene. The system being promoted involved the extensive regulation of business and/or possible take-over of businesses and natural resources.

Part of the problem also included some of the wealthy families in America looking at what assemblies of wealthy families in Europe had done by joining together to gain control of their governments and generating a fortune as a result.

In this atmosphere the free-market economy, ideas of Adam Smith were being discounted. Now collectivism, socialism, farm subsidies, government owning businesses and the sort were dominating the conversation. The breakout of World War I didn't help. The need for a strong central government just played right into the hands of the growing socialist sentiment.

Entering the 1920s, the ideas and principles of our early years as a nation were being trounced. Constitutional stability was floundering, and Adam Smith's ideas were looking ancient. John Chamberlain described the academic climate of the time this way:

> When I was taking a minor in economics as a congruent part of a history major back in the 1920s, Robert

> Hutchins had not yet started his campaign to restore a reading of the "great books" to college courses. So we never read Adam Smith's *The Wealth of Nations*. We heard plenty about it, however. The professors treated it condescendingly; we were told it was the fundamentalist Bible of the old dog-eat-dog type of businessman.
>
> The businessmen, in that Menckenian time, were considered the natural enemies of disinterested learning. We, as students, regarded them as hypocrites. They talked competition, and invoked the name of Adam Smith to bless it. Then they voted for the high-tariff Republican Party. Somehow Adam Smith, as the man who had justified a business civilization, got the blame for everything. We weren't very logical in those days, and we were quite oblivious to our own hypocrisy in making use of our businessmen fathers to pay our college tuition fees and to stake us to trips to Europe.[1]

Chamberlain, along with others of the time, came to realize that they were being brainwashed and that things weren't as they seemed. He later said:

> The depression that began in 1929 is generally considered the watershed that separates the new (collectivist) age from the old, or rugged individualist, age. Before Franklin Roosevelt, we had had the republic (checks and balances, limited government, inalienable rights to liberty and property, and all that). After 1933 we began to get the centralized state and interventionist controls of industry. Actually, however, the inner spirit of the old America had been hollowed out in the Twenties. The colleges had ceased to teach anything important about our heritage. You had to be a graduate student to catch up with The Federalist Papers, or with John Calhoun's *Disquisition on Government*, or with

> anything by Herbert Spencer, or with *The Wealth of Nations*. We were the ignorant generation.
>
> The depression began our education. But the first "great book" in economics we read was Marx's *Capital*. We had nothing to put against it. Talk of "planning" filled the air. We read George Soule and Stuart Chase on the need for national blueprints and national investment boards and "government investment." Kynes was still in the future, but his system was already being laid brick by brick. And Adam Smith was still a word of derision.[2]

Some professors spoke of what they called the "myths the Founders believed." Ever so gradually the light began to dawn, and new reading became available in Ivor Thomas's book, *The Socialist Tragedy* (New York: The Macmillan Company, 1951), explaining what socialism had done to Europe. And Max Eastman's *Reflections on the Failures of Socialism* (New York: The Devin-Adair Company, 1962), telling what socialism had done to America and the world.

A major problem in any era is the proper function of the banking system. The Founders turned the issuing of money over to a private consortium of bankers who set up a privately owned bank called the Bank of the United States. This is similar to our present Federal Reserve System. Thomas Jefferson raved about the error of doing this:

> If the American people ever allow the banks to control the issuance of their currency, first by inflation and then by deflation, the banks and corporations that will grow up around them will deprive the people of all property until their children will wake up homeless on the continent their fathers occupied. The issuing power of money should be taken from the banks and restored to Congress and the people to whom it belongs.[3]

We looked at Montesquieu as one of the influences on our new nation earlier and how his book *The Spirit of Laws* had made its mark in the world. It has been called "one of the most important books ever written" and surely takes its place among the best. In Book XI, Montesquieu sets the ingredients for a model constitution. Our Founders valued his plan enough to use a number of portions of it to guide their efforts for our Constitution. They particularly liked the principles of "separated" but "coordinated" powers. His plan helped with the concept of America's "three-headed eagle."

The separation of powers was a central theme for John Adams before the others got on board. He found himself being criticized for such a novel idea. Years later, April 12, 1809, he wrote Dr. Benjamin Rush and told his story concerning this matter:

> I call you to witness that I was the first member of Congress who ventured to come out in public, as I did in January 1776, in my "Thoughts on Government," . . . in favor of a government with three branches, and an independent judiciary. This pamphlet, you know, was very unpopular. No man appeared in public to support it but myself. You attempted in the public papers to give it some countenance, but without much success. Franklin leaned against it. Dr. Young, Mr. Timothy Matlack and Mr. James Cannon, and I suppose Mr. George Bryan were alarmed and displeased at it. Mr. Thomas Paine was so highly offended with it that he came to visit me at my chamber at Mrs. Yard's to remonstrate and even scold me for it, which he did in very ungenteel terms. In return, I only laughed heartily at him.
>
> . . . Paine's wrath was excited because my plan of government was essentially different from the silly projects that he had published in his "Common Sense." By this means I became suspected and unpopular with the leading demagogues and the whole constitutional party in Pennsylvania.[4]

Ironically, Adams had been the first of the Founders to realize the vision of Montesquieu for a self-repairing national government using the separation of powers doctrine. He actually considered good politics as a "divine science" and devoted his life to it.

In spite of the strong opposition, John Adams was actually to get his home state of Massachusetts to adopt a constitution based on separation of powers. It took a hundred years before he was recognized for the tremendous contributions he made. Ben Franklin, who had been one of the last to accept his concept, finally acknowledged that the Constitution of the United States with its separation of powers was as perfect as man could be expected to produce. He urged all the members of the Convention to sign it so that it would have unanimous support.

International Relations

I find it interesting that we presently are embroiled in an argument about how involved we should be with other countries and how we should relate to each other, as far as alliances and interaction are concerned. George Washington had some insight on that matter that I think we should consider today. He said:

Against the insidious wiles of foreign influence, I conjure you to believe me, fellow citizens, the jealousy of a free people ought to be constantly awake, since history and experience prove that foreign influence is one of the most baneful of republican government. But that jealousy, to be useful, must be impartial, else it becomes the instrument of the very influence to be avoided instead of a defense against it. Excessive partiality for one foreign nation and excessive dislike of another cause those whom they actuate to see danger only on one side and to serve to veil and even second the arts of influence on the others. Real patriots, who may resist the intrigues of the favorite, are liable to become suspected and odious, while its tools and dupes usurp the applause and confidence of the people to surrender their interests.[5]

Notes

1. Adam Smith, *The Wealth of Nations*, "Heirloom Edition," 2 vols. (New Rochelle, NY: Arlington House, n.d.), v.
2. Ibid., v-vi. ***Also,*** econlib.org/Adam Smith
3. Olive Cushing Dwinell, *The Story of Our Money*, 2nd ed. (Boston: Forum Publishing Company, 1946), 84.
4. Koch, *The American Enlightenment,* (1965), 163.
5. John C. Fitzpatrick, ed., *The Writings of George Washington*, 39 vols. (Washington: U.S. Government Printing Office, 1931-44), 35:233.

CHAPTER 15

From the Great Crash to the Great Society

Franklin Delano Roosevelt had a lot of qualities that suited a public figure well. He had a quick smile, was bold and courageous—and the family name didn't hurt. He also was lucky. He narrowly escaped an assassination attempt in Miami, then stepped into the office of president just as the repeal of prohibition cleared Congress. The sudden flow of alcohol both livened the spirits of the people after the Depression years and brought in a large flow of tax revenue from those sales.

Voters gave him a landslide victory in November 1932, with large majorities in the South and West. Roosevelt hoped he could take advantage of the collapsing economy, since he really didn't have a platform of goals to work with. He saw an opportunity to ram through a timid Congress a plan that would fundamentally rearrange the foundations of business and welfare in America. Roosevelt's programs, under the title of the "New Deal," came upon him as a quick fix-type agenda for the latest crisis. The weird absence of any internal consistency to the program has resulted in confusion over whether there were one or two New Deals.

We find that similar to the story about business failures causing the stock market collapse and subsequent recession, a similar fable popped up about FDR's New Deal program to rescue America. Eventually, most people who studied this have maintained that there were, in fact, two New Deals, not one. They have differing opinions on the direction and extent of the changes between the two.

One theory proposed that Roosevelt entered the office of president with a seriously different plan from his predecessor Herbert Hoover's "do-nothingism" and set out to restore the health of the American economy by "saving capitalism." In fact, the first phase of his master plan—mostly between 1933 and 1935—simply was an adoption of a widespread series of measures at the national level that emphasized relief, and around 1936 shifted the legislation toward reform.

A different variation had the early measures designed to keep capitalism afloat with banking legislation and an attempt to introduce planning into the economy. Rexford Tugwell agreed with this interpretation and complained that conservative elements stifled attempts to centralize control over the economy in the federal government's hands. When FDR reached the point where he felt that more radical redistributions of wealth weren't available, a second more conservative New Deal evolved that emphasized piecemeal measures.

In general, the Tugwell interpretation is endorsed by the liberal groups, which suggests that FDR saved capitalism from itself by embedding a number of regulatory measures and social programs that kept the market economy from its own "excesses."

Let's just look at a thumbnail sketch of whole New Deal and the results it generated.

Civilian Conservation Corps was to provide employment to 2.5 million and address conservation issues. The long-term effect was negligible, and it ended in 1942.

The Agricultural Adjustment Act was to control production and raise prices by offering subsidies to farmers. Farm income rose 51 percent, but didn't return to 1929 levels until 1941. Farm subsidies raised prices to consumers, benefitted large agribusinesses, and encouraged overproduction. In 1955, Congress ended most agricultural subsidies because of cost, inefficiency, and discrimination against both consumers and small farmers. Subsidies on dairy products and sugar remained.

The Glass-Steagall Act of 1935 was to separate investment banking (brokerage of stocks and bonds) from commercial banking (loans, checking, and savings accounts). It allowed financial institutions other than banks (e.g., insurance companies) to compete with banks in a wide range of services, such as checking and insurance, and limited American banks' ability to compete in world markets and to diversify.

The Tennessee Valley Authority Act was to create the TVA and provide government subsidized electric power to private citizens. It developed Tennessee Valley Authority hydroelectric dams with locks; increased government's intrusion into private sector utility operations, and fostered monopolies in electric power.

The Federal Deposit Insurance Corporation came to be in 1934 to insure all bank deposits up to $5,000 per account and to bring stability to the banking system. Their sister agency, Federal Savings and Loan Insurance Corporation (FSLIC), contributed to the collapse of the S&L industry in the 1970s and 1980s by encouraging risky investments by managers and owners. Total cost: $800 billion.

The Revenue Act of 1935 was to offset the huge federal deficits under FDR by enacting huge tax hikes and estate taxes. It accelerated progressive notions of redistribution by targeting upper classes. It did not offset deficits, but rather insured that the rich would continue to avoid taxes by being able to move money offshore or purchase tax-free municipal bonds, shifting the real burden onto the poor and middle classes. The concept remained in place until John Kennedy's and Ronald Reagan's cuts, both of which increased the amount paid by the wealthy.

The Works Progress Administration in 1935 was to create public works jobs for 9 million workers to construct bridges, sidewalks, art theaters, opera houses, and other projects. It ended in 1943 during World War II. But by 1937, unemployment had soared to 14 million. Many WPA projects were unnecessary economically and often catered to the elites (opera houses, art galleries, etc.) and were subsidized via deficits.

And the "really big one," the Social Security Act (1935) was intended to provide a "supplemental" old-age pension and emergency unemployment compensation as well as aid to families with dependent children (AFDC). The first thing that people forgot was this was never proposed to be a stand-alone retirement program. It was supposed to be a seed program that people could build their own retirement around. Now, as a result of cross-generational transfers, the Social Security Trust Fund, while solvent during the baby boom years, is projected to be in severe deficit by 2020, and depending on the economic conditions, bankrupt not long after that, even according to the most optimistic estimates. The system faces massive overhaul, with higher taxes, lower benefits, or privatization. One result of AFDC was the "illegitimacy explosion" of the 1960s-1970s, and it was substantially curtailed in 1995 as part of the welfare reform bill. Another major problem is the number categories of recipients that have been added who have never made a contribution to the program.

The Fair Labor Standards Act (1934) was meant to set minimum wages and maximum hours that could be worked. It actually raised wages in industry while reducing employment overall. New studies suggest that it might have prolonged the Great Depression considering minimum wage laws in the 1950s and 1960s were closely correlated with minority teenage unemployment at the time, suggesting the law encouraged discrimination.

Interestingly, the New Deal caused a new influx of corporate money into politics unlike anything seen before. What stands out is how little business gave to either political party prior to the Great Depression and the manipulation of the tax code that politicians wrought in an attempt to combat it.[1] Sociologist Michael Weber has conducted a study of the contributions of corporate boards of directors in 1936, finding that region and religion—not class identity—determined who gave how much to either the Democrats or the Republicans. Instead, the lesson corporate donors learned in 1936 was that government had put itself in the position of picking winners and losers in the tax code, making it critical, for the first time, to influence politicians with money.[2]

Notes

1. Michael J. Webber, *New Deal Fat Cats: Business, Labor, and Campaign Finance in the 1936 Presidential Election* (New York: Fordam University Press, 2000), 15.
2. Summary of the programs of the New Deal taken from Larry Schweikart & Michael Allen, *A Patriot's History of the United States* (New York: Penguin Group, 2004), 568-70.

WWII to Happy Days

The tragedies, pain, and sacrifices of the time of World War II are graphically illustrated and described in many volumes, and we won't cover that here. I will only make a brief comment that says how proud I was to have been a child during that period and have had many family members and neighbors who fought and died for the great cause of freedom on both sides of the world.

This dramatic time was followed by what some have called "Happy Days." It was a time when science grew by leaps and bounds, perhaps boosted by the boom of much-needed discoveries to aid the war effort. Technologies were in full bloom, and everyone enjoyed the pleasant atmosphere.

Then we jumped right into another period of upheaval in the 1960s. There was a string of events that seemed to keep the country in a state of wondering what could happen next. It included electing John Kennedy as the first Catholic president, the Cuban missile crisis, and Lyndon Johnson assuming the presidency and introducing his Great Society legislation. The Civil Rights Act was passed. Martin Luther King Jr. and Robert Kennedy were assassinated. The United States landed a man on the moon.

So many things that we could list here that happened in the world, and more specifically in this country, would begin to bore the reader and miss the point of writing this book entirely. It's time to focus on the problems and situations that I believe are destroying the very foundations of this great country.

CHAPTER 16

Liberty, Is It Worth Fighting For?

In any civil society, the citizen has rights and a duty to respect the rights of others as he expects them to respect his. In the United States, as we discussed earlier, certain rights are considered to be unalienable, such as life, liberty and the pursuit of happiness. As we grow and mature, we generally develop a particular view of society and how it should function. We are expected to follow the laws of the land, traditionally described as the "rule of law," which lays out a framework or plan for us to follow that outlines how we relate to each other and society in general.

Over the years, our society has pretty well divided itself into political groups. Conservative thinkers are, for the most part, Christian or follow some other religious belief. They believe in self-respect and self-reliance. They don't want government interfering with their lives. They don't believe in a big, overpowering central government. In other words, they still think like our Founding Fathers.

On the other hand, we have the liberal thinkers who believe that the federal government should be all-powerful and also provide for us. Can we say "nanny state"? The liberal-minded person believes in the idea of "utopia," where everyone just sits around under a shade tree and has everything they need provided for them. They believe that everyone should be treated equally and have everything be mutually shared. This brings us to Alexis de Tocqueville again. He coined the phrase "soft tyranny" to describe this situation.[1] He says that as the people in charge continue to usurp authority, this system becomes oppressive, eventually becoming a hard tyranny—similar to the totalitarianism we saw in Communist Russia.

My personal opinion about this "utopian society" where everyone is totally "equal" is simply this—we aren't "naturally equal" as the believers in this premise suggest. Everyone is different in some way. For instance, some people are ambitious and would upset the pleasant little "community" by wanting to be in charge. Others, on the other extreme of the initiative scale, would not like having the few chores or responsibilities that they would necessarily be responsible for.

As we mentioned earlier, our Founders knew that the greatest threat to human liberty is a central government with no limits. They worked tirelessly to avoid that kind of governing structure. James Madison, one of the contributors to the Federalists Papers, wrote this:

> But what is government itself, but the greatest of all reflections on human nature? If men were angels, no government would be necessary. If angels were to govern men, neither external nor internal controls on government would be necessary. In framing a government which is to be administered by men over men, the great difficulty lies in this: you must first enable the government to control the governed; and in the next place oblige it to govern itself.[2]

The liberal thinker disguises his goals or projects in moral indignation, always claiming injustice in one form or another. He projects the same image as the poor, oppressed comrades of the former USSR who owned nothing and had no future hopes of their plight improving. The Great Society in our country made all sorts of promises that were not realized any more than the utopian images that the leaders of the Communist Party made to their people. That is the reality of this type of scenario—promises of "equality for all" are realized by all, having equally nothing and walking around like zombies with no hope or ambition. The leaders, on the other hand, live like royalty.

Our brilliant Founders focused on the individual rights of man, his opportunity to be and to have all he was willing to work for—without the interference or aid of "the government." They believed that a person should be able to benefit from his own blood, sweat, and tears. Liberty to them was something that shouldn't just be dreamed about, but rather enjoyed.

Today we seem to take it for granted and don't even talk about it except in some political arena. We are so accustomed to the unusual freedom that our society offers that it doesn't make an impression on us anymore. Conservatives are more likely to recognize the importance of true liberty, where the progressives only want to give it away to the "nanny state" so it can better plan and run their life for them.

The conservative recognizes the slippery slope that we are on right now, where the rights and privileges are eroding just like they did in the ancient republics. We must return to the strict constitutional limits that the Founders provided to sustain our republic. Truly free people don't look to the government, but instead work together, cooperating to build a stronger free-market society for the good of all. Edmund Burke had a lot to say about conservative ideas:

> There is a manifest, marked distinction, which ill men with ill designs or weak men incapable of any design, will constantly be confounding,—that is, a marked distinction between change and reformation. The former alters the substance of the objects themselves, and gets rid of all their essential good as well as of all the accidental evil annexed to them. Change is novelty; and whether it is to operate any one of the effects of reformation at all, or whether it may not contradict the very principle upon which reformation is desired, cannot be known beforehand. Reform is not change in the substance or in the primary modification of the object, but a direct application of a remedy to the grievance complained of. So far as that is removed, all is sure. It stops there; and if it fails, the substance which underwent the operation, at the very worst, is but where it was.[3]

Change is one of the bywords of the "Progressive" movement. I, personally, have come to despise the word. Forgive my preacher's wording here, but I think we are "progressing" straight to hell! The progressives often justify their call for change as a way to gain new "rights." Our proper course is to retain the major "rights" and "privileges" of the free man at the birth of our nation. Our Founders knew what they were doing. The more we try and manipulate and improve on our Constitution, the less free we will be. More often than not, any change that comes to our governmental structure gives more power to the government and less to the people.

Prudence was a word more often heard during the birth of our nation than today. It simply meant that one should seriously consider the possible consequences before making any formidable decision, particularly if it would affect the masses. Jumping willy-nilly into a new and untested "change" could be calamitous and long lasting. We can't just rest on our laurels, however, and not make adjustments where they are needed. Burke said, "All that's necessary for the forces of evil to win in the world is for enough good men to do nothing."[4]

The conservative has to hold on to the idea of the Founders that passionate love of liberty goes right along with the integrity and dignity belonging to the seriously patriotic citizen.

One of the big differences between the liberal, or progressive thinker, and the conservative is the principle of equality. The liberals have fought using that one word for numerous causes over the years. In the beginning of this country, our leaders and patriots certainly believed in equality as one of the natural rights for everyone. This gave them the ability to live in an atmosphere of self-government. The ordinary citizen had the right to vote, to own property, and have equal treatment under the law. The great traditions of liberty in America make it difficult for any major changes or challenges to our unalienable rights.

The "ruling class" or "elite" that dominated the European nations were conspicuously absent during the birth of the United States. Our country was built on the "all for one and all for one" mentality.

The Meology Problem

The one attitude that began to grow from the Great Society era and has made a negative impact on our nation is called "meology." The first time I had an encounter with this was in the late 1970s when I ran for public office. Having entered the race for the state legislature, I was amazed when I approached a number of potential voters and introduced myself. To my surprise, the first thing the person said to me was, "What are you going to do for me?" They were not interested in family, community, or country! Only themselves!

This attitude, regrettably, is growing and is becoming a major factor in the political arena. This is the type of attitude the liberal crowd has fostered. The "give-away" programs that they champion have encouraged the people to look more for how they, personally, can benefit from government programs than how the country will benefit.

Traditional conservative ideology believes in freedom for all, not a selected few. This means the individual rights that our Founders fought for, not in "special rights" that some would call "government rights" since they are the result of government programs rather than the God-given unalienable rights that our nation was built on. In other words, these are rights granted to some special group instead of for the common good. This means everyone must basically be dehumanized so that they will fit into the mass utopian society plan—the drones or "worker bees" of the Great Society.

The liberally biased media is the biggest proponent of the progressive movement in that they report favorably on everything that the progressives do and negatively on anything on the right or conservative side.

C. S. Lewis once explained:

> Of all tyrannies, a tyranny sincerely exercised for the good of its victims may be the most oppressive. It would be better to live under robber barons than under omnipotent moral busybodies. The robber baron's

> cruelty may sometimes sleep, his cupidity may at some point be satiated; but those who torment us for our own good will torment us without end for they do so with the approval of their own conscience.[5]

They truly believe it is for the "greater good." After all, they have thought it through and know what's best for the society as a whole.

Basis for Our Rights

We have covered in the previous chapters what our Founders based their beliefs on. It was not some outlandish scientific or pagan theory. It was a belief in almighty God and his plan for his creation and the people involved. Burke makes another pertinent statement in saying, "There is but one law for all, namely, that law which governs all law, the law of our Creator, the law of humanity, justice, equity—the law of nature and of nations."[6] This is the law that our Founders recognized and what became the basis for all they did in establishing the society we have today. As previously stated, the Declaration of Independence clearly outlined that we live under the "Laws of Nature and Nature's God," and that we all were created by him as equals and that the Creator has endowed us with certain unalienable rights, among which are life, liberty, and the pursuit of happiness. These rights didn't come from man, but from God.

As we know, these men were very much enlightened, but not tainted by some of the ideas of the Enlightenment. Although they were some of the best educated and intelligent men of the age, they held on to a higher calling for their motivation and determination. Christianity was without a doubt the driving force for the country and was a part of the thinking and planning of everything from the household to the governmental structures.

So how did we get to the place where we are now that every idea, program, or piece of legislation becomes a battle in this country? It is primarily because of the great disparity of personal and political beliefs and ideologies that have developed over nearly a century in America.

I don't want to bore those of you who are aware of the various lines of thinking, but if you will bear with me, I believe it would be beneficial to some of the readers to be advised of these things. Briefly, let's look at the categories that the majority of our people fall into. We won't go into a lot of specifics, but basically most can be identified by the following general characteristics:

Political/Societal Definitions[7]

Secular

1 a: of or relating to the worldly or temporal <secular concerns> b: not overtly or specifically religious <secular music> c: not ecclesiastical or clerical <secular courts> <secular landowners>
2 : not bound by monastic vows or rules; specifically: of, relating to, or forming clergy not belonging to a religious order or congregation <a secular priest>

Conservative v. Liberal Beliefs

We all want the same things in life. We want freedom; we want the chance for prosperity; we want as few people suffering as possible; we want healthy children; we want to have crime-free streets. The argument is how to achieve them:

> LIBERALS—believe in government action to achieve equal opportunity and equality for all. It is the duty of the government to alleviate social ills and to protect civil liberties and individual and human rights. Believe the role of the government should be to guarantee that no one is in need. Liberal policies generally emphasize the need for the government to solve problems.

> CONSERVATIVES—believe in personal responsibility, limited government, free markets, individual liberty, traditional American values and a strong national defense. Believe the role of government should be to provide people the freedom necessary to pursue their

> own goals. Conservative policies generally emphasize empowerment of the individual to solve problems.[8]

Of course some people refuse to be "labeled" by any category, but their viewpoint and leaning becomes evident over time. As I've said before, it was pretty obvious where the Founders stood on the issues, and even though there were some differences, the same love of liberty and freedom drove them all.

Although it has been proven over and over that our Founders and the majority of the people of the time were determined to have a Christian or godly country, the battle rages on today about the "Separation of Church and State." There have been numerous court battles over this issue, and we will look at some of the specifics here. The Founders had clearly laid out the lines between the authority of the State and in the First Amendment declared that the State could not establish a state-run or state-sponsored church. It did not, however, prohibit anyone from using biblical references, saying prayers, or quoting Scriptures during the business or on the premises of state-owned property.

This premise has been the basis for many lawsuits over the years, and even the judges sometimes don't get it right. For example, in 1947, the case of Everson v. Board of Education came up at the Supreme Court, and Associate Justice Hugo Black stated while writing for the 5-4 majority ruling, "No tax in any amount, large or small, can be levied to support any religious activities or institutions, whatever they may be called, or whatever form they may adopt to teach or practice religion." He went on to say, "The First Amendment has erected a wall between church and state. That wall must be kept high and impregnable. We could not approve the slightest breach."[9]

Judge Black shows his allegiance to FDR and his liberal leanings, having been his first appointee to the court. He also had a fiercely negative opinion toward the Catholic Church. He let his own bias help the assault on religious liberty in America.

Another case where the misinterpretation of the First Amendment came into play was in 1985, when Chief Justice William Rehnquist argued in the Wallace v. Jaffree case that "(First Amendment) Establishment Clause did not require government neutrality between religion and irreligion nor did it prohibit the Federal Government from providing nondiscriminatory aid to religion. There is simply no historical foundation for the proposition that the Framers intended to build a 'wall of separation' that was constitutionalized in Everson."[10]

What the Founders intended was to disallow the establishment of a national religion that would repeat the mistakes of England, which had a government-supported church, requiring citizens to be a part of. That was the major motivation for the colonists to come to America.

This misguided idea about that the constitutional amendment forbade any mention of God or display of any Christian materials or activity on "public property" has been expanded to the point of absurdity. Professor Thomas G. West of the University of Dallas said it so well:

> The Supreme Court will allow the theology of the declaration to be taught in the classroom as long as it is understood that it belongs to a "world that is dead and gone," that it has nothing to do with the world that we live in here and now, that it is not a living faith that is holding God to be the source of our rights, the author of the laws of nature, and the protector and supreme Judge of America.[11]

Using Professor West's viewpoint, our courts today are simply acting as the puppets of the anti-Christian and secularist groups, similar to the Islamist Sharia law leaders, to restrict the religious liberties that our Founders fought and died for. What so many in the United States of America don't realize is that if we keep sitting on the sideline hoping that everything will be all right, we will soon be shaking our heads in disbelief when the nation that we once loved and respected is no more. One who was clearly aware of the importance of holding on to our Christian heritage was George Washington. In his farewell address he stated:

> Of all the dispositions and habits which lead to political prosperity, religion and morality are indispensable

> results . . . And let us with caution indulge the supposition that morality can be maintained without religion . . . That the all wise dispenser of human blessings has favored no Nation on earth with more abundant, and substantial means happiness than United America, that we may not be so ungrateful to our Creator; so wanting to ourselves; and so regardless of Posterity, as to dash the cup of beneficence which is thus bountifully offered to our acceptance.[12]

George Washington continually reminded those around him that freedom had its price—mainly for us to remember where our freedom came from and that it could not be maintained without the moral foundations of the country and its people remaining intact. In other words, freedom is not free; we must work for it and work to keep it.

Barry Goldwater, in his acceptance speech for the nomination for president in 1964 said this: "Those who elevate the state and downgrade the citizen must see ultimately a world in which earthly power can be substituted for Divine Will, and this Nation was founded upon the rejection of that notion and upon the acceptance of God as the author of freedom."[13]

Notes

1. Alexis de Tocqueville, *Democracy in America* (New York: Penguin, 2003), 226.
2. James Madison, Alexander Hamilton, and John Jay, *The Federalist Papers* (New York: Penguin, 1987), 319-20.
3. Edmund Burke, "A Letter to a Noble Lord," vol. 5 (Boston: Little, Brown, 1964), 186.
4. http://www.brainyquote.com/quotes/authors/e/edmund_burke.html#wqilzka8XourWfLi.9
5. C. S. Lewis, *God in the Dock: Essays on Theology and Ethics*, ed. Walter Hooper (Grand Rapids, Mich.: Eerdmans, 1994), 292.

6. Edmund Burke, "Speech on Impeachment of Warren Hastings," (May28,1794),http//www.notable-quotes.com/b/burke_edmund.html.
7. Merriam Webster—Online dictionary—m-w.com
8. "Conservative vs. Liberal Beliefs (Main page) (copyright 2005: revised 2010), http://www.studentnewsdaily.com.
9. Everson v. Board of Education of Ewing 330 U.S. 1; 16, 18, (1947).
10. Wallace v. Jaffree, 472 U.S. 38; 107 (1985), (Rehnquist, J., dissenting).
11. Thomas G. West, "The Theology of the United States," Claremont Institute (December 1, 2006), http://www.claremont.org/publications/pubid.30/pub_detail.asp.
12. John C. Fitzpatrick, ed., *The Writings of George Washington*, 39 vols. (Washington: U.S. Government Printing Office, 1931-44), vol.35, May 15, 1796.
13. Barry Goldwater, "Goldwater's 1964 Acceptance Speech," http://www.washingtonpost.com/wp-srv/politics/daily/may98/goldwaterspeech.htm.

CHAPTER 17

How Serious Are You?

We have just looked at some of the names that people are called or that they call themselves. Some of them are Secularist, Liberal, Progressive, and Conservative. There are some others that are being used either to compliment, insult, or just label people today. We also have Christian and Christian Fundamentalist, which can also be called extremist or radical. Moderate and extreme can be added to any of these to further describe various Muslim peoples.

One subject that I want to spend some time on is the habit of some, particularly the media, who want to add the term *extremist* or *radical* to certain religious persons, particularly if they are firm in their belief.

You may have noticed that if an explosive device is detonated in the war-torn areas of the Middle East or anywhere, the first thing you hear in the news is that it certainly must have been the work of a (1) Muslim Fundamentalist, (2) radical Islamist, or (3) Muslim terrorist. First of all, I don't condone the bombing and killing of innocent people by anyone at any time. Second, this immediately implies that anyone who is a serious believer in the Muslim faith is a terrorist and murderer. In certain cases this could be true, but in others, the person that committed this act was only following his religious teaching.

There is a lot of ignorance and confusion in the world today about religious beliefs. There is also a very diverse discipline and direction within the various religions themselves. For example, the Islamic religion is being toned down and diluted and presented to the world as a religion of "love." If you go to one of the numerous Web sites to inquire about Islamic teachings, you will not find the same thing as you would in an original copy of the Koran or Qur'an written by Muhammad, which said that everything that was being taught came directly from God to his prophet. You would also find that the writings said that people who did not believe the Qur'an and follow its teachings were "infidels." These infidels were given three choices: convert, be enslaved, or die.

Now if a person has been taught according to these principles, and they truly believe it is the truth, they can only be a "radical Islamist." I've got a surprise for you—I don't agree with the teachings, but I respect the person for being devout in their belief.

Here's another shocker for you—following the same parameters that we just set out for the Islamist believer, I am a "radical Christian." That simply means that I believe that everything in the Holy Bible is God's Word as given to his prophets and other writers. I don't go along with the Christian "leaders" who want to water down the Bible just as the Muslims who want to water down and hide the true beliefs of Islam. I believe this would be a perfect place to share a paper I wrote a couple of years ago about the "War of the Worldviews."

War of the Worldviews

Basically a worldview simply describes your philosophy, what you believe in, what you have faith in. There is an old adage that states, "If you don't believe in something, you will fall for anything." This is so true. Without a firm foundation, we can be manipulated into following any new fad or craze or political ideology that comes along. A very good example of someone who was firmly grounded is found in Joshua 24:15 where he states, "And if it seem evil unto you to serve the Lord, choose you this day whom you will serve; whether the gods which your fathers served that were on the other side of the flood, or the gods of the Amorites, in whose land we dwell: but as for me and my house, we will serve the Lord."

What we are facing in America today is a conspiracy to destroy our society from the inside. From a country that was born with a strong common belief in almighty God and the Christian faith, we are being bombarded with propaganda and lawsuits to try and build a secular society. In addition, the infusion of peoples from countries from across the globe who have different faiths and different heritages is diluting the foundation that America was built on.

Oriana Fallaci tells us in her book, *The Rage and the Pride,* how some of the European countries, burdened by huge Muslim populations, are seeing their original cultures erode. They even tried to ban her book by what she described as "intellectual terrorism." Michael Barone concluded in his analysis of the facts of the Salafists/Wahhabis in Saudi Arabia that "it may not be prudent yet to speak the truth out loud, that the Saudis are our enemies. But they should know that it is increasingly apparent to the American people that they are effectively waging war against us."

Writer and keen observer of the world scene Victor David Hanson observed that: "It is time for Washington to recognize its despotic, oil-rich "ALLY" for what it is and act accordingly." So who, you might ask, are these people that these critics are warning us about? A small group of the Wahhabi sect of Muslims formed a brotherhood (Ikhwan) in 1902, dedicated to reestablishing a purified faith by means of jihad (Holy War). A decade later, Abdul Aziz ibn Saud, ruler of the Arabian District of Najd, sponsored a "spectacular revival" of the Wahhabi sect, which gave birth to a fierce warrior brotherhood: Ikwhan ("the Brethren"). Ibn Saud built an army of true Bedouins, the greatest warriors in Arabia. By 1921 the 150,000 strong fighting men were completing the conquest of Arabia, *again.* Mohammed and his armies did the same some 1200 years before.

By 1924, a Saudi-Wahhabi conquest of Mecca turned out the Hashemite Kingdom, ensuring the Wahhabis the right to collect taxes and fees from pilgrims in Hajj. The next year they asserted power over the port of Jeddah and the Holy City of Medina. With Wahhabi in power, a global Islamic conference was called by Ibn Saud to ratify his control over the two Holy Places.

With the discovery of oil by two Americans in 1931, Saudi Arabia passed from the British to the American sphere of influence. And a year later the state of Saudi Arabia was established. The House of Saud and its religious coconspirators, the Wahhabi, were soon transformed "into the world's richest and most powerful ruling elite."

When the Americans took over the oversight of the Middle East activities, they were anxious to show that they sympathized with the Arabs, Persians, and Muslims. The message was supposed to be "America was no imperialist power with self-serving designs on the lands and wealth of other peoples." However, after sixty-plus years, the United States has no real friends in the region. Why?

According to a story by Max Boot, the US message about not being an "imperialist power" was actually seen by the Saudis as one of weakness. We may remember Osama bin Laden made the case: "When people see a strong horse and a weak horse, by nature they will take the strong horse." By the way, if you didn't know this, Osama bin Laden was a member of this wealthy ruling family. He often referred to the soft words and diplomatic actions the United States had displayed, plus the numerous events that showed Americans living a depraved and self-indulgent way of life that had made them soft and unwilling to accept military casualties that showed them to be . . . a proverbial "weak horse," bin Laden and others concluded.

I must say at this point that if all I knew about this country was what I saw in the movies, in the news and magazines, then I could certainly agree with bin Laden and the other Muslims calling the United States "The Great Satan." All you see is the immoral, sinful frivolities that dominate our society today.

Again, author Victor David Hansen explains that the terrorists hate us for who we are, not what we have done. Bin Laden and his Al Qaeda group are about assuaging (easing) "the psychological wounds of hundreds of millions of Muslims who are without consensual government, freedom and material security," said Hansen. These people can't come to grips with the dizzying . . . pace of globalization and the spread of popular western culture." For bin Laden and his hate-mongering associates, the United States is a "demonic culture that dominates the world."

"Traditional Islam seeks to teach human beings how to live in accord with God's will," Richard Pipes explains, "militant Islam aspires to create a new order." Saudi Arabia's Wahhabi cultists have no moral constraints on the death and destruction left in the wake of their drive toward building one world of puritanical Islamic rule. Theirs is a "Reverse Crusade" against the West. The Ikhwan (Brotherhood) has not forgotten its original intention of engaging jihad against the infidel, nor have they forgotten that the sacred places had not been consecrated to God but had been taken over by an earthly sovereign who named this holy territory after himself: Saudi Arabia.

The Muslim Brotherhood serves as the board of directors for the destruction of non-Islamic civilization in North America. This is hardly a new phenomenon. Israel's Dore Gold quotes Wilfred Cantrell Smith of McGill University who wrote in 1957, "Most westerners have simply no inkling how deep and fierce is the hate of the west that has gripped the modernizing Arab."

The strategic goal of the Brotherhood in North America is civilization jihad, which includes "the destruction of Western civilization through long-term civilization-killing Jihad from within . . . [by Americans and Canadian hands] and through sabotage (the hands of the believers) and, secondly, to support the global Islamic movement to establish an Islamic super-state, known as the *caliphate.* The civilization-killing process is described in a Muslim Brotherhood memorandum dated May 22, 1991, which was accepted into evidence in the U.S. v *Holy Land Foundation* trial in federal court: "The Ikhwan must understand that their work in America is a kind of grand Jihad in eliminating and destroying the Western civilization from within and "sabotaging" its miserable house by their hands and the hands of believers so that it is eliminated and Allah's religion is made victorious over all other religions."

The Muslim Brotherhood has three main civilizational tools available to satisfy these strategic goals: infiltration of supporters into America, multiculturalism as a tool for societal transformation, and denial and deception through the Wahhabi Lobby. These civilizational jihad measures are all made possible by Saudi oil money and are backed up by the threat and possible terrorist action with conventional, chemical, biological, and radiological weapons and nuclear attacks.

Look around You

The terrorist network in the United States since 1991 expanded to more than fifty US cities. Among the leading terrorist groups with a presence in multiple areas include the Muslim Brotherhood, Al-Qaeda, Hezbollah, Hamas, Armed Islamic Group (Algeria), and several American homegrown cells.

The New York and Washington, D.C. metropolitan areas accommodate nine and six terrorist groups respectively. The Muslim Brotherhood was represented in seven major urban areas in 2008. Al-Qaeda was well represented in these locations and in Florida. Hamas was popular in Texas, Louisiana, Mississippi, Missouri, Oklahoma, and Kansas. On the West Coast, Al-Qaeda maintained a presence in Washington, Oregon, and California. FBI director, Robert Mueller, said in May 2008 that the Bureau had identified small groups of Al-Qaeda terrorists in the United States.

Of the approximately 2.35 million Muslims in the United States, a survey in 2007 found that of those under thirty years of age about 25 percent condoned suicide bombings under certain circumstances, 28 percent said they didn't believe Arabs were responsible for the 9/11 attacks . . . . Over-all, Muslims in the United States lean to the Democratic Party six to one.

Despite misgivings by many in the West, Islam is not the post 9/11 enemy of the capitalist West. "Rather," Dore Gold points out in *Hatred's Kingdom,* "the problem is the extremists in the Middle East who have manipulated Friday sermons in the mosques, textbooks in the schools and state-controlled television to one end: to systematically prepare young people to condone the cold-bloodied murder of innocent civilians." The problem is that Wahhabism has been allowed to spawn in Saudi Arabia and is now a thoroughly hate-filled ideology dedicated to mass murder in the United States.

To underline the point, Mr. Gold quoted an al-Qaeda spokesman, Suliaman Abu Ghaith, as saying that "We have a right to kill 4 million Americans, 2 million of them children—and to exile twice as many and wound and cripple hundreds of thousands."

In the past the attacks by the Wahhabis were sadistic. The barbarity is seen in the current-day suicide bombings against combatants and noncombatants alike. David Horowitz wrote, "In future generations, students of history will marvel that Western civilization failed to believe that it had a right to defend itself from the sworn enemies who had proudly, unambiguously declared their genocidal intentions. They will marvel at the moral paralysis that prevented America from taking identifiable steps to prevent a recurrence of 9/11 or calamities far greater."

The tool for civilization jihad is the reversal of Western ideas about multiculturalism. Popular with those on the radical left applying Antonio Gramsci's formula for transforming American culture, multiculturalism is also a two-sided coin in the hands of the Muslim Brotherhood.

Multiculturalism in the 1980s took a meaning in North America and Europe to support the "culture war" that would lead to a progressive-socialist-Marxist society. In the early 2000s, the idea of multiculturalism shed its anticapitalist bias and assumed a revised meaning of assimilation and ethnicity. Hege Storhaug, a Norwegian specialist on Islamic integration issues, explains that multiculturalism has been transformed from the idea of economic equality to cultural equality. But, since 9/11, Europeans and Americans have come to increasingly regard immigrants, especially Muslims, one, as being cultural threats, a source of hostility to the European and American ways of life, and a potential source of inspiration of additional terrorists attacks.

Part of the radicalization is self-identification in which individuals begin to examine the fundamentalism of Wahhabism. This "religious seeking" opens the individual to new worldviews and begins shifting their identity to associate with like-minded individuals and adopt jihad ideology and values as their own.

Another important aspect of the civilization jihad is through use of multiculturalism in subverting America's schools. Stanley Kurtz, a National Review Online contributing editor, offers a simple proposition: "Unless we counteract the influence of Saudi money on the education of the young, we're going to find it difficult to win the war on terror." The young that Mr. Kurtz is referring to are those in K-12 education in the United States.

None of this information is really new as the next section that we will consider comes from an article by Rusty Wright that is dated 9/29/2003. He tells us:

If you are a Westerner, an American, a non-Muslim, or a Muslim of a different stripe than they, then some radical Muslims hate you. Why? The complex answer involves history, culture, politics, religion and psychology. Of course many—some would say most—Muslims are peace loving and deplore terrorism. Islam is quite diverse. Extremist Muslims do not represent all Muslims any more than white supremacists represent all Christians. Not all "radical" Muslims are violent or hateful. But understanding extremist Muslim hatred is essential to interpreting our post 9/11 world.

Osama bin Laden called on Muslims to "obey God's command to kill the Americans and plunder their possessions . . . to kill Americans and their allies, both civil and military . . ." He and his sympathizers want to eliminate Western influence and restore their version of Islam to the world.

Would you believe that dancing in American churches helped fuel some radical Muslim anger today? Princeton Near East scholar Bernard Lewis illustrates:

"In 1948, Sayyd Qutb visited the United States for Egypt's Ministry of education. His stay left him shocked with what he perceived as moral degeneracy and sexual promiscuity. He wrote that even American religion was tainted by materialism and consumerism. Churches marketed their services to the public like merchants and entertainers. Success, big numbers, "fun" and having a "good time" seemed crucial to American churches.

He especially deplored clergy-sanctioned dances at church recreation halls. When the ministers lowered the lights, the dances became hot. Qutb's PG description: "the dance is inflamed by the notes of the gramophone . . . the dance-hall becomes a whirl of heels and thighs, arms enfold hips, lips and breasts meet, and the air is full of lust." He cited the famous Kinsey reports as evidence of American sexual debauchery.

Qutb, who was dark-skinned, also experienced racism in America. Back in Egypt, Qutb joined the Muslim Brotherhood. Imprisonment and torture made his writings more militant. He became what Georgetown University religion and international affairs professor John Esposito calls "the architect of radical Islam."

A militant offshoot of the Muslim Brotherhood, part of the Islamic Jihad, assassinated Egyptian President Anwar Sadat. Esposito notes that Abdullah Azzam, a radicalized former Muslim Brother, significantly influenced Osama bin Laden. Former CIA Middle East case officer Robert Baer observes that a Kuwaiti Muslim Brother, Khalid Sheikh Muhammad, became a bin Laden chief. (We know him now as the architect of the 9/11 attack.)

Princeton's Bernard Lewis notes that Qutb's denunciation of American moral character became incorporated into radical Islamic ideology. For instance, he says Iran's Ayatollah Khomeini, in calling the U.S. the "Great Satan," was being consistent with the Koranic depiction of Satan not as an "imperialist" or "exploiter" but as a seducer, "the insidious tempter who whispers in the hearts of men." [The author of this article, Rusty Wright, is an author, international lecturer, and a writer for Probe Ministries (www.probe.org)].

We have been looking at the Muslim worldview. Now let us view the world from a Christian viewpoint. Dr. Paul Dean wrote the following piece that appeared on the Web on March 8, 2009. It was entitled "America & Liberty: Grounded in Christian Worldview." Dr. Dean explains in detail what this means:

Widespread is the notion among secular thinkers that liberty cannot exist in the context of government established upon Christian principles. A revisionist view of the ideas and forces that led our founders to throw off the shackles of tyranny in these United States is not only pervasive but being propagated with renewed vigor from the purveyors of political correctness. The notion that liberty is the result of enlightenment thinking has all but replaced the realty that is the polar opposite: liberty is actually grounded in the Bible.

Further, a politically correct agenda is being forced upon the American people as well as the views connected to that agenda to the exclusion of all other views. From U.S. Senator Barack Obama's recent attack [this was written before he was elected president] on the Christian right, to the Montgomery County Board of education in Maryland simply declaring in its newly approved school curriculum for children that some babies are born homosexual, to hate crimes legislation, to U.S. Senator Diane Feinstein's looking into reviving the Fairness Doctrine concerning radio broadcasters, a concerted effort to suppress all views but those deemed acceptable by the liberal elite is underway. These developments demonstrate the reality that a rejection of the biblical God is that which is destructive of liberty.

Of course, history tells a different story when it comes to the nexus of Christianity and freedom. Not only are Christian principles compatible with liberty, but true liberty cannot be sustained within any context other than a context grounded in and committed to the biblical principles that under gird that liberty. It was Nietzsche's atheism that led Hitler's totalitarian genocide supported by racism and the notion that only supermen could determine what was right for the masses. It was Marx's atheism grounded in relativism that led to any number of Communist dictatorships that counted individuals as mere pieces of property to be expended for the so-called good of the whole. After all, it was Marx who said, "Force is the midwife of every society pregnant with a new one (Gary North, Marx's *Religion of Revolution,* p. 85).

Contrast the above and the varying tyrannical regimes of which they are only representative with the United States of America, the one nation in the history of the world that dared to ground its government in biblical principles and indeed the one nation in the history of the world that had put on glorious display the biblical notions of liberty and justice for all. Americans have not always put those principles into practice as they should, but that sad truth is owing to the failure of individual men and/or generations and not the principles upon which the nation was founded. While those principles have been set aside at times, it is the principles themselves that far from quashing liberty, actually establish liberty by law.

Note the opening words of the Declaration of Independence: "We hold these truths to be self-evident, that all men are created equal, that they are endowed by their Creator with certain unalienable Rights, that among these are Life, Liberty and the pursuit of Happiness. That to secure these rights, Governments are instituted among Men, deriving their just powers from the consent of the governed . . ." The theology upon which the nation was founded is obvious

First, the truths that are mentioned in the opening line of the Declaration are "self-evident." The fact that they are self-evident means that they require no proof. They are woven into the fabric of the natural order of things and are plain for all to see and deduce. To those who believe in the biblical God, the equality of all men is self-evident. Only those who deny the biblical God deny such things. Herein is a declaration that nature and natural law are grounded in something outside of themselves, namely, "Nature's God," as the founders put it.

Second, beyond that, the notion that "all men are created equal, that they are endowed by their Creator with certain unalienable Rights, that among these are Life, Liberty and the pursuit of Happiness," is grounded in at least two biblical principles. The first principle is that all human beings are created in the image of God. As such, they have essential dignity by virtue of the image of God in them. If God created them such, then they are free moral agents and cannot be coerced by others: they have liberty. An attack on them is an attack on God Himself. The Scripture is clear: "Whoever sheds man's blood, by man his blood shall be shed; for in the image of God He made man" (Gen. 9:6).

The second principle flows from the first. The rights to life, liberty and the pursuit of happiness are not granted by government but by God. It is God who is the Creator. No man has the right to take from someone what God has given him, whether it be life or liberty. Again, the Scripture is plain: it is the Lord who gives and the Lord who takes away (Job 1:21).

Third, the role of government is limited as the Declaration says. It is limited to securing or preserving those rights that have been granted unto the citizens by God. The expansion of government into other areas is an expansion that goes beyond the bounds of Scripture and cannot be anything other than destructive of the liberty that government is charged to preserve. Biblical natural law addresses all issues including abortion, taxes, homosexual marriage, welfare, schools and school curriculum, religion in the public square, establishment, the fairness doctrine, free speech, etc. The only way to understand any of these things rightly is to understand the principles upon which a free society can exist. And the only way to understand those principles is to apply the Scriptures to civil society and civil government. A failure to make that application will necessarily and ultimately lead to the loss of that free society.

Fourth, the fact that government derives its just power from the consent of the governed is grounded in the unalienable rights granted by God to men. If no man has the right to take the life of another, then a man may defend himself or his family if attacked. Self-defense is a biblical principle (Lk. 22:36) that does not negate other biblical concepts of martyrdom, accepting the plundering of one's home joyfully (Heb. 10:34), or turning the other cheek (Matt. 5:39). It is the fact that individual men have a right to self-defense or self-preservation that undergirds the role of government to defend or preserve a citizenry. The people have a right to enlist a government to serve as their agent in such a task. The concepts of unalienable rights granted by God, individual liberty, and limited government as an agent of the people enables a free and civil society rather than a chaotic civil society by tyranny to exist.

Each of these four dynamics is grounded in the reality of God and His revelation to us. If Americans who are not Christians and indeed Christians who are Americans, cherish the notion that "our fathers brought forth on this continent, a new nation, conceived in Liberty, and dedicated to the proposition that all men are created equal," and we are resolved "that government of the people, by the people, for the people, shall not perish from the earth," and we don't want these high soundings words to be just that (as they were/are merely to even some who utter them), they must not only repeat the words, but embrace the principles upon which the words are founded and live by them. Let us understand from which our freedom comes and let us teach it to our children and pray for our government "that we may lead quiet and peaceable lives in all godliness and reverence," free from tyranny (1Tim. 2:2).

Thank you, Dr. Dean for a powerful wake-up call for American citizens.

CHAPTER 18

Rebirth of a Phenomenon

"The people should never rise, without doing something to be remembered—something notable and striking. This destruction of the tea is so bold, so daring, so firm, intrepid and inflexible, and it must have so important consequences, and so lasting, that I can't but consider it as an epocha in history." This is from the diary of John Adams, December 17, 1773. He wrote in a letter to James Warren the same day, "The Dye is cast: The People have passed the River and cut away the Bridge: last Night Three Cargoes of Tea, were emptied into the Harbour. This is the grandest, Event, which has ever yet happened Since, the Controversy, with Britain, opened! The Sublimity of it, charms me!"[1]

He was excited by the events related to the Boston Tea Party. Most everyone who has studied the early history of our country knows something about this controversial event, but not the fact that this is only a part of the story. I only recently discovered myself that there were actually *ten* tea parties. Shocking, isn't it?

> "What discontents, what dire events, From trifling things proceed? A little Tea, thrown in the Sea Has Thousands caused to bleed."
>
> —*Anonymous New Hampshire Poet*

It was more than just a little tea, however. This tea that the group of patriots dumped into the Boston Harbor on this chilly morning of December 16, 1773, was actually more than 92,000 pounds. Huge piles of it floated across the bay. Many of the British observers wondered if the colonists had gone mad.

These same people had, on average, consumed 1,200,000 to 2,000,000 pounds of tea per year previously. A large contingent of the American populace normally drank tea twice a day. And now they just dump it in the bay? But this was only the starting point to what would soon spread beyond Massachusetts and all down the eastern seaboard, from York, Maine to Charlestown, South Carolina. The beleaguered colonists dumped, burned, and boycotted tea. This all as a revolt against the Tea Act that Great Britain had recently passed to benefit its pet business, the East India Tea Company. The company had been allowed to avoid the import tax they had been paying, select the few distributors in America to deal with, and pass the taxes on to the colonists.

They didn't expect the reaction they got. Ben Franklin wrote to his friend Thomas Cushing, regarding the matter, "They have no idea that any people can act from any principle but that of [self-] interest, and they believe that threepence on a pound of tea, of which one does not drink perhaps ten pounds a year, is sufficient to overcome the patriotism of an American." Most of the people in the colonies were upset that the threepenny tax was earmarked to pay the salaries of the very colonial administrators they considered oppressors, including Governor Hutchinson. The colonial merchants were also enraged that the East India Company had effectively cut them out of the supply chain, awarding huge shares of the market to Loyalist merchants who buddied up to them.

A handbill posted in Boston stated, "The hour of destruction, or manly opposition to the machinations of tyranny, stares you in the face."

The October 18, 1773, issue of the *Boston Gazette,* which was the paper of record for the patriots, announced that a large shipment of cheap Bohea tea was headed for Boston. It gave some pertinent details of the current political climate:

"It is the current Talk of the Town that Richard Clarke, Benjamin Faneuil, and the two young Messers Hutchinson are appointed to receive the Tea allowed to be exported to this place. This new scheme of Administration lately said to be so friendly to the Colonies, is at once so threatening to the trade, and so well calculated to establish and encrease the detested TRIBUTE, that an attempt to meddle with this pernicious Drug would render men much more respected than they are . . . obnoxious." I might mention that the paper was not liked by the loyalists, who called it "the weekly dung barge."

The patriots gathered and discussed various strategies to combat the problem. Then on November 28, the first shipment arrived in Boston on the *Dartmouth.* She was carrying 144 chests of tea. The next morning, patriotic handbills appeared all over the city: "Friends! Brethren! Countrymen!—That worst of plagues, the detested tea, shipped for this port by the East India Company, is now arrived in the harbor; the hour of destruction, or manly opposition to the machinations of tyranny, stares you in the face."

There were shipments bound for other ports and the pressure was on the Boston Sons of Liberty, who were considered the leaders of the protest, to do something. The patriots in Philadelphia, New York and Charleston were expecting their own shipments soon and they were looking to Boston to set the example.

A letter from a Philadelphia activist was printed in the *Boston Gazette.* It read, "All that we fear, is that you will shrink at Boston . . . we fear you will suffer this to be landed." And a newspaper from New York echoed the sentiment: "If you touch one grain of this accursed tea, you are undone. America is threatened with worse than Egyptian slavery."

On the cold, dark, rainy afternoon of December 16, 1773, a crowd of more than five thousand gathered in Boston's Old South Church, in what to date was the largest town meeting in the city's history. The people packed the church to the rafters, crowding together to stay warm, with only candles to illuminate the speakers. More were huddled outside beneath the windows. While they were listening to the updates in the situation, they learned that the nearby town of Lexington had, in a show of solidarity, gathered all its tea and burned it. This actually gave Lexington, Massachusetts the distinction of staging America's *first* "tea party." When the news reached the gathering in Boston, the crowd erupted in a raucous cheer. The *Massachusetts Spy*, newspaper wrote that the citizens of Lexington "had unanimously resolved against the use of Bohea tea of all sorts, Dutch or English importation" and to prove their sincerity, gathered all their tea and burned it in public.

Meanwhile, back at the meeting in Boston, speakers continued to speak and things looked to be getting ugly. In a moment of prescience, Josiah Quincy warned that the coming events were likely to "bring on the most trying and terrible struggle this country ever saw."

Then John Adams rose suddenly and announced: "This meeting can do nothing more to save this country." At that very moment, the assembly heard war whoops coming from the street. A band of about thirty young men, appearing, as one writer reported, "to be Aboriginal Natives from their complection," materialized in the church's front doorway. The timing was so precise that some historians believe Adam's statement was in fact a signal for the "Indians" to arrive. One thing is certain; none of them was wearing the elaborate costumes and feathered headdresses you might see in some of the pictures or depictions today. The one thing certain is that they did make a commotion and stir the crowd into a frenzy. The shouts from the crowd showed that something had been planned by the Sons of Liberty; such as "Boston Harbor a tea pot tonight!," "Who knows how tea will mingle with salt water!," "Hurrah for Griffin's Wharf!" The "Indians" proceeded to the harbor with the crowd in tow. One bystander later wrote, "You'd thought that inhabitants of the infernal regions had broken loose."

Despite later rumors to the contrary, Sam Adams, John Hancock and other prominent (and highly recognizable) patriots did not participate in the events that night. They had set the Tea Party in motion and now it was time for the "people of the lowest rank" to carry it off. Led by the supposed "Mohawks," the crowd marched to Griffin's Wharf. The core group of thirty disguised men was joined by fifty to one hundred young men who smeared soot or coal dust on their faces as an impromptu disguise. Most people would be surprised to know just how young some of these men were. The crowd included a fifteen-year-old blacksmith's apprentice named Joshua Wyeth and thirteen-year-old Peter Slater, an apprentice rope-maker. Some were acting under the direct orders of their masters; others were apprenticed to Loyalists but had sneaked out to participate in the hoopla.

"Captain Ayers . . . ought to have known our people better than to have expected we would be so mean as to suffer his rotten tea to be funneled down our throats with the Parliament duty mixed with it." From *The Committee for Tarring and Feathering.*

"What think you, Captain, of a Halter around your neck—ten Gallons of liquid Tar decanted on your Pate—with the Feathers of a dozen wild Geese laid over that to enliven your Appearance? Only think seriously of this—and fly to the Place from whence you came—fly without Hesitation—without the Formality of a Protest—and above all, Captain Ayres, let us to advise you to fly without the wild Geese feathers."

This broadside was addressed to Captain Ayres of the British ship *Polly,* which was laden with 697 chests of East India Company tea and moored in Chester, Pennsylvania, a few miles south of Philadelphia, on the Delaware River. It was signed: "Your friends to serve. THE COMMITTEE OF TARRING AND FEATHERING."

The day was December 25, 1773, and the handbill represented an unwelcome Christmas card for the weary sailor. His ship had departed London on September 27, along with the other East India Company vessels, carrying tea to Boston, but adverse weather had disrupted his passage. The good captain and his crew spent almost three months aboard the tiny, bucking craft. He was certainly taken aback by the handbill and then members of the group demanding to be let aboard the ship.

For those who are not familiar with the practice of "tarring and feathering," it is a practice whereby a large pot of tar is heated up, usually outside with wood placed around it for fuel. It is then applied to the body of the victim and feathers spread over the tar. Then, in most cases, the subject is set straddle a rail (wooden fence post) and carried out of town ("ridden out of town on a rail"). This practice was started in Europe during medieval times and was used up until the 1930s or so in the United States. My father had witnessed the practice.

Having been at sea for months, Ayres was likely surprised by the hostile reception, especially since he was unaware of the destruction of tea that had happened in Boston and Lexington. He may have even been expecting a friendly welcome—after all, Philadelphia was a city whose very name spoke of tolerance and civility. It was the City of Brotherly Love, as William Penn had named it by combining the Greek words *philos* (love) and *adelphos* (brother).

And, more to the point, Philadelphia was the American city closest to British hearts, a city they considered much more genteel than the brawling Boston. In spite of this, the residents were highly upset about the tea situation and a handbill was posted stating their case to the merchants with this headline—"By uniting we stand, by dividing we fall." The message was: "You need not be surprised that the eyes of ALL are now fixed on you: as on men, who have it in their power to ward off the most dangerous stroke, that has ever been meditated against the liberties of America . . . . It is in our power and you are now warn'd of it to save yourselves much trouble, and secure your native Country from the deadly Stroke now aimed in your persons against her."

It was signed *Scaevola,* the name of the celebrated Roman soldier who had been taken captive and, in an act of bravery, burned his hand over a flame to show the Etruscan king that he was unafraid of torture. To aid the cause, William Bradford, owner of the London Coffee House and publisher of the *Pennsylvania Journal,* stepped up to assure a group of patriots worried about failing to organize a boycott. He said, "Leave that business to me—I'll collect a town meeting for you—prepare some resolves [and] . . . they shall be executed." Bradford used his connections and conviction to arrange a meeting with several influential Philadelphians, including Charles Thomson, Thomas Mifflin, Dr. Benjamin Rush, and Dr. Thomas Cadwalader.

After much wrangling, meetings with Ayres and the making of an agreement, Ayres weighed anchor and took his cargo back to England. Philadelphia managed to rid itself of the largest consignment of tea the

East India Company tried to foist upon the colonies, showing that it was no longer England's metropolis, but America's.

The next tea party episode happened well to the south, South Carolina that is. If you were a young, well-to-do American male in the 1700s who liked to live it up, then the place to be was Charles Town, South Carolina. This was the fourth largest colonial port, after Philadelphia, New York, and Boston and known for its numerous taverns and inns. Elizabeth Carne, who owned one of these establishments, advertised that "Entertainment for Men and Horse" was available at her place.

Charles Town, whose name gradually morphed into Charleston, was founded in 1670 by English settlers, many of whom had emigrated from Barbados.

Initially, pirating was a primary occupation in the area, but by 1700 the people found that good money could be made by planting rice indigo and trading and owning slaves. The population was mainly made up of wealthy land and slave owners and slaves and the poor whites were not doing very well.

The same Josiah Quincy from Boston that we mentioned before, visited the city of Charleston in 1773 and commented that "nothing I saw raised my conception of the mental abilities of this people." There was one man who defied the stereotype of the rich, lazy plantation owner. His name was Christopher Gadsden. He was one of the least recognized patriots in the history of the colonies. Born in Charleston, he inherited a large fortune from his father and became a successful import-export merchant. He was also very active in the local chapter of the Sons of Liberty. Charleston had protested the Stamp Act like the other colonies had, but the local Sons of Liberty went one step further by hanging the stamp collector in effigy and trashing his home.

They organized a highly effective boycott of British goods, which soon began to pile up, unwanted, on the city's wharves. Gadsden himself would patrol the harbor at night "to see if anything was moving among the shipping." After the British repealed the Stamp Act and introduced the Townshend Acts, Gadsden led another, even more effective boycott, causing British imports to drop by 50 percent.

Then, in the fall of 1773, the British dispatched seven ships full of underpriced East India Company tea across the ocean. The *London,* captained by Alexander Curling, carried 257 chests bound for Charleston. After an uneventful voyage, the vessel arrived in the harbor on December 1. Charleston was the second colonial port, after Boston, to receive one of the hated tea ships. The day the tea arrived, handbills appeared all over town inviting residents to a meeting on December 3 in the Great Hall of the city's famous Old Exchange mercantile building.

The meeting, organized by Christopher Gadsden and the Sons of Liberty was, as the *Charles Town Gazette* stated, for people "who thought it would be criminal tamely to give up any of our essential rights as British subjects, and involve our posterity in a state little better than slavery." The majority agreed not to accept any further shipments of tea (either from East India Company or from smugglers) in return for a provision allowing them, for the next six months, to continue selling the tea they already had on hand.

Gadsden was disappointed in the overall result, but got some satisfaction for being able to head up the efforts to collect and send 194 whole barrels and 21 half-barrels of rice to Boston where they were beginning to feel the pinch of the Port Act. Gadsden wrote to John Adams: "We depend on your Firmness, and that you will not pay for an ounce of the damn'd Tea." In the coming months, several other ships were boarded by the Sons of Liberty and some "tar and feathering" happened.

On to New York

On December 17, the day after the Boston Tea Party, the New York Sons of Liberty called for a huge meeting at town hall. Several thousand attendees listened as speakers read letters from Boston and Philadelphia expressing their solidarity with the people of New York. Next, the mayor, Whitehead Hicks, delivered a message from the governor. He told the crowd that Governor Tryon agreed that any tea that arrived should be returned, but that it should be stored first until orders could be received from Parliament allowing for the return.

The crowd wasn't pleased with this as they knew that as soon as the tea left the ship, the hated threepence tax would have to be paid. The Sons of Liberty were left to wrestle over their next move.

Before a decision could be reached, Paul Revere came riding into the city with an electrifying story. Patriots in Boston had stormed aboard the tea ships and tossed the cargo overboard! Thomas Smith wrote that the news "astonished the town," and tension ran high as the New York Sons of Liberty made plans to host a tea party of their own.

A huge public meeting, scheduled for April 23, was designed to be a spectacular bit of propaganda for the Sons of Liberty—a way to demonstrate their influence without any risk of violence. It was a win-win situation for Loyalists and patriots alike, until something completely unexpected happened: *Another* tea ship, the *London*, showed up.

After unloading its cargo of tea in Charleston in December, the *London* had traveled up the coast under a different commander, one James Chambers. Chambers had a bit of checkered history in New York. A longtime sea captain, he had delivered the first Stamp Act stamps to the city back in 1765. Now the Sons of Liberty received word (probably through contacts in Philadelphia) that Chambers was carrying eighteen chests of (probably smuggled) tea, which he planned to sell for his own personal profit.

When the *London* arrived at Sandy Hook, Chambers denied that he had any tea aboard and thus was allowed to continue on and dock at Murray's Wharf (at the foot of present-day Wall Street), which he reached at about 4 p.m. on April 22. Once again, he was queried by citizens whether his ship carried tea, and he answered vehemently that it did not. But Chambers had underestimated the temperature of the times, for the crowd was far too angry and persistent to be put off. Summoned by shouts and cries, hundreds of people poured aboard the *London* and began tearing apart the cargo.

By this point, Chambers was confessing to anyone who would listen that, yes, he did have eighteen chests of tea on board, but the event had already descended into chaos. Some people smeared on war paints in homage to the Boston Mohawks; others hoisted up the tea chests, cracked them open and dumped their contents overboard. In the confusion, Chambers decided wisely to make himself scarce.

Chestertown Tea Party

Chestertown is a sleepy maritime center of some five thousand residents located on Maryland's Eastern Shore. The Chester River, a calm and wide tidewater stream, flows past its handsome, red-brick eighteenth-century houses and out into the reaches of Chesapeake Bay. The *Chestertown Spy,* a local online newspaper, reports happenings under such old-timey headings as "Occurrences," "Disturbances," and "Fortnightly." In the summer, well-heeled vacationers arrive from Annapolis and Philadelphia to boat and swim and fish; in the winter it reverts to a sleepy little town.

At one time each year, Memorial Day weekend—Chestertown explodes with visitors. The population swells by thousands, the town's quaint B and B's are booked for months in advance. There are wine tastings, a five-kilometer run/walk, a parade and a garden show—typical Memorial Day fare, you might think, except for one unique addition: Men dressed up like colonial era patriots storm aboard a replica of an eighteenth-century brigantine called the *Geddes* and throw chests of tea into the Chester River, all in honor of an event that took place on May 23, 1774—The Chestertown Tea Party.

Many of the historic cities commemorate their tea parties each year, but Chestertown has the biggest party. Its motto is "Often imitated, never equaled . . . since 1774." *Everyone* dresses in colonial dress, people of all ages, and the ritual of throwing the tea into the river is usually accompanied by sailors from the *Geddes* jumping overboard into the river.

Some say this event never happened, but the story that is told goes like this: On May13, 1774, the Sons of Liberty stormed out of Worrell's and marched down High Street in broad daylight. They boarded the *Geddes,* catching its crew off guard and threw the chests of tea overboard, along with several sailors who resisted the assault. Crowds lining the Chester River cheered boisterously as both sailors and tea hit the water. No official records exist to verify these events, but the natives celebrate with great vigor and reverence.

Another Charlestown

An orderly town of small houses with lawns divided by picket fences, Charlestown, Massachusetts was the original Puritan settlement on the Boston peninsula, affording sweeping views of the city from its hilly prominences. The local artisans and middle-class shopkeepers hated the British with a passion. The feeling was mutual—after the bloody battle of Bunker Hill in June of 1775, vengeful Redcoats put the town to the torch, destroying a large portion of it. But some eighteen months earlier, on December 28, 1773, according to the *Boston Gazette*: "The inhabitants of Charlestown, agreeable to a unanimous Vote of said Town the Tuesday preceding, on Friday last bro't *all* their TEA into the public Market Square, where it was committed to the Flames at high Noon-Day."

Provincetown's Party

On the night of December 10, 1773, the brig *William,* one of the four original tea ships that the East India Company had sent to Boston, ran aground in the treacherous waters off Cape Cod. Aboard the ship were 300 street lamps and 58 chests of tea destined for consignee Richard Clarke. The ship's captain, Joseph Loring, managed to offload all the chests safely. On December 16, the day of the Boston Tea Party, Richard Clarke's son Jonathan left his place of safety with the British on Castle Island, secretly stole away to the Cape Cod location where Loring had hidden the tea, and paid laborers to cart the chests to Provincetown.

From there, the persuasive young Clarke managed to convince the captain of a fishing vessel to carry the tea into Boston Harbor, where it was stored safely in the army fort on Castle Island. Upon receiving the news, Sam Adams and the rest of the patriots fumed.

The affair offered a certain consolation, however. While in Provincetown, Jonathan Clarke had sold several chests of the tea to his cousin, a Wellfleet justice of the peace named John Greenough, whose father and half-brother David were prominent Boston patriots. Upon hearing the news, David wrote urgently:

> Dear Brother,
> The report was brought here today by some credible men from Truro, that very much surprised me as well as all other of your friends, that you were going to bring one or two chests of that cursed tea to Wellfleet itself, which I earnestly beseech you as your friend and brother, as you value your own interest and the credit of your family, not to concern yourself in anyway with the tea. If you have bought any I advise you rather to sink it in the sea than to bring any of it here. For my part I can hardly believe that such a good friend to your country as you always professed to be will shift sides so quickly at the prospect of a little profit.

It was too late. Seven "Indians" showed up at the house in Provincetown where Greenough had hidden one chest of tea; the men seized and burned it. Later, at a town meeting in Wellfleet, the Sons of Liberty demanded and received the other two chests and likewise destroyed them.

Extremely upset, John Greenough wrote to his father in Boston: "Can we imagine a more absolute state of Tyranny and outrageous cruelty than when every private gang of Plunderers and Assassins may wreek their vengeance against any Person or their Property?"

Dorchester's Turn

On December 17, 1773—the day after the Boston Tea Party—an elderly laborer named Ebenezer Withington was walking along the salt marshes of a Dorchester beach when he spied a half chest of tea bobbing in the water. Withington knew nothing about either the tea party or the boycott and merely considered himself extraordinarily lucky to have found such a bonanza. Snatching up the chest, he headed home, although not before encountering a group of Loyalist gentlemen who asked him if he had been "picking up the Ruin," that is, scavenging for any tea that might have floated to shore.

A puzzled Withington asked "if there was any Harm" in what he was doing, to which the gentlemen merely laughed, saying that he had nothing to fear "except from [his] Neighbors." Still perplexed, Withington went home with the tea, drank some, and apparently sold a portion to a few neighbors. The Sons of Liberty heard about his dealings pretty quickly. On December 31, dressed as Narragansett Indians, they raided a home belonging to Withington's two sons. After a search turned up nothing, they continued to Withington's house, which, according to the *Boston Gazette,* was located "at a place called Sodom." They found the offending weed, seized it, and carried it to Boston. There, in an account provided by prominent Boston merchant John Rowe, the Indians "brought [the tea] into the Commons of Boston & Burnt it this night about eleven o'clock. This is supposed to be part of the Tea that was taken out of the Ships & floated over to Dorchester."

Boston, Again

On March 6, 1774, the brig *Fortune*, arrived from London carrying twenty-eight and a half chests of Bohea, which was consigned to various Boston merchants including the 120-year-old importing firm of Davison Newman & Co., Ltd. This tea was not shipped directly by the East India Company but rather by other London merchants and apparently the *Fortune's* captain Benjamin Gorham and the consignees believed that this technicality would keep their cargo from being destroyed by patriots.

No such luck. As the *Boston Gazette* crowed: "The SACHEMS must have a talk upon this matter." They didn't talk long. On March 7, according to a petition for redress that the firm of Davison Newman later sent to King George, "persons, all unknown to the Captain, armed with axes" boarded the *Fortune* "and with force threw the tea in the

Water whereby the same was wholly lost and destroyed." The event became known as the Second Boston Tea Party.

Yorktown, Virginia

In August 1774, in response to the Boston Tea Party and subsequent Intolerable Acts, Virginia formed a Revolutionary Council that adopted a motion to refuse to purchase any English goods, including tea. In late October, a shipment of tea from London reached Yorktown aboard the brig *Virginia.* When patriot leaders learned about the cargo, they took quick action. According to the *Virginia Gazette*:

> The inhabitants of York having been informed that the *Virginia*, commanded by Howard Esten, had on Board two Half Chest of Tea, shipped by John Norton, Esq; and Sons, Merchants in London, by Order of Mess. Prentis and Company, Merchants in Williamsburg, assembled at 10 o'clock this Morning, and went on Board said ship . . . they immediately hoisted the Tea out of the Hold and threw it into the River, and then returned to the Shore without Damage to the Ship or any other Part of her Cargo.

In May 1775, John Norton, the owner of the *Virginia*, defended his actions in a letter—written from the safety of London—published in the same paper. Briefly, he stated that he believed that Great Britain had no right to tax America and he respected their liberty.

The Cambridge Party

The episode in Cambridge was far from spectacular. It was a reprimand noted in Harvard College's faculty records on March 1, 1775:

> A Disorder having arisen this morning in the Hall [Harvard Hall] at breakfast between some of the Students, respecting the drinking of India Tea: & some of the Utensils for breakfast having been broke; the Parties having been heard—

Resolved 1: We disapprove of the conduct on both sides as imprudent.

Resolved 2: That the regulation of the Hall belongs exclusively to the Government of the College & consequently that no Students have the right to interpose with regard thereunto . . .

Resolved 3: Since the carrying of India Tea into the Hall is found to be a Source of uneasiness and grief to many of the Students and as the use of it is disagreeable to the People of the Country in general; & as those who carried Tea into the Hall declare that the drinking of it in the Hall is a matter of trifling consequence with them; that they be advised not to carry it in for the future, & in this way that they, as well as the other Students in all ways, discover a disposition to promote harmony, mutual affection, and Confidence, so well becoming Members of the same Society . . . whatever convulsions may unhappily distract the State abroad.[2]

Notes

1. *John Adams, Revolutionary Writings, 1755-1775*, Gordon Wood, ed. (New York, Library Classics of the United States, Inc., 2011), 288.
2. With great appreciation to Joseph Cummins, *Ten Tea Parties, Patriotic Protests That History Forgot* (Philadelphia, PA: Quick Books, 2012), portions of entire text.

CHAPTER 19

What Is Our Foundation?

Everything that has a life must have a foundation to endure. We, as a people, have to have standards, rules, laws to guide us, protect us, and give us a reason to exist. The United States was founded on principles that have kept it strong, and until lately, it has been envied and admired by the rest of the world. Lately, we seem to have lost our way. The principles that have guided us have come under question and a large contingent of our citizens seems to be lost and confused, with no direction and no purpose.

One of the main purposes for this book is to illustrate what our roots are and why we should be looking back to regenerate the hope and dreams of our Founders by realigning with their inspiration. Many want to deny the truth about what our country was founded on. They can't deny the facts.

Extension of the Capital

The U.S. Capitol was enlarged by an act of Congress; and on the Fourth of July, 1851, in the presence of an immense audience, President Fillmore laid the corner-stone, and Daniel Webster, Secretary of State, delivered the commemorative oration. Beneath the stone, among other things, is deposited, in Mr. Daniel Webster's own handwriting, the following record:

> On the morning of the first day of the seventy-sixth year of the independence of the United States of

America, in the city of Washington, being the Fourth of July, 1851, this stone, designed as a corner-stone of the extension of the Capitol, according to a plan approved by the President, in pursuance of an act of Congress, was laid by

Millard Fillmore,
President of the United States,

. . . assisted by the Grand Master of the Masonic Lodges, in the presence of many members of Congress, of officers of the Executive and Judiciary Departments—National, State and District—of officers of the army and navy, the corporate authorities of this and neighboring cities, many associations—civil, military, and masonic—members of the Smithsonian Institution and National Institute, professors of colleges and teachers of schools in the District of Columbia, with their students and pupils, and a vast concourse of people from places near and remote, including a few surviving gentlemen who witnessed the laying of the corner-stone of the Capitol by President Washington, on the 18th day of September, A.D. 1793.

If, therefore, it shall be hereafter the will of God that this structure shall fall from its base, that its foundation be upturned, and this deposit brought to the eyes of men, be it then known that on this day the union of the United States of America stands firm, that their Constitution still exists unimpaired and with all its original usefulness and glory, growing every day stronger and stronger in the affections of the great body of the American people, and attracting more and more the admiration of the world. And all here assembled, whether belonging to public life or to private life, with hearts devoutly thankful to Almighty God for the preservation of the liberty and happiness of the country, unite in sincere and fervent prayer that this deposit,

> and the walls and arches, the domes and towers, the columns and entablatures, now to be erected over it, may endure forever!
>
> God save the United States of America!
> Daniel Webster,
> *Secretary of State of the United States.*

Mr. Webster, standing on the spot where Washington stood fifty-eight years before, in his address said,

> This is the New World! This is America! This is Washington! And this, the Capitol of the United States! And where else among the nations can the seat of government be surrounded, on any day of any year, by those who have more reason to rejoice in the blessings which they possess? To-day we are Americans, all, and are nothing but Americans. Every man's heart swells within him; every man's port and bearing become somewhat more proud and lofty as he remembers that seventy-five years have rolled away and that the great inheritance of liberty is still his—his, undiminished and unimpaired, his, in all its original glory, his to enjoy, his to protect, and his to transmit to future generations. This inheritance which he enjoys to-day is not only an inheritance of liberty, but of our own peculiar American liberty.
>
> And I now proceed to add that the strong and deep-settled conviction of all intelligent persons among us is that, in order to preserve this inheritance of liberty, and to support a useful and wise government, the general education of the people and the wide diffusion of pure morality and true religion are indispensable. Individual virtue is a part of public virtue. It is difficult to conceive how there can remain morality in the government when it shall cease to exist among the people, or how the aggregate of the political institutions, all the

> organs of which consist only of men, should be wise and beneficent and competent to inspire confidence, if the opposite qualities belong to the individuals who constitute those organs and make up that aggregate.
>
> If Washington actually were among us, and if he could draw around him the shades of the great public men of his own day, patriots and warriors, orators and statesmen, and were to address us in their presence, would he not say to us, "Ye men of this generation, I rejoice and thank God for being able to see that our labors and toils and sacrifices were not in vain. You are prosperous, you are happy, you are grateful; the fire of liberty burns brightly and steadily in your hearts, while duty and the law restrain it from bursting forth in wild and destructive conflagration. Cherish liberty, as you love it; cherish its securities, as you wish to preserve it. Maintain the Constitution which we labored so painfully to establish, and which has been to you such a source of inestimable blessings. Preserve the union of the States, cemented as it was by our prayers, our tears, and our blood. Be true to God, to your country, and to your whole duty. So shall the whole eastern world follow the morning sun to contemplate you as a nation; so shall all generations honor you as they honor us; and so shall that Almighty Power which so graciously protected us, and which now protects you, shower its everlasting blessings upon you and your posterity."

The paintings and statuary which adorn the rotunda and the halls of Congress are all suggestive symbols of scenes in the history of our Christian civilization, and of the triumph of our principles of civil liberty and government. The nine large paintings in the rotunda represent De Soto's Discovery of the Mississippi, the Landing of Columbus, the Baptism of Pocahontas, the Embarkation of the Pilgrims at Delft, the Landing of the Pilgrims on Plymouth Rock, the Signing of the Declaration of Independence, the Surrender of Burgoyne at Saratoga, the Surrender of Cornwallis at Yorktown, and the Resignation of

Washington at Annapolis. Groups of sculpture, representing scenes in our early Christian history and in the westward march of civilization, adorn the various parts of the Capitol, while similar symbols suggest Christian ideas and scenes on the eastern portico, in front of which is an area of ten acres or more, in the center of which is a statue of Washington, large as life, and on its pedestal inscribed "First in War; First in Peace; First in the Hearts of his Countrymen."

The Washington Monument is a massive structure, the corner-stone of which was laid on the 4th of July, 1848, in the presence of the President of the United States and an immense concourse of citizens, and with masonic and Christian ceremonies. Robert C. Winthrop, Speaker of the House of Representatives, delivered a commemorative oration on Washington, in which he traced his exalted goodness and greatness to the educating influence of the Christian religion, which was followed by a consecrating prayer by Rev. J. McJilton, of which the following are the concluding sentences—

> And now, O Lord of all power and majesty, we humbly beseech thee to let the wing of thy protection be ever outspread over the land of Washington! May his people be thy people! May his God be their God! Never from beneath the strong arm of thy providence may they be removed; but, like their honored chief, may they acknowledge thee in peace and in war, and ever serve thee with a willing, faithful, acceptable service! Hear our prayer, we beseech thee, that the glory of this nation may never be obscured in the gloom of guilt; that its beauty may never be so marred by the foul impress of sin that the light of its religious character shall be dimmed. Open the eyes of the people, and let them see that it is their true interest to study thy laws, to seek thy favor, and to worship thee with a faithful worship.[1]

When the U.S. Senate vacated its old Chamber, in 1959, Vice President John C. Breckinridge gave this address to describe the situation: "Let us devoutly trust that another Senate, in another age, shall bear to a new and larger chamber this Constitution vigorous and inviolate, and that the last generation of posterity shall witness the deliberations of the representatives of American States still united, prosperous, and free."

The attainment of the highest prosperity and true glory of the republic can be secured only by the choice of upright, moral, Christian men to administer the government. *Ours is a Christian nation*, and all our civil institutions rest on the Christian religion; and hence duty demands, as does the very genius of our institutions, that all who administer the civil affairs of the nation should be men who will legislate and act in their official functions in harmony with the principles on which our institutions were founded by our Christian fathers.

"Our republic," says Dr. Lyman Beecher, "in its Constitution and laws, is of heavenly origin. It was not borrowed from Greece or Rome, but from the Bible. Where we borrowed a ray from Greece or Rome, stars and suns were borrowed from another source—the Bible. There is no position more susceptible of proof (the proof is in this volume) than that as the moon borrows from the sun her light, so our Constitution borrows from the Bible its elements, proportions, and power. It was God that gave these elementary principles to our forefathers as the 'pillar of fire by night and the cloud by day,' for their guidance. All the liberty the world ever knew is but a dim star to the noonday sun which is poured on man by these oracles of Heaven. It is truly testified by Hume that the Puritans introduced the elementary principles of republican liberty into the English Constitution; and when they came to form colonial constitution and laws, we all know with what veneration and implicit confidence they copied the principles of the constitution and laws of Moses. These elementary principles have gone into the Constitution of the Union and of every one of the States; and we have hence more consistent liberty than ever existed in all the world, in all time, out of the Mosaic code."

The Christian statesman and philosopher Thomas S. Grimké, of South Carolina, states the same fact of the harmony of our civil institutions with the Bible. "If ever," he says, "a political scheme resembled the Divine Government, it is ours, where each exists for the whole, and the whole for each. As in the planetary world, so in our system, each has its own peculiar laws; and the harmonious movement of the whole is but a natural emanation from the co-operative influence of the parts."[2]

Biblical Descriptions of Christian Rulers

A Christian nation whose civil institutions thus harmonize with the Divine government should have in its seat of legislation men whose faith and official acts and private lives harmonize with the purposes and principles of a Christian government. The Bible, out of which rose the forms as well as the spirit of our civil institutions, enjoins this policy on the part of the people.

"The God of Israel said, the rock of Israel spake to me, He that ruleth over men must be just, ruling in the fear of God." "Thou shalt provide out of all the people able men, such as fear God, men of truth, hating covetousness, and place such over the people to be rulers." (Exodus 18:21) And to designate the exalted character which civil rulers should possess, they are spoken of in the New Testament as "ministers of God for good;" (Romans 13:4) "for they are God's ministers, attending continually upon this very thing" (Romans 13:6). The influence of the administration of such rulers upon national virtue and prosperity is described under such emblems as these—

> "He [a Christian ruler] shall be as the light of the morning, when the sun riseth, even a morning without clouds; as the tender grass springing out of the earth, by clear shining after rain."(2 Samuel 23:4)
>
> "He shall come down like rain upon the mown grass; as showers that water the earth. In his days shall the righteous flourish, and abundance of peace so long as the moon endureth." (2Samuel 23:3)
>
> "Then shall thy light break forth as the morning, and thy health shall spring forth speedily; and thy righteousness shall go before thee; the glory of the Lord shall be thy reward." (Isaiah 58:8)

> "Thou shalt be like a watered garden, and like a spring of water, whose waters fail not. Then shall thy light rise in obscurity, and thy darkness be as noonday, and the Lord shall guide thee continually."
>
> Isaiah 58:10-11)

Washington felt the importance of having all the offices filled with such men. Writing to Gouverneur Morris in 1797, he said, "The Executive branch of this Government never has suffered, nor will suffer while I preside, any improper conduct of its officers to escape with impunity." Himself one of the noblest types of a Christian ruler, he desired to see all the civil offices filled with upright, honest, able men. Each department of the Government has had those who have filled their offices as Christian men, acting in the fear of God; but a Christian people should be vigilant at all times to have the administration of their Government conducted by rulers who will rule in the fear of the Lord, and harmonize the legislation of the nation with the law of God.

The Capitol of the republic has witnessed the rites of religion in both branches of its legislature, and daily and Sabbath services have had a gracious influence in directing the deliberations of Congress and in calming the heated excitements of the hour.[3]

Christian Judges

"Of all places," said Daniel Webster, "there is none which so imperatively demands that he who occupies it should be under the fear of God, and above all other fear, as the situation of a judge."

The judiciary of England had an illustrious Christian judge in Matthew Hale. In entering upon his official duties he drew up, for the government of his official life, the following rules—"1. That in the administration of justice I am intrusted for God, the king, and the country; and, therefore, 2. That it be upright. 3. Deliberate. 4. Resolutely. That I rest not upon my own understanding or strength, but implore and rest upon the direction and strength of God." This eminent English judge was a strict observer of the Sabbath.

The incorruptible chief-justice of England, at the time of Cromwell and the Commonwealth, could not be seduced to desecrate the Sabbath by the example of crowned heads or by the influence of learned divines. Neither a Puritan nor a Cavalier, he was an honest Christian man, and an upright jurist. In his instruction to his children Sir Matthew Hale says:

> I have, by long and sound experience, found that the due observance of the Lord's day, and the duties of it, has been of singular comfort and advantage to me; and I doubt not it will prove so to you. God Almighty is the Lord of our time, and lends it to us; and as it is but just we should consecrate this part of that time to him, so I have found, by a strict and diligent observation, that a due attention to the duty of this day hath ever joined to it a blessing upon the rest of my time, and the week that hath so begun hath been blessed and prospered to me; and, on the other side, when I have been negligent of the duties of this day, the rest of the week hath been unsuccessful and unhappy to my own secular employments; so that I could early make an estimate of my success in my secular engagements the week following, by the manner of my passing of this day; and this I do not write lightly or inconsiderately, but upon a long observation and experience.

American Judges

The judicial history of the American courts corresponds, in its Christian features, to the earlier ages of the republic, in the other departments of the Government. Before recording the decision of the courts of the United States in favor of the Christian religion being the religion of the Government as well as of the nation, it will be instructive to notice the eminent Christian characters of a number of the chief judges.

Eminent on the list of Christian judges is John Jay. He was the first chief justice of the Supreme Court of the United States, and presided as such with unsurpassed integrity and wisdom, Webster, in alluding to him, said that "when the spotless ermine of the judicial robe fell on John Jay it touched nothing less spotless than itself." Like Mansfield and Hale, of England, he ever sought "that wisdom that cometh down from above" to guide him in all his official investigations and decisions.

"If the character of this eminent man," says his biographer, "is beautiful in its simplicity and its moral purity, it becomes still more interesting when regarded as a bright example of Christian virtue. The tone of his mind was always serious. He regarded religious meditation and worship as no unimportant duties of life." He was a member of the Protestant Episcopal Church. "This," says Judge Story, "was the religion of his early education, and became afterwards that of his choice. But he was without the slightest touch of bigotry or intolerance. His benevolence was as wide as Christianity itself. It embraced the human race. He was not only liberal in his feelings and principles, but in his charities. His hands were open on all occasions to succor distress, to encourage enterprise, and to support good institutions."

Associated with Jay on the Supreme Bench were James Wilson, a Christian patriot and judge—"of great learning, patient industry, and uprightness of character,"—William Cushing of Massachusetts, John Blair, Jr. of Virginia, James Iredell of North Carolina, William Paterson of New Jersey, and Bushrod Washington, a nephew of President Washington. These were all men distinguished for their legal accomplishments and Christian virtues. Of Judge Washington it was said that "the love of justice was a ruling passion, it was the master-spring of his conduct. He made justice itself, even the most severe, soften into the moderation of mercy."

> "There was," said Judge John Story, "a daily beauty in his life, which won every heart. He was benevolent, charitable, affectionate, and liberal, in the best sense of the terms. He was a Christian, full of religious sensibility and religious humility. Attached to the Episcopal Church by education and choice, he was one of its most sincere but unostentatious friends. He was as free from bigotry as any man, and, at the same time he claimed the right to think for himself, he admitted

> without reserve the same right in others. He was, therefore, indulgent even to what he deemed errors in doctrine, and abhorred all persecution for conscience' sake.
>
> "But what made religion most attractive in him, and gave it occasionally even a sublime expression, was its tranquil, cheerful, unobtrusive, meek, and gentle character. There was a mingling of Christian graces in him, which showed that the habit of his thoughts was fashioned for another and a better world."

Also among the most eminent of American judges was Chief-Justice John Marshall, of Virginia. He will ever be venerated as one of the brightest intellects of the country, and as having shed the most lucid light on the constitutional and legislative jurisprudence of the Government. His logical intellect, severe simplicity of character, legal knowledge, purity of life, and Christian faith, form one of the richest treasures of the American nation. He was, in public and private life, continued to a venerable age, loyal to his God, the Constitution of his country, his own conscience, and the Christian religion.

"He had," says one, "a pure and childlike religious faith. The hard, muscular intellect had not built up its strength on the ruins of the heart. It is related of him that he once chanced to be present at a discussion between two or three young men upon the evidences of the Christian religion. They indulged freely in sneers, and, at the end of their argument, turned indifferently to the chief-justice—whom they took, from his poor and plain costume, for some ignorant rustic—and asked him, jocularly, what he thought of the matter.

> "If," said the narrator of the incident, "a streak of lightning had at that moment crossed the room, their amazement could not have been greater than it was at what followed. The most eloquent and unanswerable appeal was made for nearly an hour, by the old gentleman, that he ever heard. So perfect was his recollection that every argument used by the opponents

> of the Christian religion was met in the order in it was presented. Hume's sophistry on the subject of miracles was, if possible, more perfectly answered than it had been done by Campbell. And in the whole lecture there was so much symmetry and energy, pathos and sublimity, that not another word was answered. An attempt to describe it would be an attempt to paint the sunbeam."

This deep-rooted religious faith never wavered. Marshall continued to repeat, night and morning, in his serene old age, the prayer which he had been taught at his mother's knees; and, at a period when skepticism was fashionable among cultivated men, he never uttered a word calculated to throw a doubt on the Divine origin of Christianity. A lesson of the deepest reverence for everything holy was, on the contrary, taught by his daily life; and he died, as he had lived, trusting in the atonement of Jesus. This great jurist and eminent Christian man regarded it as among the highest honors of his life to be a teacher in the Sabbath-school. Here he was found, for many years of his life, on every Sabbath, with his class, expounding to them the law of God and the sublime truths of the gospel of Christ.

Judge Joseph Story, of Massachusetts, for many years Associate Justice on the Supreme Court of the United States, was eminent for his judicial and literary attainments and his Christian virtues. He said this about the Christian religion:

> One of the beautiful traits of our municipal jurisprudence is, *that Christianity is a part of the common law*, from which it seeks its sanction of its rights and by which it endeavors to regulate its doctrine. And, notwithstanding the specious objection of one of our distinguished statesmen, the boast is as true as it is beautiful. There has been a period in which the common law did not recognize Christianity as lying at its foundation. For many ages it was almost exclusively administered by those who held its ecclesiastical dignities. It now repudiates every act done in violation

> of its duties of perfect obligation. It pronounces illegal every contract offensive to its morals. It recognizes with profound humility its holydays and festivals, and obeys them as dies non juridici. It still attaches to persons believing in its Divine authority the highest degree of competency as witnesses.

Justice John McLean, of Ohio, adorned the judicial department of our Republic, by his eminent talents, learning, and civic virtues, for more than a generation. He became in early life a sincere and humble Christian, and for more than half a century gave a most beautiful illustration of the pure and exalted virtues of the Christian religion both in public and in private life. Not one suspicious breath of Corruption ever soiled his fair fame, or diminished the purity and power of his fame and influence. He was in the highest degree a Christian statesman and an upright judge. His views of the need and importance of Christianity to civil government are expressed in the following words:

> For many years my hope for the perpetuity of our institutions has rested upon Bible morality and the general dissemination of Christian principles. This is an element which did not exist in the ancient republics. It is a basis on which free governments may be maintained through all time.
>
> It is a truth experienced in all time, that a free government can have no other than a moral basis; and it requires a high degree of intelligence and virtue in the people to maintain it. Free government is not a self-moving machine. It can only act through agencies. And if its aims be low and selfish, if it addresses itself to the morbid feelings of humanity, its tendencies must be corrupt and weaken the great principles on which it is founded.
>
> Our mission of freedom is not carried out by brute force, by canon law, or any other law except the moral

> law and those Christian principles which are found in the Scriptures.

He was for many of the last years of his life President of the American Sunday-School Union, an institution whose beneficent influence has been felt in every department of Church and State. In accepting the Presidency of the American Sunday-School Union, Judge McLean wrote the following letter:

> Cincinnati. April 10, 1849.
>
> Dear Sir—
> Whilst I consider myself honored by the Board of Officers and Managers of the American Sunday-School Union in being placed nominally at their head, I cannot repress a fear that, in accepting the position, I may stand in the way of someone of higher merit and greater usefulness.
>
> The more I reflect upon Sabbath-schools, the more deeply am I impressed with their importance. Education without moral training may increase national knowledge, but it will add nothing to national virtue. By a most intelligent and able report, made some years ago by Guizot, it appeared that in those departments of France where education had been most advanced, crime was most common. And, by later reports, it is shown that in Prussia, Scotland, and England, where the means of education has been greatly increased—especially in Prussia and Scotland—criminal offences have increased. Making due allowance for the growth of population and the aggregation of individuals in carrying on various useful enterprises, the principal cause of this is *a want of moral culture.*
>
> Knowledge without moral restraint only increases the capacity of an individual for mischief. As a citizen, he is more dangerous to society, and does more to corrupt

the public morals, than one without education. So selfish is our nature, and so prone to evil, that we require chains, moral or physical, to curb our propensities and passions.

Early impressions are always the most lasting. All experience conduces to establish this. Who has forgotten the scenes of his boyhood, or the pious instructions of his parents? Who does not carry these with him all along the journey of life? However they may be disregarded and contemned by an abandoned course, yet they cannot be consigned to oblivion. In the darkest hours of revelry, they will light up in the memory and cause remorse. And this feeling will generally, sooner or later, lead to reformation.

Whatever defect there may be of moral culture in our common schools, it is more than supplied in our Sabbath-schools. Here the whole training is of a moral and religious character, entirely free from sectarian influences. The child is instructed in his duty to God and to his fellow-beings, and for which he must answer in the great day of accounts. He becomes familiar with the Scriptures by his Bible lessons, which are fixed in his memory by his answer to questions propounded. In deed, the whole exercises of the school are eminently calculated to interest and elevate his mind . . . .

Compare it with the motives which lead to other lines of action and with their results. The aspiration of the mere politician begins and ends in himself.

The benefits (if benefits they may be called) conferred on his supporters have no higher motive than this. The same remark will apply to many who are engaged in the pursuits of commerce, or in the prosecution of enterprises which ordinarily lead to the accumulation of individual and national wealth. They may become great

> in this respect, and advance the wealth of their country, without being exemplary themselves or increasing the public virtue. And so of professional renown. How empty is that bauble which entwines the brow of the orator in the senate, at the bar, or in the pulpit, whose heart is not full of the kindly feelings of humanity and who does not endeavor to mitigate the sufferings and increase the happiness of his race!
>
> If we desire to make our nation truly great, and to transmit to posterity our institutions in their primitive simplicity and force, we must imbue the minds of our youth with a pure and an elevated morality, which shall influence their whole lives. And I know of no means so well calculated to produce this result as Sabbath-schools. Whether we look to the good of our country, or to a future immortality, these schools are recommended by considerations of the deepest importance.
>
> I regret that my public duties will prevent my being present at your annual Meeting.
>
> With the greatest respect, I am, dear sir, faithfully yours,
> John McLean.

The Supreme Court of the United States, and the judges who sat on its bench in 1827, received a just tribute from Thomas S. Grimké, in a speech he delivered in the Senate of South Carolina, December 17, 1827. He says:

> It is emphatically a court of the whole people and of every State, of the Government of the Union and of the Government of every State. It is as independent of the President and Congress as of the Governor and Legislature of South Carolina. Its members are selected from different States, and its bar gathers within its bounds the talents and learning, the courage, virtue, and patriotism, of the East and the West, of the North

> and the South . . . . No one, indeed, can possibly read the judgments of this tribunal—equally beneficent and illustrious—and not be deeply impressed with its wisdom and learning, its moral courage and justice, its high sense of duty, its love of peace and order, its independence, dignity, and patriotism. I know not any body of men who are entitled to more enlightened admiration, more sincere gratitude, more profound respect for their talents, learning, virtues, and services. Theirs is indeed a parental guardianship, full of moral dignity and beauty, sustained by the energy of wisdom and adorned by the simplicity of justice and truth.

The brief sketches contained in this book of some of the eminent men who have adorned the judicial history of the republic and shed such light on the profound and important science of jurisprudence, and who in their private character illustrated so nobly the Christian virtues, were prepared, as they did in the administration of justice and law, to practically believe and carry out that true and admirable exposition of law, as given by the venerable and learned Hooker, a prominent Puritan leader, who has been called the "Father of the Constitution."

He says:

> Of law there can be no less acknowledged than that her seat is the bosom of God, her voice the harmony of the world. All things in heaven and earth do her homage; the very least feel her care, and the greatest are not exempt from her power. Both angels and men, and creatures of what condition soever, though each in a different sort and name, yet all with one uniform consent admire her as the mother of their peace and joy.
>
> In giving practical form to this sublime eulogy on law and its benignant power and results, the minds of many of the most eminent judges of the State and national Governments were illuminated, through prayer, with

> wisdom from heaven. They kneeled before the Infinite Judge of the Universe and humbly entreated that in the administration of earthly justice and law they might be inspired and guided of God. This fact is historic in the Christian lives of many American judges.[4]

Court Decisions on Religion

In 1824, the Supreme Court of Pennsylvania reviewed the subject most thoroughly and extensively, and the decision of the court deserves a thoughtful perusal. The trial was on an indictment for blasphemy, founded on an act of Assembly passed in 1700. The decision may be found in Sergeant & Rawle's Reports, page 394, and is as follows—

The court said that, even if Christianity was not part of the law of the land, it is the popular religion of the country, an insult on which would be indictable as directly tending to disturb the public peace. Christianity, general Christianity, is, and always has been, a part of the common law of Pennsylvania; not Christianity founded on particular religious tenets; not Christianity with an established Church, and tithes, and spiritual courts; but Christianity with liberty of conscience to all men. The first legislative act in the colony was the recognition of the Christian religion, and the establishment of liberty of conscience. It is called "the Great Law," and is as follows—

> Whereas the glory of Almighty God and the good of mankind is the reason and end of government, and therefore government itself is a venerable ordinance of God, and forasmuch as it is principally devised and intended by the Proprietary and Governor and freemen of Pennsylvania and territories thereunto belonging, to make and establish such laws as shall best preserve true Christian and civil liberty, in opposition to all unchristian, licentious, and unjust practices, whereby God may have his due, Caesar his due, and the people their due; "Resolved, therefore, that all persons living in this Province, who confess

> and acknowledge the one Almighty and Eternal God to be the Creator, upholder, and ruler of the world, and who hold themselves obliged in conscience to live peaceably and justly in civil society, shall in no wise be molested, &c.

The court, after quoting the whole law at length, further says:

> Thus this wise legislature framed this great body of laws for a Christian country and a Christian people. Infidelity was then rare, and no infidels were among the first colonists. They fled from religious intolerance to a country where all were allowed to worship according to their own understanding.
>
> Every one had the right of adopting for himself whatever opinion appeared to be the most rational concerning all matters of religious belief; thus securing by law this inestimable freedom of conscience, one of the highest privileges and greatest interests of the human race. We see that the Christianity of the common law is incorporated into the great law of Pennsylvania; and by this it is irrefragably proved that the laws and institutions of this State are built on the foundation of reverence for Christianity.
>
> On this the Constitution of the United States has made no alteration, nor in the great body of the laws, which was an incorporation of the common-law doctrine of Christianity, as suited to the condition of the colony, and without which no free government can long exist. Under the Constitution penalties against cursing and swearing have been enacted. If Christianity was abolished, all false oaths, all tests by oath in common form by the book, would cease to be indictable as perjury. The indictment must state the oath to be on the Holy Evangelists of Almighty God.

The Court Continues

After reviewing a series of decisions made in Pennsylvania and elsewhere, the court continues this way: "It has long been firmly settled that blasphemy against the Deity generally, or an attack on the Christian religion indirectly, for the purpose of exposing its doctrines to ridicule and contempt, is indictable and punishable as a temporal offence. The principles and actual decisions are that the publications, whether written or oral, must be malicious, and designed for that end and purpose." After stating that the law gave free permission for the serious and conscientious discussion of all theological and religious topics, the court said:

> A malicious and mischievous intention is, in such a case, the broad boundary between right and wrong, and that it is to be collected from the offensive levity, scurrilous and opprobrious language, and other circumstances, whether the act of the party was malicious; and, since the law has no means of distinguishing between different degrees of evil tendency, if the matter published contains any such evil tendency it is a public wrong . . .
>
> No society can tolerate a willful and despiteful attempt to subvert its religion any more than it would to break down its laws—a general, malicious, and deliberate attempt to overthrow Christianity, general Christianity. This is the line of indication where crime commences, and the offences become the subject of penal visitation. The species of offence may be classed under the following heads;
>
> 1. Denying the Being and Providence of God. 2. Contumelious reproaches of Jesus Christ; profane and malevolent scoffing of the Scriptures, or exposing any part of them to contempt and ridicule. 3. Certain immoralities tending to subvert all religion and morality, which are the foundations of all governments. Without these restraints no free

> governments could long exist. It is liberty run mad to declaim against the punishment of these offences, or to assert that their punishment is hostile to the spirit and genius of our Government. They are far from being the friends to liberty who support this doctrine; and the promulgation of such opinions, and the general receipt of them among the people, would be the sure forerunner of anarchy, and, finally, of despotism. No free government now exists in the world unless where Christianity is acknowledged and is the religion of the Country.

Do you think this could be said today?

Supreme Court of Massachusetts Decision

The Supreme Court of Massachusetts, Judge Parsons presiding, gave a similar decision in favor of Christianity. It was a case in which a Christian Church in Falmouth had occasion to vindicate the Third Article of the Constitution of the State, respecting religion and its support. Judge Parsons, who delivered the opinion of the court, was regarded by men of legal learning as the equal of Hale, Holt, Mansfield, Marshall, Kent, and Story. His decision, so luminous and full, in reference to Christianity and its relations to civil government, is, therefore, of the highest authority. The article of the Constitution of Massachusetts, on which the decision is based, is as follows:

> Art. 3. As the happiness of a people and the good order and preservation of civil government essentially depend on piety, religion, and morality; and as these cannot be generally diffused throughout the community but by the institution of a public worship of God, and of public institutions in piety, religion, and morality; therefore, to promote their happiness, and to secure the good order and preservation of their Government, the people of this Commonwealth have a right to invest their Legislature with power to authorize and require, and the Legislature shall from time to time authorize

> and require, the several towns, parishes, precincts, and other bodies politic, or religious societies, to make suitable provision, at their own expense, for the institutions of the public worship of God, and for the support or maintenance of public Protestant teachers of piety, religion, and morality, in all cases where such provision shall not be made voluntarily.

The decision made by Judge Parsons was:

> The object of a free government is the promotion and security of its citizens. These effects cannot be produced but by the knowledge and practice of our moral duties, which comprehend all the social and civil obligations of man to man, and the citizen to the state. If the civil magistrate in any state could procure by his regulations a uniform practice of these duties, the Government of that state would be perfect.
>
> To obtain that perfection, it is not enough for the magistrate to define the rights of the several citizens, as they are related to life, liberty, property, and reputation, and to punish those by whom they may be invaded. Wise laws, made to this end, and faithfully executed, may leave the people strangers to many of the enjoyments of civil and social life, without which their happiness will be extremely imperfect. Human laws cannot oblige to the performance of the duties of imperfect obligation; as the duties of charity and hospitality, benevolence, and good neighborhood; as the duties resulting from the relation of husband and wife, parent and child, of man to man as children of a common parent; and of real patriotism, by influencing every citizen to love his country and to obey all its laws. These are moral duties, flowing from the disposition of the heart, and not subject to the control of human legislation . . . . Civil government, therefore, availing itself only of its own powers, is extremely defective; and unless it

could derive assistance from some superior power, whose laws extend to the temper and disposition of the human heart, and before whom no offence is secret, wretched indeed would be the state of man under a civil constitution of any form.

This most manifest truth has been felt by legislators in all ages; and as man is born not only a social but a religious being, so in the pagan world, false and absurd systems of religion were adopted and patronized by the magistrates, to remedy the defects necessarily existing in a government merely civil.

On these principles, tested by the experience of mankind and by the reflections of reason, the people of Massachusetts, in the frame of their Government, adopted and patronized a religion which, by its benign and energetic influences, might co-operate with human institutions, to promote and secure the happiness of the citizens, so far as might be consistent with the imperfections of man.

In selecting a religion, the people were not exposed to the hazard of choosing a false and defective religious system. Christianity had long been promulgated, its pretensions and excellencies well known, and its Divine authority admitted. This religion was found to rest on the basis of immortal truth; to contain a system of morals adapted to man in all possible ranks and conditions, situations and circumstances, by conforming to which he would be ameliorated and improved in all the relations of human life; and to furnish the most efficacious sanctions, by bringing to light a future state of retribution. And this religion, as understood by Protestants, tending by its effects to make every man submitting to its influences a better husband, parent, child, neighbor, citizen, and magistrate, was, by the

> people, established as a fundamental and essential part of their Constitution. [5]

As we have seen, on the idea of laws, the American Founding Fathers would have agreed with Aristotle rather than Plato. Plato looked at law strictly from a standpoint of a code of negative restraints and prohibitions. Aristotle and the Founders considered law to be a positive rules by which they could be assured the opportunity to enjoy their unalienable rights and provide protection for themselves, their family and their property. In other words, law was a positive good rather than a necessary evil.

John Locke had the same idea when he said: "The end of law is not to abolish or restrain, but to preserve and enlarge freedom. For in all the states of created beings, capable of laws, where there are no laws there is no freedom. For liberty is to be free from restraint and violence from others, which cannot be where there is no law."[6]

Notes

1. Benjamin F. Morris, *The Christian Life and Character of the Civil Institutions of the United States* (Powder Springs, GA: American Vision, Inc., 2007), 774-78.
2. Ibid., 782-88.
3. Ibid., 784-85.
4. Ibid., 798-812.
5. Ibid., 813-21.
6. John Locke, *Second Essay Concerning Civil Government* Great Books of the Western World, vol. 35 (Chicago: Encyclopedia Britannica, Inc., 1952), p. 37, par. 57.

CHAPTER 20

The All-Important Question

The title of this book asks a question: "America, have you lost your mind, or is it your soul?" This may have seemed a bit harsh or intrusive, but we have reached a point in time where it has to be asked. We stand at a crossroads on the journey of life and we must—both individually and as a nation—make a decision concerning the path we will take. I have tried to present the facts pertaining to where we came from, who our forefathers were, and what made us the most admired and revered nation in the world for more than two centuries.

In this final chapter, I will present more facts and then ask the question again. I hope at that point you will have all the information you need to decide who you are in relation to the United States of America and what you would like to say in response to that question.

Early in 2005, Brooke Allen wrote an article called "Our Godless Constitution" in which she claims that this country was not founded on Christian principles but on Enlightenment principles.[1] I have touched on this subject before, but for those who have not studied that era, let's look at it briefly now.

The Enlightenment is the title that was given to a period in eighteen-century Europe and America (primarily Europe) when reason was coupled with recent advances in science and pronounced as the principal source of intellectual and moral authority. An idea or subject had to be argued rationally and demonstrated empirically to be proven true. "Enlightenment thinkers rejected the idea that religion can be a source of truth, and believed instead that the application of reason to the evidences of the senses is the sole source of truth."[2]

Almost every modern critic of America's Christian heritage argues that America was founded by deists on Enlightenment principles. To prove their point, they name Benjamin Franklin, George Washington, Thomas Jefferson, and others. I sincerely hope that the evidence that has been presented in this book has proven this argument to be utterly absurd.

Gregg Singer has this reply:

> A Christian world and life view furnished the basis for this early political thought which guided the American people for nearly two centuries and whose crowning [achievement] lay in the writing of the Constitution of 1787. This Christian theism had so permeated the colonial mind that it continued to guide even those who had come to regard the Gospel with indifference or even hostility. The currents of this orthodoxy were too strong to be easily set aside by those who in their own thinking had come to a different conception of religion and hence government too.[3]

For example, the following words appear on panel three of the Jefferson Memorial: "God who gave us life gave us liberty."[4] Jefferson then asked, "Can the liberties of a nation be secure when we have removed a conviction that these liberties are the gift of God?"[5]

In an address to the military on October 11, 1798, John Adams stated that "we have no government armed with power capable of contending with human passions unbridled by morality and religion . . . Our Constitution was made only for a moral and religious people. It is wholly inadequate to the government of any other."[6] *Perhaps that's why we have so many wanting to change it now!*

In a letter to Thomas Jefferson, Adams wrote the following:

> The general Principles, on which the [founding] Fathers Achieved Independence, were the only Principles in which that beautiful Assembly of young Gentlemen could Unite, and these Principles only could be intended by them in their Address, or by me in my Answer. And what were these general Principles? I answer, the general Principles of Christianity, in which all those Sects were united: . . . Now I will avow, that I then believed, and now believe, that those general Principles of Christianity, are as eternal and immutable, as the Existence and Attributes of God; and that those Principles of Liberty, are as unalterable as human Nature and our terrestrial, mundane System.[7]

George Washington warned the American people in his farewell address, "Of all the dispositions and habits which lead to political prosperity, religion and morality are indispensable supports . . . Let us with caution indulge the supposition that morality can be sustained without religion . . . Reason and experience both forbid us to expect that national morality can prevail in exclusion of religious principle."

Physician Benjamin Rush affirmed Washington's assessment that religion is the prerequisite for morality, virtue, and liberty:

> The only foundation for a useful education in a republic is to be laid in Religion. Without this, there can be no virtue, and without virtue there can be no liberty, and liberty is the object and life of all republican governments . . . [A]ll [of Christianity's] doctrines and precepts are calculated to promote happiness of society, and the safety and well-being of civil government.[8]

R. J. Rushdoony writes that Madison "denied the Enlightenment faith in the objectivity of reason, which, in Christian terms, he saw as inalienably tied to self-love. Man's reasoning is thus not objective reasoning; it is personal reasoning and will be thus governed by 'the nature of man' rather than an abstract concept of reasoning."[9]

Manifest Destiny

It has been said that the United States has a Manifest Destiny to be an Example and a Blessing to the Entire Human Race. The majority of historians agree that the original colonists had a sense that what they were doing in coming to this New Land was preordained by a higher power and that they would be blessed beyond measure in it. John Fiske wrote:

> They believed that they were doing a wonderful thing. They felt themselves to be instruments in accomplishing a kind of "manifest destiny." Their exodus [from Europe] was that of a chosen people who were at length to lay the everlasting foundations of God's kingdom on earth . . . This steadfast faith in an unseen ruler and guide was to them a pillar of cloud by day and of fire by night.
>
> It was of great moral value. It gave them clearness of purpose and concentration of strength, and contributed towards making them, like the children of Israel, a people of indestructible vitality and aggressive energy.[10]

The term and idea of "manifest destiny" has endured over time and has been heard in presidential speeches and other places many times. However, John Adams cautioned about the error of misinterpreting the true meaning of it: "I always consider the settlement of America with reverence and wonder, as the opening of a grand scene and design in Providence for the illumination of the ignorant, and the emancipation of the slavish part of mankind all over the earth."[11]

Thomas Jefferson had this opinion of how the development of freedom under the Constitution would affect the world. He felt it was "the world's best hope" and wrote to John Dickinson in 1801 that what had been done in the United States "will be a standing monument and example for the aim and imitation of the people of other countries, and I join with you in the hope and belief that they will see, from our example, that a free government is of all others the most energetic; that the inquiry which has been excited among the mass of mankind by our revolution & its consequences, will ameliorate the condition of man over a great portion of the globe."[12]

The Founders were careful to emphasize the responsibility they had put on themselves to perform the unenviable task of being the example to the world. John Adams was in England during the preparation of the Constitution and wrote: "The people of America have now the best opportunity and the greatest trust in their hands that Providence ever committed to so small a number."[13]

Alexander Hamilton also felt the weight of the matter of influence the Constitution would have on the world. He said:

> "It has been frequently remarked that it seems to have been reserved to the people of this country, by their conduct and example, to decide the important question, whether societies of men are really capable or not of establishing good government from reflection and choice, or whether they are forever destined to depend for their political constitutions on accident and force."
>
> He went on to say that if the people of the United States failed in this mission, it would contribute to "the general misfortune of mankind."[14]

John Adams had a similar feeling of responsibility and stated that if the people abandoned the freedom gained by the adoption of the Constitution, it would be "treason against the hopes of the world."[15]

John Jay had some thoughts about the aftermath of the task of putting the Constitution together. Establishing a truly free people he believed had seen a manifestation of divine approbation which was too obvious to be denied. He wrote:

> It has often given me pleasure to observe that independent America was not composed of detached and distant territories, but that one connected, fertile, wide-spreading country was the portion of our western sons of liberty. Providence has in a particular manner blessed it with a variety of soils and productions and watered it with enumerable streams for the delight and accommodation of its inhabitants. A succession of navigable waters forms a kind of chain round its borders, as if to bind it together; while the most noble rivers in the world, running at convenient distances, present them with highways for the easy communication of friendly aids and the mutual transportation and exchange of their various commodities.
>
> With equal pleasure I have often taken notice that Providence has been pleased to give this one connected country to one united people—a people descended from the same ancestors, speaking the same language, professing the same religion, attached to the same principles of government, very similar in their manners and customs, and who, by their joint counsels, arms, and efforts, fighting side by side throughout a long and bloody war, have nobly established their general liberty and independence.
>
> This country and this people seem to have been made for each other, and it appears as if it was the design of Providence that an inheritance so proper and convenient for a band of brethren, united to each other by the strongest ties, should never be split into a number of unsocial, jealous, and alien sovereignties.[16]

The main theme throughout this volume has been to debunk and discredit the large and growing group of people who want to claim that this country is not and never has been a Christian nation. Well I hope that I, with the help of the actual words and deeds of our Founding

Fathers have proven otherwise. And in that effort, I want to share some quotes and data on a man who represented the heart of this nation while serving as our president and who was also misunderstood.

Ronald Reagan—Man of God

Many biographers have had a misguided opinion of Ronald Reagan. They see him as an old movie actor who lived in the Hollywood atmosphere and was a worldly man. They didn't see the man of a vibrant Christian faith and great love for his country. Ronald Wilson Reagan had an old-fashioned love for the Lord and believed that he had a calling from God; he truly wanted to fulfill that calling.

Mary Beth Brown, who wrote *Hand of Providence,* a Reagan biography, said that Lyn Nofziger told her that Reagan was "born again." He was quoted as replying to a question about his faith: "Having accepted Jesus Christ as my Savior, I have God's promise of eternal life in heaven, as well as the abundant life here on earth that he promises to each of us in John 10:10."[17]

In 1964, a man named Holmes Tuttle asked Reagan to make a fund-raising speech for presidential candidate Barry Goldwater at the Ambassador Hotel in Los Angeles. The speech was a huge success and well received. Henry Salvatori, a businessman and later Reagan Kitchen Cabinet member, paid to have the speech televised nationally, causing a wellspring of support for Goldwater from all over the country.

In the speech, Reagan challenged Americans when he said:

> Alexander Hamilton warned us that a nation which can prefer disgrace to danger is prepared for a master and deserves one . . . If we are to believe that nothing is worth the dying, when did this begin? Should Moses have told the children of Israel to live in slavery rather than brave the wilderness? Should Christ have refused the Cross? Should the patriots at Concord Bridge have refused to fire the shot heard round the world? Are we to believe that all the martyrs of history died in vain?"

> You and I have a rendezvous with destiny. We can preserve for our children this, the last best hope for man on earth, or we can sentence them to take the first step into a thousand years of darkness. If we fail, at least we can let our children, and our children's children, say of us we justified our brief moment here.
>
> We did all that could be done.

Goldwater went on to eventually lose to Lyndon Johnson and fade from public consciousness, but no one would soon forget that speech, and Reagan found himself at the center of the conservative movement.

On January 3, 1967, Reagan became the thirty-third governor of the state of California, and took his oath of office on a four-hundred-year-old Bible brought to California by Father Junipero Serra, an immigrant from Spain. (Father Serra was the Catholic priest who founded the missions up and down the coast of California during the eighteenth century.)

After giving a four-minute speech, Reagan turned to the minister who had participated in the ceremony and said, "I am deeply grateful for your presence because you remind us, and bring here, the presence of someone else, without whose presence I certainly wouldn't have the nerve to do what I'm going to do."

Someone back in our history, I think it was Benjamin Franklin, said, "If ever someone could take public office and bring to public office the teachings and the precepts of the Prince of Peace, he would revolutionize the world and men would be remembering him for a thousand years. I don't think anyone could ever take office and be so presumptuous to believe he could do that or that he could follow those precepts completely. I can tell you this, I'll try very hard."

Later that week; the new governor made these comments at a prayer breakfast:

> Faith in God is absolutely essential if a person is to do his best. Sometimes we're afraid to let people know

> that we rely on God. Taking this stand just seems to be a logical and proper way to begin. Belief on the dependence on God is essential to our state and nation. This will be an integral part of our state as long as I have anything to do with it.

The Reagan family attended worship services together at the Bel Air Presbyterian Church, where Reagan often sought guidance from Reverend Donn Moomaw. Reverend Moomaw said in an interview that he and Reagan "have spent many hours together on their knees." And a History Channel program revealed that Reagan would say in prayer, "God, I want to follow your will, not my will."[18]

Reagan believed strongly in intercessory prayer, and in one letter he thanked a couple for "telling me about the people of your church and your prayers for me. I believe very much in His promise that 'where two or more gather in My name, there will I be.' I think I have known and felt the power and help of those prayers."

Years later, after Sister Mary Ignatius had written Reagan to congratulate him on his reelection, the president wrote back to her thanking her for her prayers, saying, "I believe in intercessory prayer and know I have benefitted from it. I have, of course, added my own prayers to the point that sometimes I wonder if the Lord doesn't say, 'here he comes again.'"

In a 1973 letter to the Cleavers, the parents of his high school sweetheart and minister of his church in Dixon, Illinois, Reagan wrote:

> One thing I do know—all the hours in the old church in Dixon (which I didn't appreciate at the time) and all of Nelle's faith, have come together in a kind of inheritance without which I'd be lost and helpless. During my first months in office, when day after day there were decisions that had to be made, I had an almost irresistible urge—really a physical urge—to look over my shoulder for someone I could pass the problem on to. Then without my quite knowing how it happened,

> I realized I was looking in the wrong direction. I started looking up instead and have been doing so for quite a while now. My faith is unshakable, and because all of you were so much responsible, I thank you for a peace beyond description. Love, Dutch.[19]

Reagan's letter to the Cleavers echoes what the apostle Paul emphasized in Philippians 4:6-7: "Be anxious for nothing, but in everything by prayer and supplication, with thanksgiving, let your requests be made known to God; and the peace of God, which surpasses all understanding, will guard your hearts through Christ Jesus."

In writing about God's creation while serving as governor of California, Reagan said, "Somehow I've never had any trouble reconciling spiritual and scientific versions of creation. God's miracles are to be found in nature itself, the wind and waves, the wood that becomes a tree—all these are explained biologically, but behind them is the hand of God. And I believe this is true of creation."

He taught his daughter, Patti, "God is all around—everywhere, all the time. He just waits for us to turn to Him."

He loved to go to his retreat, Rancho del Cielo, where he could think, talk to God, and fully experience his majestic creation.

"He once called it his 'open cathedral,'" says Judge Bill Clark, a close friend and advisor of Reagan's. "He'd come out of his house and look at the sky and not say a word. The Great Communicator didn't talk a lot in those circumstances. Many don't understand that, but he would just look about him with that great grin." The ranch was where Reagan liked to go to "recharge his batteries," and his days and nights there allowed him to withdraw from worldly affairs and spend time in prayer and meditation, seeking God's will and listening for his voice.[20]

In her book, *Angels Don't Die,* Patti writes that her father taught her prayer was simply talking to God, having a conversation with him. Reagan proved to Patti, through advice and example, that prayer was very easy and uncomplicated, like talking to a friend.

During the 1976 presidential campaign, Reagan did a nationwide TV special that invoked the biblical themes that called on Americans to keep their "rendezvous with destiny." In the speech, he asked citizens to help him "make this land the shining, golden hope God intended it to be." Journalist Frank Van der Linden reported in *The Real Reagan* that Reagan met with George Otis of High Adventure Ministries during the campaign. When Otis asked him, "Do you really believe somebody is listening up there?" Reagan replied, "Oh my! If I didn't believe that, I'd be scared to death!"[21] In January 1977, Reagan met with a group of conservatives. One of the statements he made was concerning the opinion that liberals had toward conservatives. He said:

> When we are maligned as having little thought or compassion for people, let us denounce the slander for what it is . . . Concern for people is at the very heart of conservatism. Concern for the dignity of all men; that those in need shall be helped to become independent . . . concern that those who labor and produce will not be robbed of the fruit of their toil or their liberty. Concern that we will not forfeit the dream that gave birth to this nation—the dream that we can be as a shining city upon a hill.[23]

Reagan often referred to America as "The Shining City on a Hill," a phrase that is found in Matthew 5:14: "You are the light of the world. A city that is set on a hill cannot be hidden."

What most people didn't understand about how Reagan appealed to the so-called Reagan Democrats was not economic issues, but moral issues. Polish, Irish, Lithuanian, Italian, and Cuban voters liked Reagan's stand against abortion and his hard line toward communism. They saw him as a "moral savior" who had come to restore the moral consensus that had grasped and lead this country for more than two hundred years. They shared the same moral compass as the Evangelical Christians.

In his acceptance speech for the nomination in 1980, he said:

> It is impossible to capture in words the splendor of this vast continent which God has granted as our portion of His creation. There are no words to express the extraordinary strength and character of this breed of people we call Americans . . . Some say the American spirit no longer exists. But I have seen it . . . The spirit is still there, ready to blaze into life if you and I are willing to do what has to be done; the practical, down-to-earth things that will stimulate our economy, increase productivity, and put America back to work.[24]

After finishing his speech, he paused and said, "I have thought of something that is not a part of my speech, and I'm worried over whether I should do it. Can we doubt that only Divine Providence placed this land, this island of freedom, here as a refuge for all those people in the world who yearn to breathe freely?" His face cracked, and he continued, "I'll confess that I've been a little afraid to suggest what I'm going to suggest—I'm more afraid not to—that we begin our crusade joined together in a moment of silent prayer." The once noisy convention hall became quiet. Then speaking softly, he ended with, "God bless America."[25]

After he sent the US Marines to invade the island nation of Grenada on October 25, 1983, he wrote in his autobiography about the valiant men rescuing the students and neutralizing the Marxists, and he gave all the credit to the Lord. He wrote, "Success seems to shine on us and I thank the Lord for it. He has really held me in the hollow of His hand."

Journalist Trude Feldman wrote in the *World Tribune* about an interview she had with Reagan shortly before his seventy-fifth birthday. It happened to fall on the day the space shuttle *Challenger* exploded. When they sat down in the Oval Office, Reagan had just finished paying tribute to the fallen astronauts.

Reagan was distraught over the loss of the men and women and said, "I draw strength from my belief in God and His teachings. That belief and faith in the Almighty helps me to cope with a tragedy like this."

Reagan finally steered the conversation around to his birthday and made this comment: "The anniversaries of my birth aren't important. What is important is that I have tried to lead a meaningful life, and I think I have."

On the National Day of Prayer in 1982, President Reagan told his audience:

> "I also believe this blessed land was set apart in a very special way, a country created by men and women who came here not in search of gold, but in search of God. They would be free people, living under the law with faith in their Maker and their future.
>
> Sometimes it seems we've strayed from that noble beginning, from our conviction that standards of right and wrong do exist and must be lived up to. God, the source of our knowledge, has been expelled from the classroom. He gives us his greatest blessing—life—and yet many would condone the taking of innocent life. We expect him to protect us in a crisis, but turn away from him too often in our day-to-day living. I wonder if he is waiting for us to wake up."[26]

In a White House ceremony to celebrate that National Day of Prayer in 1982, Reagan said:

> Today prayer is still a powerful force in America, and our faith in God is a mighty source of strength. Our Pledge of Allegiance states that we are "one nation under God," and our currency bears the motto, "In God We Trust." [27]
>
> The morality and values such faith implies are deeply embedded in our national character. Our country embraces those principles by design, and we abandon them at our peril. Yet in recent years, well-meaning Americans in the name of freedom have taken freedom

> away. For the sake of religious tolerance, they've forbidden religious practice in our public classrooms.
>
> How can we hope to retain our freedom through the generations if we fail to teach our young that our liberty springs from an abiding faith in our Creator?
>
> Thomas Jefferson once said, "Almighty God created the mind free." But current interpretation of our Constitution holds that the minds of our children cannot be free to pray to God in public schools. No one will ever convince me that a moment of voluntary prayer will harm a child or threaten a school or state. But I think it can strengthen our faith in a Creator who alone has the power to bless America . . .
>
> Just as Benjamin Franklin believed it was beneficial for the Constitutional Convention to begin each day's work with a prayer, I believe it would be beneficial for our children to have an opportunity to begin each school day in the same manner.

Again, speaking at the National Religious Broadcasters Convention in 1982, Reagan called for the need to have traditional values reflected in public policy and posed the question: "Do we really think . . . God will protect us in a time of crisis even as we turn away from him in our day-to-day life?"[28]

Ronald Reagan knew that the only way to be truly free was through the Lord, through the blood of Christ, and paradoxically, through the sovereign hand of God. Throughout his life, Reagan could see God's invisible hand leading him, guiding him—God's tender grace was a place of refuge. The Bible makes many references to "God's hand" and the "hand of God," and in Isaiah 49:16, the Lord uses this imagery to tell the believer how important he is to him: "See I have inscribed you on the palms of my hands." Reagan was very fond of this image too—this hand of God, this hand of Providence—and it provided him an everlasting peace.[22]

Notes

1. Brooke Allen, "Our Godless Constitution," *The Nation* (February 21, 2005).
2. Herbert Kohl, *From Archetype to Zeitgeist: Powerful Ideas for Powerful Thinking* (Boston: Little, Brown and Company, 1992), 65.
3. C. Gregg Singer, *A Theological Interpretation of American History* (Philadelphia: Presbyterian and Reformed, 1964), 284-85.
4. This originally appeared July 1774; see note 5.
5. The original phrase "And can the liberties of a nation be thought secure when we have removed, their only firm basis, a conviction in the minds of the people that these liberties are of the gift of God?" appears in Jefferson's *Notes on the State of Virginia*(Boston: Lilly and Wait, 1832), 170.
6. John Adams, *The Works of John Adams, Second President of the United States,* Charles Francis Adams, ed. (Boston: Little, Brown, and Company, 1854), 9:229, October 11, 1798.
7. Lester J. Cappon, ed., *The Adams-Jefferson Letters: The Complete Correspondence between Thomas Jefferson and Abigail and John Adams* (Chapel Hill, NC: The University of North Carolina Press, 1988),. 338-340. John Adams to Thomas Jefferson, June 28, 1813.
8. . "Benjamin Rush (1746-1813)," University of Pennsylvania, http://www.archives.upenn.edu/people/1700s/rush_benj.html. Retrieved August 20, 2011.
9. Rousas J. Rushdoony, *The Nature of the American System* (Nutley, NJ: The Craig Press, 1965), 73.
10. John Fiske, *The Beginnings of New England* (2004) 304-5.
11. Quoted in Conrad Cherry, *God's New Israel* (Englewood Cliffs, NJ: Prentice-Hall, 1971), 65.
12. Albert Ellery Bergh, ed., *The Writings of Thomas Jefferson*, 20 vols. (Washington: Thomas Jefferson Memorial Association, 1907), 10:217.
13. Koch, *The American Enlightenment,*(1965), 257.
14. Alexander Hamilton, James Madison, and John Jay, *The Federalist Papers* (New York: Mentor Books, 1961), No. 1, p. 33.
15. Koch, *The American Enlightenment,* (1965), 367.
16. Hamilton, *Federalist Papers*, No. 2, p. 38.

17. Mary Beth Brown, *Hand of Providence* (Nashville, TN: WND Books, 2004), xiv.
18. Ibid., 137-38.
19. Ibid., 143.
20. Ibid., 148-49.
21. Ibid., 159-160.
22. Ibid., 195.
23. Ibid., 162
24. Ibid., 166
25. Ibid., 167
26. Ibid., 184
27. Ibid., 184
28. Ibid., 187

CHAPTER 21

Conclusion

My dear readers, we have covered a lot of material in this volume. I have done my best to document most of the major events that have happened over the years to bring us to this point. All this was to bring us to a point where we could examine what happened in the early seventeenth century to bring to life a nation unlike any other in history. The people who came to America, as Ronald Reagan put it, were not coming here in search of gold; it was something much more precious. It was freedom. They came from places where they were used and abused, tortured and deprived of the very rights that we in America take for granted.

Not only do we take them for granted, but some want to destroy our whole system and model it after the failed systems of the past or even some that are in existence today which in no way can compare with what we have.

Part of the problem lies in the fact that a lot of our own people don't even know what a republic is. You hear people all the time talking about our "democracy." I heard several yelling on television the other night that certain legislative proposals were going to destroy our democracy. I hope that some of the material that I have placed in this book will help to "enlighten" some of them.

We were warned of the disintegration of our modern society in the 1940s by Robert Weaver, University of Chicago professor and father of modern-day conservatism, in his book, *Ideas Have Consequences.* He questioned whether we would continue to believe in the existence of a "source of truth higher than, and independent of self" or choose our own self-created version of morality and philosophy.[1] He proposes that how we answer that question, as a society, will affect the health and stability of our nation. His concern was that we have a growing focus on material things and are letting our unique Western civilization values decay.

He posits that the decay comes from a denial of universal truths, which in turn, leads us to deny accountability to any higher form of authority, such as almighty God. Instead of displaying any respect for our Founders or the ideals that they set up, our society is coming to see itself as the final arbiter of truth.

This man's opinion from that far back is certainly evident today when we see America endorsing and adapting to ungodly behaviors and even encouraging the poorer nations that we have influence on to endorse these unbiblical standards. Forgetting our once-revered position as a world leader, we now copy and emulate the laws and customs of other nations. This is "progress" to some. No longer are we recognized as a "standard setter" in the world, nor do we embrace our Christian heritage.

So we come to a very important question that lingers in many minds but seldom gets asked:

What Role Should Religion Have in Politics?

The 2012 presidential campaigns are in high gear, and several times the issue of religion has risen to the surface, only to be dragged back down into the depths of "it shouldn't matter." But how important is religion to politics and the office of the president, and should it really be an issue or held as something personal and private?

When we turn to the history given us in the Bible, we see that God raised up a nation that worshipped him and whose rulers relied upon him for wisdom and guidance. Whenever the rulers and people turned away from God and his teachings, the nation was brought down and destroyed. We read about this pattern being repeated over and over again.

When our Founding Fathers sacrificed everything to establish America, they did so by God's statutes and teachings. If you read the writings of these men, you will see that they turned to the Bible more than any other reference in establishing the documents and laws our nation was founded upon. The architects of American law quoted the Bible more than four times more often than any other reference. Upon George Washington's swearing in as the first president of the United States, the first thing he did was to march the delegation to the local church where he worshipped God and gave thanks for his sovereignty and hand in helping them secure their freedom.

For the first two centuries, America remained faithful to God and kept him at the center of the nation's life. But in the 1960s, things changed. Just as the Israelites did time and time again, America turned away from God and replaced him with hedonistic, self-pleasuring secularism. And you can study any social statistic you want, and they will all show a decline in the positive social attributes and a rise in the negative social and moral attributes of the American people and government.

Today, America is far more hedonistic and secular than they are God-fearing, and the decadence of our society shows it. Abominable lifestyles that were punishable by death in the Old Testament are being legislated and given privileged status by our federal and state governments. Just as the first three chapters of Romans explain when talking about sinful behavior: these things are not only done but approved by the leaders.

Jedidiah Morse (1761-1826) was a pioneer American educator, clergyman, geographer, and father of Samuel Morse, inventor of the telegraph and Morse code. After the American Revolution, he taught school to earn money while a graduate student at Yale. The students needed a good geography text, so he wrote *Geography Made Easy* and published it in 1784. It was the first geography book published in the United States and went through over twenty-five editions. Morse later published other American and world geographies, earning the informal title of "Father of American Geography."

While at Yale, Jedidiah studied for the ministry. In 1789, he accepted a call to the First Church of Charlestown, Massachusetts, one of the oldest churches in America. He was highly alarmed by how far the Boston clergy had moved away from doctrinal orthodoxy as well as by the growing influence of European rationalism in the United States. In 1799, he preached an insightful election sermon: "If the foundations be destroyed, what can the righteous do?" In it he said:

> Our dangers are of two kinds, those which affect our religion, and those which affect our government. They are, however, so closely allied that they cannot, with propriety, be separated. The foundations which support the interest of Christianity are also necessary to support a free and equal government like our own . . . To the kindly influence of Christianity we owe that degree of civil freedom, and political and social happiness which mankind now enjoys. In proportion as the genuine effects of Christianity are diminished in any nation, either through unbelief or the corruption of its doctrine, or the neglect of its institutions; in the same proportion will the people of that nation recede from the blessings of genuine freedom, and approximate the miseries of complete despotism. I hold this to be a truth confirmed by experience. If so, it follows, that all efforts made to destroy the foundations of our holy religion, ultimately tend to the subversion also of our political freedom and happiness. Whenever the pillars of Christianity shall be overthrown, our present republican form of government, and all the blessings which flow from them, must fall with them.[2]

"If the foundations are destroyed, what can the righteous do?" (Psalm 11:3 NIV). *Does this scenario sound familiar?* And people wonder why America is on the verge of ruin and collapse.

If we turn to history, we will readily learn that the *only* way to turn America around and save our nation is to turn to God and his precepts. And that has to start with the leadership of the nation. It is imperative that we elect strong Christian leaders who will rule the nation in the fear of God Almighty. These leaders then must appoint equally strong and committed Christians to key positions such as judgeships, cabinet posts, etc. Then the people as a whole need to kneel down, confess their sins, ask for forgiveness and repentance, and turn their faces toward God and follow his statutes. I can't tell you how strongly I feel about this, that the only way to save America is to follow 2 Chronicles 7:14 (NIV) that says, "If my people, who are called by my name, will humble themselves and pray and seek my face and turn from their wicked ways, then I will hear from heaven, and I will forgive their sin and heal their land." Are you willing to get on your knees for America's sake?

So when we take the time, as we have here, to look at the work, sweat, blood, tears, and prayers that our Founders put into this one-of-a-kind nation, how can anyone look you in the eye and say we have to change this country into something better? Remember the question we started with?

America, have you lost your mind, or is it your soul?

If we don't recognize, appreciate, and try to preserve the wonderful republic our Founders gave us, then we have lost our minds. And if we don't recognize it was a gift from God, then our souls are in danger. I pray that this collection of material has been beneficial to you and that you will join the fight to save this country.

God Bless America!

Notes

1. Carol Swain, *Be the People* (Nashville, TN: Thomas Nelson, Inc., 2011), 127.
2. Richard Lee, *The American Patriot's Bible* (Nashville, TN: Thomas Nelson, Inc., 2009), 607.

Bibliography

1. *The Real Thomas Jefferson.* Andrew M. Allison, National Center for Constitutional Studies, 2009.
2. Brown, Mary Beth, and Michael Reagan. *Hand of Providence: The Strong and Quiet Faith of Ronald Reagan.* Nashville, TN: WND Books, 2004.
3. Cummins, Joseph. *Ten Tea Parties.* Philadelphia, PA: Quick Books, 2012.
4. Chaplin, Joyce E. *Benjamin Franklin's Autobiography.* New York, NY: W. W. Norton & Co., Inc., 2012.
5. DeMar, Gary. *America's Christian History.* Powder Springs, GA: American Vision, Inc., 2010.
6. Etheredge, Robert C. *The American Challenge.* Orinda, CA: Mira Vista Press, 2011.
7. Freiling, Thomas. *Walking with Lincoln.* Grand Rapids, MI: Revell/ Baker Publishing, 2009.
8. Hill, Jonathan. *Zondervan Handbook to the History of Christianity.* Oxford, England: Lion Publishing Plc., 2006.
9. *Thomas Jefferson Writings,* Literary Classics of the United States. New York, NY: Literary Classics of the United States, 1984.
10. Lee, Richard. *The American Patriot's Bible.* Nashville, TN: Thomas Nelson, Inc., 2009.
11. Lillback, Peter. *George Washington's Sacred Fire.* Bryn Mawr, PA: Providence Forum Press, 2006.
12. Morris, Benjamin F. *The Christian Life and Character of the Civil Institutes of the United States.* Powder Springs, GA: American Vision, Inc., 2007.
13. Schweikart, Larry, and Michael Allen. *A Patriot's History of the United States.* New York, NY: Penguin Group, Inc., 2004.

14. Skousen, W. Cleon. *The 5000 Year Leap.* (1981) National Center for Constitutional Studies, 1981.
15. Stearns, Robert. *No, We Can't.* Bloomington, MN: Chosen Books, 2011.
16. Wood, Gordon, ed. *John Adams: Revolutionary Writings 1755-1775.* New York, NY: Library Classics of the United States, Inc., 2011.